# THE SELF IN SCHOOLING: THEORY AND PRACTICE

## How to Create Happy, Healthy, Flourishing Children in the 21st Century

*Henry G. Brzycki, PhD*

The Self in Schooling: Theory and Practice—How to Create Happy, Healthy, Flourishing Children in the 21st Century. Copyright © 2013 by Henry G. Brzycki. All rights reserved.

Printed in the United States of America. No part of this book may be used or reproduced in any manner without written permission except in the case of brief quotations embodied in critical articles and reviews, and in scholarly research. For information address Dr. Henry G. Brzycki, 2352 Park Center Boulevard, State College, PA 16801.

This publication is designed to provide accurate and authoritative information in regard to the subject matter covered. It is sold with the understanding that the author and publisher are not engaged in rendering legal, accounting, psychological, medical, or other professional service. If expert assistance is required, the services of a competent professional person should be sought.

Cover and Interior Design by Scribe

**Library of Congress Cataloging-in-Publication Data**

Henry G. Brzycki, 1955–
    The Self in Schooling: Theory and Practice—How to Create Happy, Healthy, Flourishing Children in the 21st Century.
    Includes bibliographical references and index.
    ISBNs: 978-0-9887161-0-0 (paper); 978-0-9887161-1-7 (Nook); 978-0-9887161-2-4 (Apple); 978-0-9887161-3-1 (Kindle)
    Educational psychology. 2. Psychological and physical well-being. I. Title.
    LCCN: 2012923693            2013

Imprint Name: BG Publishing, State College, PA

Printed in the United States of America

**To my wife, Elaine, with all my love.**

Elaine has dedicated her life to empowering all who know her to express their wisdom and higher purpose in life in order to make the world more beautiful. I have been the recipient of her powerful force for good and love. Elaine's constant support is what made this book possible. All who read this book will be impacted by Elaine's vision of a more beautiful world.

# Contents

|  |  |  |
|---|---|---|
| *Acknowledgments* | | ix |
| *Preface* | | xi |

### Section 1: Theory

| Chapter 1 | Interdisciplinary View of Complex Problems | 3 |
|---|---|---|
| | Urgent Needs | 7 |
| | Humanity Is Hurting | 8 |
| | 21st-Century Problems With Solutions That Are Beyond Our Present Mind-Set | 9 |
| | A Lever for Change: The iSelf Model | 10 |
| | The Whole Self | 11 |
| | Well-Being and Education | 12 |
| | A New Tool for Learning | 14 |
| | Theory and Practice | 16 |
| | Symptoms When People Lack Self-Understanding | 18 |
| | A Deeper Look at Self | 22 |
| | Internal and External Selves | 22 |
| | Increasing Potential | 24 |
| Chapter 2 | A Possible Copernican Shift | 25 |
| | The iSelf Model at the Center of Psychology and Education | 25 |
| | Issues in Cognitive Psychology | 26 |
| | Is This the Best We Can Do? | 28 |
| | Social Construction of Reality | 29 |
| | Evolution of Mind | 30 |
| | Teaching and Learning | 32 |
| | Positive Psychology | 34 |
| | Academic and Well-Being Outcomes | 36 |

| | | |
|---|---|---|
| Chapter 3 | A New Kind of Mind | 41 |
| | Creativity | 43 |
| | Pedagogy That Empowers | 44 |
| | Education Aligned With Psychology | 45 |
| | The Standards Based Paradigm Is Ineffective | 47 |
| Chapter 4 | The Integrated Self-Model Description | 49 |
| | Why Teach Self-Knowledge in Schooling? | 50 |
| | iSelf Model Attributions | 51 |
| | Character | 52 |
| | A Model of Self Developed From the Research Data | 54 |
| | Self-System Attributes Defined | 55 |
| | Positive Psychology Attributes | 60 |
| | An Expanded Definition of Well-Being | 63 |
| | Revisiting the Nature Versus Nurture Debate | 66 |
| | iSelf Model and Information Processing | 67 |
| | Emotions and Learning: I Feel, Therefore I Learn! | 69 |
| | Evolution of the Mind | 72 |
| | The Self and Neurological Research | 81 |
| | The Self and Emotions | 82 |
| | Emotions and Health Research | 84 |
| | Mind-Body Connections and the NIH | 85 |
| | Education Research | 86 |
| | Self-Schema and Learning | 87 |
| | Self-Knowledge and Schooling | 89 |
| | Empowering Adolescent Well-Being and Academic Performance Through Schooling | 91 |
| Chapter 5 | The Purpose of Education in the 21st Century | 93 |
| | Beyond the Information Age | 94 |
| | Paradigm Crisis or Not? | 97 |
| | NCLB: Cognitive Focus and Results | 99 |
| | NCLB and Business Models | 101 |
| | Forces for Change | 103 |
| | Humanistic Education | 104 |

**Section 2: Practice**

| | | |
|---|---|---|
| Chapter 6 | Curriculum | 109 |
| | Connecting Academic Subjects to the Self | 112 |
| | The Self Across the Curriculum | 115 |

|  | Levels of Consciousness Through Schooling | 119 |
| --- | --- | --- |
|  | Process of Transforming the Self | 122 |
|  | Applications of SAC in K–16 Schooling | 122 |
|  | Teaching Educational Psychology Best Practice | 123 |
|  | Three Examples of Self Across the Curriculum | 123 |
|  | Analysis and Reflection | 131 |
| Chapter 7 | Personalized Learning | 133 |
|  | Learner-Centered Psychological Principles | 135 |
|  | Realization of Importance: Good Intentions Are Not Enough | 141 |
|  | Need for a Framework: Searching for Best Practices | 142 |
|  | Teachers Unions' Views Inhibit Personalized Learning | 143 |
|  | Teachers and Personalized Learning | 146 |
|  | Shift to Coaching | 147 |
|  | Personalized Learning and Potential | 150 |
|  | Eight Conditions to Empower Student Potential | 150 |
|  | The Role of Technology | 151 |
|  | Transforming Learning Environments With Technology | 152 |
|  | Personalized Learning Plans | 154 |
| Chapter 8 | Well-Being and Protective and Risk Factors | 159 |
|  | Well-Being: Obesity | 161 |
|  | Well-Being: Psychological | 173 |
| Chapter 9 | New Models: Future Possibilities | 199 |
|  | Educational and Health Policies Return on Investment | 199 |
|  | Déjà Vu | 200 |
|  | Real-World Learning Model | 201 |
|  | Flipped Classrooms | 204 |
|  | New Approach to College Success | 204 |
|  | Future Possibilities | 205 |
|  | Which Reality to Create? | 207 |
|  | *References* | 209 |
|  | *Index* | 227 |
|  | *About the Author* | 237 |

# Acknowledgements

I have realized that writing this book has changed me. I am clear that many people have helped inspire me to a higher vision for what is possible, for each of us and for all. Others have guided me to implement these ideas, while many of my students and counseling clients have demonstrated the effectiveness of these new approaches and methods.

I cannot thank all my students and counseling clients enough. They have provided substantive input into my work for the past 30 years and have all contributed to my life as much or more than I ever did to theirs. My counseling clients trusted that my methods would work to empower them to live happy, healthy, flourishing lives through one-on-one interactions and relationships. My students at Franklin Pierce University, Pennsylvania State University, and Clarion University helped affirm that the idea of producing better people through schooling processes is important and does work in practice. Many colleagues have guided me in a long personal and professional journey to seeing and manifesting my own unique purpose in life. My family instilled lifelong values and a family culture of how to live a life of happiness, health, and flourishing.

From my heart and for very personal and individual reasons I would like to acknowledge these great people for their contributions to my life and work, and to this book: Marie F. Brzycki, Henry R. Brzycki, Beverly Gladwin, Dr. Janet Dowding, Barbara Brzycki White, Norman J. Brzycki, Kathy Condon, Elaine Brzycki, Amy Sikora, Crystal Murray, Gina-Marie Thompson, Linda Thompson, Beth Sommers, Michelle Koerner, Pam Allen, Joshua Samuel Almes, Mr. Philip Blum, Karen Kugel, Lynda Haessler Hauman, Nina Pattison, Jerry Kocher, Dr. Greg Goodman, Dr. David P. Baker, Deborah Meier, Dr. Analucia Schliemann, Dr. Barbara Brizuela, Dr. Kathleen Weiler, Dr. Martha Trudeau Tucker, Dr. Howard Gardner, Dr. Israel Scheffler, Ataan Kurgun, Holly Chiancola, Dr. Paul Dimattia, Gary Kanavos, Jeanne R. Lind, Ryan Brown, David Brown, Mary Brown, Dr. Roger Brooks, Dr. Bill Clark,

Fred Bramante, Dr. Deborah Jameson, Dr. Tammy Woody, Jackie Haines, Lisa Hedrick, Dr. Frederick Brown, Heather Morrell, Carol Black, Megan Roach, Edmund Twining IV, Leslie Long, Corrine Callahan, Dr. Jocelyn Smrekar, Dr. Barrie Brancato, Dr. Tarajean Yazzie-Mintz, Dr. Ethan Mintz, Elizabeth West, Cassandra Grace Mosier, Laura Altobelli for her professional editing, and Rachel Paul McGrath for her publishing expertise.

# Preface

Francis W. Parker, the father of progressive education at the beginning of the 20th century, expressed a desire to improve the human condition *through* education—a desire that I have emulated throughout my life and career as a teacher and counselor. When I read his work, his positive vision of humanity inspired me to a higher level of consciousness, a calling to my life's purpose. His perspective drove me to explore the psychological paradigms that make a difference in the quality of our individual and collective lives: "If I should tell you any secret of my life, it is the intense desire I have to see growth and improvement in human beings. I think that is the whole secret of my enthusiasm and study, if there be any secret to it, my intense desire to see mind and soul grow" (Giffin, 1906, p. 133).

As you read this book, my goal is for you to better see how the *mind and soul grow*, empowering *you* to foster *growth and improvement* in human beings and in our human condition. This book is written from an interdisciplinary perspective to move outside traditional boundaries to serve students of educational psychology and public health, new and seasoned teachers, education and health policy makers, psychological counselors, and medical professionals and epidemiologists alike. Grounded in scholarly research, these chapters are written for use by undergraduate and graduate preservice teachers and counselors and in professional development courses for master teachers, counselors, mental and physical health professionals, and other practitioners. I also hope this writing will be accessible to parents and professionals working in any field—anyone who cares about empowering children and adults to flourish personally and professionally so they may realize their full potential.

While writing this book, I hoped to distinguish it from others in this genre by not only discussing theory but also providing practical examples that will add value to your personal and professional development. I present a comprehensive model of self that represents, so to speak, the DNA of the inner life of each person. In addition, I give examples of ways to apply both the theory and the self-model in the classroom or at home—examples that I hope will inspire your own creative ideas. My goal is for you to come away with

- a thorough understanding of a researched psychological model of self that will help you both assess and intervene for your students', patients', and clients' well-being;
- a comprehensive model of self that represents the DNA of the inner life of each person;
- a fresh perspective on steps the educational system could be taking to move beyond our current model, still mired in 19th-century sensibilities, and address the myriad 21st-century needs; and
- a clear and accurate picture of the dire well-being condition of our children, adolescents, and young adults, as well as the economic costs that society is bearing as a result of inaction by policy makers and human services practitioners.

It is my highest hope, and an overarching theme throughout this book, that you will be able to step outside of your usual ways of thinking about the well-being of our youth and reevaluate the systems that we have in place to support them in living a flourishing life. While reading this book, think about the problems presented and the proposed solutions. Ask yourself, "What if we *did* set up our schools and our society using the theory presented?" In doing so, I hope you come away inspired by a new vision and sense of what is possible.

# Section 1

# THEORY

## CHAPTER 1

# INTERDISCIPLINARY VIEW OF COMPLEX PROBLEMS

The "self" may be defined as the essential or particular qualities that distinguish one person from another, such as personality traits or talents. However, it can be even more useful in teaching, learning, and counseling to think of the self as a holistic system with three major components: the body, the mind, and the soul. Further, learning about the self is really the same in both traditional classroom educational settings and therapeutic counseling, in that the pathway to learning is through psychological processes that are personally meaningful. In both environments, the goal is similar: to lay the groundwork for a flourishing life. The root of the word *psychology*, "psyc," comes from the Greek word *psyche*, which means *soul*. In the context of psychiatry, the mind is "an organic system reaching all parts of the body and serving to adjust the total organism to the demands of the environment" (Friend & Guralnik, 1953, p. 1175). All these aspects of the person unite as the self. The self is important to know and understand because it mediates the inner life with the outer life to determine our realities and shape a positive life course.

During my own journey to discover greater meaning, life purpose, and mental and physical well-being in my life, and through my commitment to give back to others, I have studied the self in K–16 classroom learning and therapeutic counseling contexts. I realized every one of my breakthroughs in my own understanding of my life occurred because I had access to a new level of self-understanding and higher consciousness. The quality of my life soared every time I examined my life and learned more about myself. At one transformative moment that came to me well into my adult years, when I felt at one with the goodness of humanity, it occurred to me that others might find this process of self-discovery as valuable and enlightening as I had. I then began to think about my own education through the public school system and which lessons helped me live a high-quality life and manifest my unique potential during and after my schooling. In particular, I examined which lessons I learned—or had not learned—about my own self.

Certainly, I learned much about the usual academic content (and I enjoyed most), although I did not understand *why* I was learning much of it. While I was reading, for example, *The Catcher in the Rye* or *Walden* in English literature class in high school, I did not know how to make these brilliantly meaningful works, with their deep and meaningful thoughts and concepts, relevant to me and my life, to my own self-understanding. As a developing adolescent, I was hungry for this type of meaning. I was not getting what I needed from my teachers to appreciate the depth of the academic content, nor was I learning how to apply these meanings to my own personal development and life-course trajectory. Then, during senior year, my physics teacher started off the first semester by asserting that we did not need him, that all that we needed to learn was already in ourselves and our textbook. Well, after 12 years of schooling during which I was taught to be reliant if not dependent on teachers for my future success, this myth and belief system was shattered, thankfully.

I remember the first time I experienced a transformation in my own understanding of my unique journey toward self-actualization: I was sitting in a freshman organizational psychology class. Simply upon seeing Maslow's Hierarchy of Needs (1954), I felt as though my head exploded. I learned that powerful personal development can occur through the teaching of academic content.

On the basis of these discoveries, I was compelled to design a series of educational courses that transformed the lives of my counseling clients through self-understanding. With numerous years of successfully transforming the lives of my clients, healing their psychological conditions, and using this model of personal transformation to flourish personally and professionally, I realized that our educational system could be better utilized to empower young people to live a high quality of life, filled with personal meaning, positive life directions, and psychological and physical well-being. If we included these goals in our education system, then, just maybe, we could make the world a better place.

Who among us has gone through life without knowing who we are, or without having a paradigm to guide us in understanding who we are and why we do the things we do? Perhaps if we had known who we were, we could have accessed deeper experiences in our relationships. We could have had more accomplishments academically and better job prospects that more closely mirrored our innate nature and talents. By gaining a more thorough understanding of our unique potential, we can find a more direct pathway to reaching it as we navigate this fast-paced modern life, characterized by rapid change. During the times in which overwhelming personal and professional crises threaten our mental and physical health, we must find the psychological and emotional tools we need to get through these periods.

I have dedicated my life to studying and empowering the self from numerous perspectives. In my K–16 teaching and in my counseling practice, I have worked with clients seeking guidance to choose a college, change careers, conquer substance abuse, overcome marriage and family dysfunction, and recover from sexual abuse. The one common denominator that I have found in all cases is that the pathway to success—whether it be academic and career success, emotional and psychological healing, or inner peace and love—is through a better understanding of one's self and making one's self-awareness a high priority.

As counselors and teachers, we must be interested in studying how to make a difference in the lives of the young people in our care and how to empower them through our work. This is where these two human service professions come together at the mission level—to educate and to help individuals become themselves. We share a mission to empower the life course in terms of health and well-being, and these are learned and manifest through personally meaningful experiences.

I want to connect and deepen the processes that these two professions use in their respective strategies for reaching people: counselors' interventions and teachers' lesson activities. The common factor to producing successful results in both domains—whether a student is learning academic content in a classroom or a client is experiencing a productive session on how to be happy and experience authentic emotions in a therapist's office—is self-understanding. Over the years, I became aware that my professional effectiveness in both professional arenas was based on my ability to help both my students and clients learn about themselves.

The research is compelling and persuasive about the causal links between the psychology of the self, psychological and physical well-being, and academic achievement. Numerous studies from the psychological and medical professions demonstrate the direct causal relationship between self-esteem and depression and obesity, purpose in life and emotional well-being, and self-efficacy and positive life-course trajectories, among other examples presented throughout this book (Bandura et al., 2001; CDC, 2012; Cohen, 2006; Goetz et al., 2003; Locker & Cropley, 2004; Mann et al., 2004; Orth et al., 2012; Ryan & Deci, 2000; Ryff & Singer, 1998a; 1998b; Ternouth et al., 2009). One particularly important research study that also takes a similar approach to my own research, known as the ACE (Adverse Childhood Experiences) study, provides an interdisciplinary view when researching the causal relationship between adverse childhood experiences, social-emotional and cognitive impairment, adverse or health risk behaviors, disease, disability and social problems, and life expectancy (Felitti et al., 1998; Felitti & Anda, 2009).

This book draws upon research and best practices in a wide variety of disciplines where the self is studied or considered an important risk or protective factor. Examples include medicine and the problems of obesity and obesity-related illnesses and the correlations between self-esteem and emotional profiles to physical health. Important work is emerging in the field of positive psychology and strengths-based counseling that holds promise for the new personalized learning model and a teaching and learning method known as the "flipped classroom" from the field of education. Also included are perspectives from evolutionary, developmental, educational, cognitive, and positive psychology that inform a new model of mind that can be taught through our schooling processes. Exciting new developments in mind, brain, and education (MBE) also offer fMRI proof of the complex dynamics inherent in developmental and learning processes. This book draws upon the latest innovations in thinking about 21st-century learning and proposes a new theory of education for modern times, so to, hopefully, provide a framework for transforming our present 19th-century system of education to reflect our growing needs. All these interdisciplinary perspectives have been studied and included in this book because they offer important insights into the need for a comprehensive model of self in schooling.

As we teach numerous distinctions about the self in our classrooms, children should emerge from their schooling experiences more able to be well, with a greater understanding of what it means to be healthy—emotionally, physically, spiritually, intellectually, and psychologically. Academic learning and success will stem from student well-being and contribute to it, rather than being the sole purpose of schooling or occurring without regard to larger humanistic concerns.

All too often, scholars only think deeply and thoroughly about their particular fields of expertise, rarely daring to cross over into another body of knowledge at the risk of marginalizing their influence and reputations that take so long to build. Our world is changing rapidly and growing in complexity. We need to think about our problems from numerous perspectives and draw upon the best insights from each in order to create a breakthrough in our abilities to solve many acute problems. This is why this book takes an interdisciplinary view to solve problems: to hopefully create a breakthrough that will empower humanity to be better, in a way that is consistent with our highest visions for what is possible.

As you read this book, I recommend that you reference the topics discussed back to three themes that are woven into the discussion regarding the importance of self-knowledge and the cultivation of a new kind of mind for creating personal meaning in today's modern society: (1) defining a new psychological paradigm for learning and well-being, (2) integrating education with new developments in psychology, and (3) aligning education's purpose with a new pedagogy for the 21st century.

### Urgent Needs

I hope that this book puts into a proper and effective context the urgency of the psychological and physical well-being problems and the extent and depth of these problems for anyone who cares about children: students, parents, teachers, policy makers, mental health counselors, medical professionals, epidemiologists, and health policy leaders. The situation is critical, and our health care and education systems lack a cohesive strategy to combat the problems. We continue to use a fire extinguisher to put out a five-alarm blaze. It is my intention to put into one place a well-researched, scholarly work that can be used to impact the psychological and physical well-being problems, hopefully at a systemic level, at their base or root. This needs to happen sooner than later, as we are beyond the tipping point.

These psychological and physical well-being problems are not even on the radar screens of educators, nor are the possible solutions. They actually *are* on the radar screens of mental health professionals, but the U.S. Department of Health and Human Services (HHS) is without a serious national or societal strategy or set of programs to address them. Even by its own reporting, HHS efforts are poor at best in reducing childhood and adult obesity and numerous prevalent depressive disorders.

While researching this book, it became very evident that the Centers for Disease Control and Prevention (CDC), U.S. Department of Health and Human Services (HHS), U.S. Department of Education (DOE), National Institutes of Health (NIH), National Institute of Mental Health (NIMH), and numerous other policy-setting bodies do not talk to one another or collaborate on a set of effective strategies to successfully address growing health and well-being issues among our children, adolescents, and adults.

Not only do I paint a clear picture of the mental and physical health problems in our country, but I offer a serious, research-based strategy for solving these problems at a very systemic level, to transform our system of education so as to release students' full potentials—academic, career, and life—for all future generations.

Is it any wonder that the United States has lost its position in the world as a model society, when in international comparisons we do not measure up in terms of well-being or academic performance? At a time when educators in the United States are debating the merits of blogging for 3rd graders, or extending the school day or year to thereby place even more stressors upon our youth, Europe is funding research on best practices on human flourishing as an ideal aim of education and investigating conceptual and normative ethical questions about education for the good life in a diverse society. I hope this book inspires action that allows us to catch up to our colleagues in those enlightened European countries.

## Humanity Is Hurting

Everywhere you look—in schools, on the television, within family homes, in social media, and in doctors' offices—there is an overwhelming amount of evidence that something isn't working, that the way in which we understand our selves, each other, and the world is not quite right. Why else would people be in such ill mental and physical health? If we take a snapshot of the condition of human beings in 2012, taken as a whole picture, the evidence is both staggering and deeply depressing. Here are just a few statistics from recent studies to underscore the magnitude of our nation's health and well-being problems:

- More than 14 million children and adolescents have mental health issues.
- Approximately 20% of all youth are impacted by a mental disorder to the extent that they have difficulty functioning.
- About 80% of these children with mental disorders do not get the help they need.
- Depressive disorder is the leading cause of disability among Americans age 15–44.
- Antidepressants are the second most prescribed type of drug in the United States, right behind pills for high cholesterol, according to data from IMS Health. Last year, 255 million prescriptions for antidepressants were dispensed in the United States, a 2% increase from 2009.
- In 2010, approximately 160,000 children missed school every day out of fear of being bullied.
- 15% of all students who don't show up for school report that it is due to their fear of being bullied while at school.
- Approximately 71% of students report bullying as an ongoing problem.
- Suicide is one of the leading causes of death among children under the age of 14 in the United States.

- In Louisiana, 56% of students had a healthy body mass index (BMI), with 44% having an unhealthy BMI. About 22% are obese, with only 37% of students meeting the minimum standard for cardiovascular fitness.
- Obesity has increased from 13% to 34% in the past 50 years.
- More than 60% of America's children are overweight, with approximately 20% obese.
- More than one-third of U.S. adults (35.7%) are obese. Approximately two-thirds of U.S. adults are overweight.
- Since 1980, obesity prevalence among children and adolescents has almost tripled.

Source: U.S. Department of Health and Human Services, 1999; Kataoka, Zhang, & Wells, 2002; National Institute of Mental Health, 2010; http://www.bullyingstatistics.org; The Center for Evaluation and Education Policy, Indiana University School of Education; http://whatworks.wholechildeducation.org; CDC, 2012a, http://www.cdc.gov/obesity/data/adult.html.

These statistics do not represent the complete picture. Additional statistics are presented and discussed throughout this book and in particular in the well-being chapters within the practice section.

## 21st-Century Problems With Solutions That Are Beyond Our Present Mind-Set

Acute 21st-century problems are beyond our present ability to solve because we do not have the mind or psychological mind-set to solve them. They are too complex, with too many forces, too many stakeholders, and no clear set of priorities of what is important. Throughout this book, we will follow the data compiled when defining the problem and possible solutions. In the practice section, I share further statistics so there is no misunderstanding of the scope and depth of the problems discussed or the necessity of the theory and the applications proposed.

The statistics include percentages of obesity rates now and in the future for children, adolescents, and adults; adults on prescription drugs and addicted to prescription drugs; adolescents and adults treated for depression; adults on depression medications; adolescents who commit suicide; health complications from obesity; and adolescent suicides and childhood bullying. Further, I discuss expenditures for obesity and obesity-related illnesses; health care; public education nationwide; No Child Left Behind (NCLB) testing; drug and alcohol addiction for adolescents and adults; and behavior-based illnesses in adolescents and adults. When each of these expenditures is viewed from a specific industry or domain or collectively, we can conclude that we are not getting a sufficient return on our investments.

## A Lever for Change: The iSelf Model

The most direct path to making humanity healthier, happier, and more successful is to empower a shift, putting the self of the person at the center of our educational system and, more broadly, all modern life. I want to identify the most acute problems we are confronted with in the 21st century and then offer a framework to solve these. I am putting together in one place a clear picture of the human well-being realities and a pathway to the future in the spirit of Archimedes's vision, "Give me a lever long enough and a fulcrum on which to place it, and I shall move the world," where the fulcrum is the education system and the lever is an integrated model of the self-model—called the iSelf model—applied to our system of education and all schooling processes.

The iSelf model is a new paradigm of an integrated self that I developed during my research on recent scholarly works in psychology and education that leads to improved academic and well-being outcomes (Brzycki, 2009; 2010). The iSelf model also draws upon my numerous clinical experiences where the model of self, the theoretical applications, and actual transformations support the ideas presented and discussed.

The iSelf model is short for *integrated self-paradigm*. The iSelf model integrates component parts from self-system and positive psychology attributes. It is a paradigm for teaching self-knowledge. This iSelf paradigm can be used as a framework for epidemiologists, medical practitioners, pediatricians, mental health counselors, school counselors, K–16 teachers, teacher education and psychology professors, college and university academic and first-year experience advisors, and career counselors. Most importantly, it can be a lever of change in the U.S. education system. I present the iSelf model in context in Chapter 2, in more detail in Chapter 4, and with application to K–16 classrooms in Chapter 5.

As a counselor and educator who has applied the ideas presented here in this book, with transformational results in terms of the quality of people's lives and their psychological and physical well-being, I believe that the idea of teaching self-knowledge to all through public schooling to improve mental and physical well-being represents a breakthrough in what it means to be human, with all the inherent possibilities for a better life, for all. In short, focusing on the self in schooling is an idea whose time has come. In the context of well-being outcomes (in terms of academic knowledge and mental and physical health), learning about and through the self is the most direct and impactful pathway to ensure positive outcomes for individuals and society.

## The Whole Self

The direct correlation between the mind and body (mental and physical health) has been known since ancient Greeks philosophized and built systems of education that improved this connection. Just now, as the 21st century unfolds, we can deliver on the long held promise that human beings through sound mind can take control over their own health destinies. Plato, in his theory of the *Phaedo*, said, "The soul becomes involved with a body because it desires to live in a way in which it only can if it has a body of suitable kind" (Broadie, 2001). In other words, in order to express our souls fully and completely during our lifetimes, we require a healthy body to carry out this expression.

Throughout this book, I will be defining an integrated self as the combination of body, brain, mind, and soul. By *mind* I mean "human consciousness that originates in the brain," as distinguished from the *soul*, by which I mean a core "animating and vital principle in human beings," to allow for more immaterial emotional and spiritual self-conceptions (Webster's Dictionary, 1972). In addition, I use two important distinctions when discussing the self and the self in schooling: transformed mind-set and untransformed mind-set.

A *transformed mind-set* (or simply *transformation*) is a deep change at a being level within a human being. It is a fundamental, systemic change in the conscious awareness of self and all. It is a change in the DNA of one's consciousness, understanding of numerous self-components, and freedom to be who one really is, not who one "should" be or is expected to be. It impacts mind, body, and soul dimensions. It is usually characterized by having achieved a state of self-actualization, a new understanding that includes examining and changing deeply held, unconscious beliefs and knowing one's purpose in life as a higher calling in life to give back to others. A transformed mind-set has experienced all the iSelf model distinctions. An *untransformed mind-set* is the opposite: one has no motivation to achieve self actualization, no motivation to examine or change beliefs, and no interest in discovering a higher calling in life, and one does not have an interest in learning about the self or any self-attributions common to all yet unique to each.

The self is not separable from mind, soul, or body, and is conceptualized as a holistic organism where each component reinforces the other. In this way, if we take care of our souls, then we will take care of our minds and bodies. Hence we have the thesis that we should be teaching children and adolescents about self-knowledge as a strategy to mental and physical well-being.

The demands of modern life have taken us away from our sense of self, our understanding of who we are, and our knowledge of what is important to us. Archetypal psychologist Thomas Moore (1992) puts into context the importance of proactively teaching the self to children, adolescents, and young adults: "The great malady of the twentieth century, implicated in all of our troubles and affecting us individually and socially, is loss of soul [self]. When soul [self] is neglected, it doesn't just go away; it appears symptomatically as obsessions, addictions, violence, and loss of meaning" (p. xi).

Throughout this book, I will be discussing a model of self that is holistic and can be implemented through schooling. The iSelf model, when implemented in schooling, proactively addresses human beings at the being level or the level of our souls.

In her own medical research into the mind-body connection and how to help people live more fully, founder of Harvard University's Mind-Body Clinic, Dr. Joan Borysenko (1995), asserts what is common to all human beings is a core self that seeks emotional, psychological, and physical healing:

> Despite our differences, we're all alike. Beyond identities and desire, there is a common core of self—an essential humanity whose nature is peace and whose expression is thought and whose action is unconditional love. When we identify with that inner core, respecting and honoring it in others as well as ourselves, we experience healing in every area of life.

Therefore, with the spirit of this quote—that we can heal in every area of life through identification with our inner core—I hope that we and the young people in our care can learn to love ourselves and each other more deeply through the ideas and discussions in this book.

## Well-Being and Education

There is such a lack of emphasis placed upon well-being and a lack of policies and practices to both intervene into and prevent the conditions and highlight the lack of rigor and commitment in the fields of education, psychology, and medicine. At present, the studies of "health and well-being," "education and schooling," and "psychological counseling" are three separate and distinct bodies of work and fields of study. One middle school research study on self-knowledge best practices (Brzycki, 2009), which includes a model of an integrated, whole person, attempts to bridge these fields and merge them into a cohesive whole. The fundamental assumption and common denominator is that all three involve people and that we can do more and need to do more for human well-being at this critical time in human history. Therefore, doing all that we can to empower the full potential of people in our society is the issue for our time. Clearly there have been numerous technical breakthroughs in physical health care, yet human behavior remains the obstacle to changing health-related outcomes (Schroeder, 2007).

Many of those who have an interest in making our world better will state that global warming and sustainability are the issues of our time. Others will state that it is the wide and growing disparity of wealth in the United States and internationally. When viewed from the present paradigm of thinking, these are true statements. Within the present paradigm of reality and of how we see human beings, the external-to-human perspective dominates.

Throughout this book I will be discussing whether or not we need a new paradigm—one that better frees and releases human potential and allows children, adolescents, and young adults to flourish. Primarily, our thinking needs to shift from the external to the internal, to what is going on inside human beings, as our first consideration as a pathway or strategy toward implementing a new mind-set—a transformed mind-set. From this transformed mind-set, the societal and educational focus is on the integrated self and psychological and physical well-being. From this transformed mind-set, there is an abundance of wealth for all people in the United States and worldwide. The problems of global warming and sustainability will be addressed and will be solved because in the new paradigm the internal well-being of each person is the priority, and we will take care of the planet and our environment due to self-interest and raised consciousness. People's health and well-being and therefore their quality of life are affected dramatically by lifestyle behaviors such as smoking, use of drugs and alcohol, poor diet, and lack of physical activity, all of which, according to leading health and well-being researchers, involve behaviors that are potentially controllable by the individual (Deci & Ryan, 2008).

All learning in life and in and out of the classroom require learning about one's self—one's professional competencies and interests and contributions to the greater good to empower our society and all people. I will be taking a hard look at the psychological approaches that could be used to empower the well-being of people in our society to improve the quality of life for individuals and families and for society as a whole. Woven throughout this discussion about psychological approaches will be arguments made and evidence supplied that serve to demonstrate the need for a new way of thinking about ourselves and our world, for a 21st-century paradigm change. In addition, in these times of economic uncertainty, where policies are put into place at federal, state, and local levels based on affordability, I discuss the economics of our educational policies and our health care policies in terms of value or returns on investment.

## A New Tool for Learning

The thesis of this book is that we need a new kind of mind or a new psychological tool to meet the demands of the 21st century, with a new theory that the most effective place to implement this new tool is through schools and schooling, using the iSelf model.

The study of the self in cognitive developmental psychology has taken on heightened importance due to the increasing awareness of the central, functional role that the self plays in development across the life-span. But although the importance of studying the self has grown recently in cognitive developmental psychology, there exists very little acknowledgement of this importance in education, medicine, or psychological counseling.

We know that young people today are feeling many stresses associated with modern life. Research has shown that these stressors produce issues of concern such as drugs, depression, obesity, alcohol, eating disorders, suicide, bullying, and cutting, among others. Young people need new strategies to deal with these concerns while going through them. We also know that young people today want to lead a meaningful life, to empower the fullest expression of their best and highest selves, and to enhance their abilities to experience more fully love, pride, happiness, self-respect, and joy.

K–16 schooling plays a dominant role in the lives of young people where they get to learn all these attributes. Much like adults use work and marriage to learn about and express these attributes, young people need opportunities to learn about and express these attributes as well. Where better than the place they spend approximately 8 hours per day?

In my counseling practice, I often hear a client say something to the effect that they want to be happy, or "my well-being is not where I want it to be." My interventions usually consist of transforming the paradigm of understanding that the client brings to our work through a process of finding meaning (Frankl, 1984). This approach is grounded in the following Rogerian (1980; 1989) paradigm: individuals have a future potential to be happy, to enhance well-being, to discover their own reasons for living a full life. This means that all individuals have it within themselves to create the life they can imagine.

A developmental outcome that is important to a positive life-course trajectory is *subjective well-being*, defined as "a person's cognitive and affective evaluations of his or her life" (Diener et al., 2002, p. 63). This important attribute is seldom measured in either studies of psychopathology or education, and yet, this is certainly one important measure teachers and counselors alike should utilize to assess their effectiveness.

The engaged life consists of using one's strengths and talents to meet challenges; our young people want to live an engaged life. It is of primary importance to educators and counselors to be able to teach our young people how to construct a self as the mediator between their inner life and external life, so as to be able to assess and take control of their subjective well-being. *Personal meaning* is where the self-system and positive psychology come together—the nexus of teaching and learning in schooling and psychotherapeutic contexts.

*Personal meaning* is an attribute from the positive psychology literature. It is important to consider that teaching and learning do not merely occur in K–16 classrooms or families. Children are on a constant quest for personal meaning. Once our children reach school age, other powerful forces compete as primary sources of learning, such as social media, peer groups, YouTube and other Internet sites, television, and others. Therefore, learning is ubiquitous and omnipresent and contributes to the social construction of reality. As individuals, we do not necessarily create our realities in a vacuum; creating reality is an interplay and complex dynamic among inner self and brain processes and external influences that draw out and call us toward the greater social good or, too often, toward the negative, where the mind of each self is the mediator or nexus of these dynamic processes. If young people learn from and interact with external elements without the tools for self-understanding, then their reality is pulled in the direction of those powerful external forces. Without a tool for self-understanding, young people grow up thinking that all learning is external without valuing their own inner strengths and talents and resources to create the life of their dreams. One implication of this belief is that they will not be of sound mind or body. This is why the self in schooling contributes to a new reality for a new society at this important time in our human history. We need this type of discussion and breakthrough in our abilities to understand a new kind of mind for the 21st century.

Take, for example, the recent development at the university level to address the well-being of 18- to 25-year-old young adults in their college educational experiences by hiring a well-being professional, as in this employment listing from Middlebury College for a director of health and wellness education:

> Middlebury College is seeking qualified candidates for a new position in our Dean of Students office. The Director of Health and Wellness Education will develop, implement and evaluate a broad-based health and wellness education program with a focus on alcohol and drug use, sexual assault prevention and response, stress management, and bystander intervention programs. (HigherEdJobs.com, accessed June 27, 2012)

Note the emphasis placed upon wellness education programs is likely reacting to mental and physical health crises, with a focus upon alcohol and drug use, sexual assault, and stress management. If throughout schooling we are teaching young people self-knowledge and how to create a paradigm shift in their abilities to experience life and create the life of their calling, we would then teach preventively and prior to college how to find inner peace and understanding of the stressors of modern life. The emphasis could be placed upon teaching self-knowledge using the iSelf model as a significant protective factor for use over one's life-span. Consider that all human beings go through numerous experiences that require us to have a solid foundation of self to draw upon that provides a prism and compass for overcoming impacts to our psyche, such as childhood sexual abuse, family divorce, job loss, and post-traumatic stress disorder (PTSD) for those serving in our wars, to name a few. Additionally, that this function now exists on university campuses is a strong indication that K–12 schooling is producing people who do not have the abilities to manage their own behaviors, underscoring the need to emphasize self-knowledge and self-determination so students can design the life they are meant to live, consisting of psychological and physical well-being.

My focus is on K–16 schooling in that self-esteem is the number one protective factor for all children, adolescents, and young adults in these grades. According to one important study on the importance of self-esteem when developing psychologically from adolescents to young adulthood, "growth curve analyses indicated that self-esteem increases from adolescence to middle adulthood, reaches a peak at about age 50 years, and then decreases in old age" (Orth, Robbins, & Widaman, 2012, p. 1), underscoring the need to teach self-knowledge and the iSelf model throughout K–16 schooling. Further, this same study found strong correlations between self-esteem and strong relationships, professional career success, and job satisfaction and health.

## Theory and Practice

This book includes both theory and practice. I want to emphasize both as being equally important and highlight the distinction that we often, in our discourse when discussing the condition of modern society, fail to place our thoughts and actions in the proper theoretical framework. This framework provides context and space for contemplation and thoughtful responses.

For example, in the summer of 2012 on CNN, Senator McCain was espousing the failures of the Obama administration's policies in the Middle East, and Syria in particular, as a failure in leadership. He asserted that the United States has lost its leadership position in the world. If viewed from an on-the-ground reality that too many Syrians are being killed needlessly, then this is a true statement: The United States, the world community, and the United Nations are not taking action to prevent killings at the hand of a repressive government. However, when viewed from the context or theoretical frame of neoconservatives' understanding of leadership, this means the use of power and military force are policy preferences.

Another leadership frame would be the use of and priority given to diplomatic processes to affect desired outcomes. This theoretical frame emerges from an understanding that the use of force through military might are proving to be ineffective means to a real positive outcome, as recent experiences in both Iraq and Afghanistan demonstrate. Yet in the "Muslim Spring," another leadership frame would call for empowering the individual as the means for societal transformations in the Middle East countries. This is evidence of the transformations occurring at the initiative and for the benefit of each individual in society; even ones that are repressed and have been for generations. Moving forward, how we act and determine policy depends on our theoretical framework.

As a culture, we do not place enough adequate emphasis on thoughtful inquiry with responses and conversation to make conditions better and jump too easily to reducible, immediate solutions that place confidence in technological solutions above human relations and cooperation. The word *theory* means looking at, viewing, reflecting, and referring to contemplation or speculation, as opposed to action. Therefore, theory is about creating something new, a new way of viewing circumstances or frame of thinking, as contrasted with applying that new way of thinking to change the circumstances. Theories are formed by observing and putting into context through language a body of evidence that depicts actual circumstances or the current realities. *Practice*, in short, means to implement or take steps to apply an idea or theory.

As an example of the distinctions between theory and practice, medical theory involves attempting to understand the causes and nature of health and sickness, while the practice of medicine attempts to make people healthy. These two things are related but can be independent, because it is possible to research health and sickness without curing specific patients, and it is possible to cure a patient without knowing how the cure worked. Education works the same way. Educational theory attempts to help us understand why education works or does not and what forces are at work that necessitate the thinking about new and important changes in the field, while teachers and other practitioners attempt to impact young people in their care in their day-to-day work. An effective teacher may not know the theories that shape his or her work and may yet indeed produce outstanding results.

The iSelf model is effective as an educational psychology and philosophy and best practice method to empower 21st-century skills in academics, improve psychological and physical well-being, or both. The iSelf model forms the theoretical frame for 21st-century learning in academic domains in that it deepens learning and teaches creativity, teamwork, career interests, and real-world problem solving, all by shifting the responsibility for learning to the student. From a transformed perspective, internal human emotions and psychological considerations come first, *a priori*, with external or circumstances secondary.

The untransformed view of our world and human beings places the external circumstances first. One recent view asserts that people are suffering from panic, depression, and psychosis due to connection addiction to the Internet and technology, or what *Newsweek* magazine called "iCrazy" (*Newsweek*, July 16, 2012) to characterize our human condition in modern times. People would not be "iCrazy" if they did not need something internally: whether to emotionally fill a relationship need, or feel a sense of belonging, or relieve a fear of not being able to survive economically, or psychologically understand the constant barrage of information and changes in the world, or to feel a connection to the greater consciousness and a spiritual connection to other human beings and the human condition.

In terms of state government policy, in Pennsylvania, the governor advocated that teachers in our public schools and state workers accept large cutbacks including reduction of pensions, while proposing $1.7 billion in tax cuts for oil and gas companies who reported $7.3 billion in quarterly profits for the first quarter 2012 (Levy, Associated Press, June 18, 2012). In this example, the human considerations clearly take a backseat to the economic, corporate-centric views that drive our thinking and policies in numerous domains. Through a human-centric, inner-self, or iSelf lens, those acute educator interests and views would be considered first because they directly affect the well-being of young minds, and we can use oil and gas profits and interests to serve these.

## Symptoms When People Lack Self-Understanding

I have worked with numerous types of people with a wide array of mental and physical illnesses and a wide array of intellectual capabilities and talents. It is helpful here to categorize people with symptoms that often remain under the radar of the typical Diagnostic and Statistical Manual (DSM-IV) categories and diagnosis. In fact, DSM-IV (2000) categories very often do not capture these subtle symptoms that can be identified and for which preventative interventions can be taken. These symptoms can be seen in children, adolescents, young adults, and adults of all ages. The critical variable is not age but rather the stage of consciousness and well-being.

I create these categories in an attempt to place them at the center of our transformed, inner-focused view of the world and because these capture most people in modern society, meaning we are all experiencing some or many of these symptoms. These categories describe everyday, normal people, not special or privileged people or those diagnosed with mental illnesses or serious physical conditions. As an expression of hope, the people in these categories can transform their lives to one of psychological and physical well-being and happiness.

Once you understand the power of paradigm shifts and transformed mind-sets on the world and reality, seeing the world through the lens of paradigms, ontological and otherwise, is rewarding because you see more of the underlying dynamics that are creating changes in our society.

Therefore, from a transformed mind-set, the following sections describe types of people who could benefit from greater self-knowledge.

### Uncomfortable in Your Own Skin

I had just gone through a series of personal transformation workshops during my 30s where my views of myself and others were changing rapidly and dramatically—a transformation at the level of my being, or ontological. I had stopped at a school crossing per instructions of the crossing guard where upon I looked to my left and walking on the sidewalk were groups of middle-school-aged children on their way home from school. All were talking excitedly, most highly animated, and having fun as schoolmates are apt to do after a full day of classroom learning, playground activities, and lunchroom friendships. One girl, skinny, fair haired, loaded down with a heavy knapsack of books and computers, was trailing one group of similar aged girls. They were busy laughing and putting their heads close as if they were talking about someone. Following behind, rushing to catch up was our loaded down girl, who had a crunched up, uncomfortable look on her face, uneasy in her skin and self, knowing at some level that she was being ditched by the other group of girls, her friends she thought, but did not know better. At that moment I committed myself to developing a personal development, self-understanding, and self-esteem program that would empower young people to feel better about themselves so that they would not feel so uncomfortable if not included or would not exclude in such a mean manner. I empathized with this young girl and immediately put myself in a time and place where I felt similar uncomfortableness with myself and my understanding of everyday relationships and life. In short, I knew that I could help young people through this developmental stage.

## A Little Off

Years ago there was a Matchbox Twenty song "Unwell" with these lyrics: "But I'm not crazy; I am just a little unwell. I know right now you can't tell. But stay awhile and maybe then you'll see a different side of me. I am not crazy, just a little impaired." In my more than 30 years of teaching and counseling adolescents and young adults, this lyric best captures the essence of their state of being. Not requiring mental health assistance, nothing really to diagnose, maybe borderline personality disorder, but most likely not. Yet clearly a person in this state of being is not manifesting, or on the path toward manifesting, his potentials, academic or others. Something is a little off regarding well-being, emotionally and psychologically. Teachers would not recognize the inner states of the children in front of them; their concern has been and continues to be on students' academic performance. A parent would not suggest that their child see a mental health professional for fear of stigmatizing their child and thus creating a mind-set of a self-fulfilling prophecy that they are indeed mentally ill. Clearly this would be an overreaction. Yet astute parents would most likely see or sense that something was off about their child. Other parents might not see it in that they themselves can't recall going through a similar phase, or they are just too busy living modern life, which is most likely the case. Counselors would be trained to diagnose a mild DSM-IV borderline personality disorder, evidenced with symptoms of not being motivated, not making friends, not excited about life, or even making friends with "shadows on the walls." They would recommend a series of sessions where talk of growing up or adjustments or other issues would be identified, but most likely, and I've seen this played out often, they would not have a model of assessment or intervention that would allow the patient/client to see for himself what is going on and develop a self-system to move past this temporary stage without harming dysfunctions impacting his identity development.

## Clueless

Some young people are completely unaware they have a self, complete with their own feelings, interests, needs, ways of processing, unique purpose in life, or other attributions. They may realize they are a part of a family, with a family dynamic made up of mother and or father, siblings, and possible pets. They do what they are told, dutifully go to school, do well enough academically; socially they have friends, participate in sports, modern culture, and life. Externally they are doing all right by all measures and from numerous perspectives—parents, teachers, coaches, relatives, and maybe even themselves. Yet they do not know that they have their own inner life, separate from the family or friends or culture. They internalize that what happens to their family members also is happening to them, or they do not know that they have their own feelings separate from others or that it is acceptable to have different views and feelings. Take a case where a parent is suffering from cancer and both parent and child keep their emotions bottled up, not realizing that they have these or unable to express these.

### Under Potentiality

Some people by all accounts are filled with potential, extraordinary capabilities, but for whatever reason or reasons are not manifesting them. Take, for example, the person who is a talented pianist, or artist, or intellectual (such as a scientist), or writer, or athlete who does not have the courage to participate in those activities that would bring out or encourage the expression of these gifts. Often external supports do not exist in either the family, school, or community for this person. This person, gifted as she might be, could potentially suffer in silence and just do what is easy for her, follow the existing rules, patterns, and steps.

Later in this book I will present a model of manifesting one's potential using the power of vision or dreams. This includes becoming clear about the present realities and circumstances, contrasted with what is possible or the potential that the person senses or knows. When discussing a personalized learning plan or personalized learning, I will discuss including personal potential into the plan. Much like Vygotsky's zone of proximal development (ZPD), the potential zone incorporates a number of self-attributions, such as a sense of purpose, motivation, self-efficacy, accomplishments, service to others, and so on.

How many of us live a life of quiet desperation hoping to one day being able to manifest our unique and full potentials in life? This is the major underlying antecedent to drug and alcohol abuse, a sense of resignation that our potential will never be manifest.

### Preharming

We all know the person who chooses a self-destructive lifestyle: that person who once got or gets perfect grades, starred or stars on the athletic field, and who was or is a perfect child at home, then turns to drugs, alcohol, aggressive behavior, cutting, or suicide. Once this person starts harming, then a DSM diagnosis can be made if this person seeks help. But brewing before self-destructive behaviors manifest is usually a lack of a feeling of self-esteem or self-knowledge in one of the dimensions in the iSelf model. Most directly, those who actually do self-harm or harm to others are not aware of their unique life purpose or dreams for their life and do not know how to access either. Therefore they blame others or themselves for their feeling of being stuck in a state of not being able to feel, with severe dissociation.

## A Deeper Look at Self

It is one of my goals that iSelf will do for educators, counselors, and health professionals what the theory of multiple intelligences (Gardner, 1993) did when first introduced—provide for a deeper look at the person in their care. It is also my goal to inspire human service professionals, teachers, counselors, physicians, pastors, and so on, to see their roles differently. Additionally, I would like the iSelf model to be used as a framework for a new model of education to replace No Child Left Behind 2001 (NCLB) and the reauthorization of Elementary and Secondary Education Act (1965; ESEA).

Knowledge of the self is the single most important competency to impart to children and adolescents to ensure health, well-being, and a positive lifecourse trajectory. The self, and in particular the iSelf model, is a lens through which to view and understand the condition of human being and the reality we have created. This new model focuses on ways in which education helps people reach their full and unique potentials in life. The iSelf model is situated at the intersection of psychology and education, and it challenges scholars and practitioners alike to forge new views and methods that will improve the quality of our lives.

## Internal and External Selves

Another important distinction to make that will enhance the readers' ability to understand and use the information in this book is that of "internal" or "inner" self, or what occurs within the mind of the person, and "external" or "outside" self, or what circumstances occur outside the mind of the person but within his or her realm of experience. This is important in that the majority of studies conducted in numerous fields that teachers and counselors draw upon for validation of new concepts address the external or circumstantial variables to the self. It is my hope that iSelf will inspire new research focusing on the inner life of the mind.

From the external circumstantial view, we discuss school reform by saying that our schools need to do more to change the system because of international competition or test score gaps among socioeconomic classes of students, or that companies will not have enough workers to fill our offices and factories. From the internal or inner-self and human-centric view, we sense the need for changes or reforms in our system of education because we feel that the potential of people is not being manifest; we see that we are not taking care of the highest species on this planet, human beings. We keep doing more of the same thing, expecting a different result.

The iSelf model is a lens for understanding young people who are not seeing or achieving their unique and full potentials in life. Contemporary schooling is the major obstacle because of our view or perspective.

The current purpose of the study or focus upon human capital is to increase the economic standing, not the well-being of society. Our reality is, therefore, an economic-centric view versus a person-centered view of the world. An economic-centric view of human capital places the focus upon external factors, such as the productivity of each person to produce goods and services to improve measures of gross national product (GNP). This view, however, minimizes the understanding of and focus upon the human condition, the inner state of people in our society, or a human-centric view. When we take the inner view over the external view (certainly not to disregard the external, but to make it subservient or secondary), we are taking an ontological or transformed view of human beings, and we understand that we actually create our realities and the external circumstance in life.

Some studies of human capital and child well-being are beginning to understand and underscore a combined, causal view (Bourdieu, 1985; Coleman, 1988; Putnam, 1993) that social capital leads to human capital and is an important protective factor in the lives of children. Situating the iSelf between these two bodies of work, child well-being and human capital, enhances the theoretical frames of both and could lead to further developed, better crafted strategies and comprehensive policies that strengthen society by helping individuals realize their full potentials.

Human capital is defined from the field of economics as "the abilities and skills of any individual, especially those acquired through investment in education and training that enhance potential income earning" (Collins Dictionary, 2003). Social capital is defined from the field of sociology as "the network of social connections that exist between people, and their shared values and norms of behavior, which enable and encourage mutually advantageous social cooperation" (Collins Dictionary, 2003).

Primary driving motivations for all human beings are to see and achieve their full and unique potentials in life, to matter, to make an impact, to live a good life. Therefore, from economics, sociology, psychology, education, and all points of view, it is important to ask the following questions: Why don't people achieve their full potentials in life? And what pathways to potential are available to us as human beings?

## Increasing Potential

As individuals, we are all concerned about understanding our potentials in life, to live a good life—it is our primary motivator. Scholars from economics and sociology consider the idea of potential from the point of view or perspective of economics and society, not from individual psychological and physical well-being, as we are discussing throughout this book. Even from the disciplines of psychology and medicine, external risk and protective factors are considered most often, before the inner self, which might not even be considered at all.

The iSelf model is a philosophy of education that situates the self of the student at the center of a new educational paradigm that has the possibility of transforming education and our world by teaching each school-aged young person self-knowledge.

Recent advances in educational psychology and psychology in general have come together into education in the form of teaching and learning that could serve to transform our system of education and schooling, yet psychology is not used widely or well in education settings. Additionally, the thesis of this book is that we need a new paradigm of education that serves people's needs and the needs of our society in the 21st century and beyond. From this view, this book is really about the psychological well-being of people and how this leads to physical health, which is a direct function of learning.

From the iSelf lens, therefore, psychological and physical well-being are a function of learning about the self. But where in our society does this learning occur? And where should it occur? School and schooling processes are the most direct applications for learning about the self and are at the heart of the iSelf model.

# CHAPTER 2

# A Possible Copernican Shift

Nicolaus Copernicus (1473–1543), author of *On the Revolutions of the Celestial Spheres* (first edition 1543 in Nuremberg), was the modern scientist who hypothesized that the sun was the center of the astronomical universe and not the earth. The self in schooling calls for a Copernican shift in our externally focused perspectives to an inner-self-focused, human-centric universe. This shift is a transformation in creating for yourself meaning—from who you are told you should be to whom you are meant to be. I believe that the iSelf model, when implemented in schooling processes, will create this Copernican shift, and that we have evolved cognitively as a human species to the point that we now want this shift and need this shift. Further, as we end one age, the current "information age," and seek to label the next wave of change that characterizes more fully where we are as people, the iSelf model will prove to be the framework that allows for the "integration age" to emerge and be analyzed and substantiated (described further in Chapter 5).

## The iSelf Model at the Center of Psychology and Education

This book is about wellness, the health and well-being of our children, and prevention of mental and physical health issues such as obesity, depression, cutting, drug and alcohol, anxiety, and so on.

The iSelf model depicted in Figure 1 both incorporates and informs numerous fields in psychology and education: teaching and learning methods; school reform initiatives such as 21st-century skills and next-generation standards, known as the *Common Core*; cognitive and positive psychology; and new counseling methods.

Figure 1 represents the iSelf model both informing these fields and being informed by them. The self is at the center of these, indicating a lens that

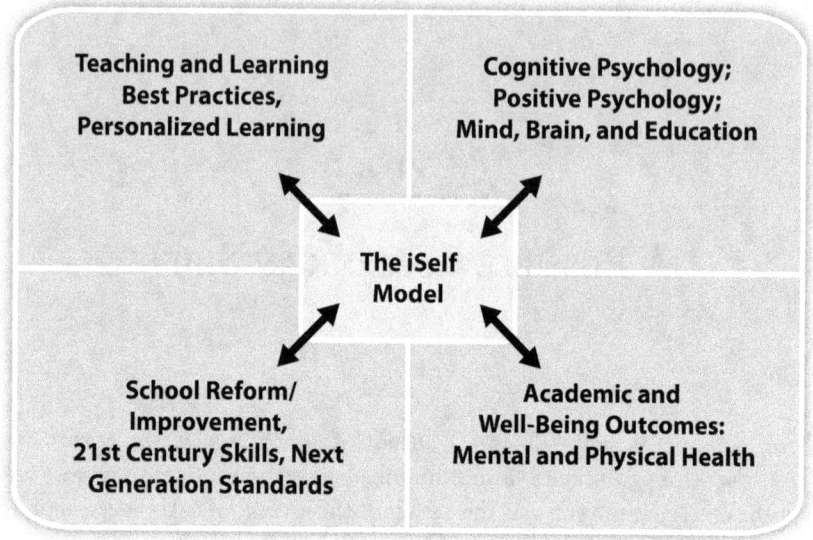

**Figure 1.** The Integrated Self at the Center of Psychology and Education

will enhance the practices and results in each of these fields. The integrated self-model (iSelf) should be at the center of all four fields and can potentially impact each.

## Issues in Cognitive Psychology

There is a growing acceptance that individuals have a significant degree of control over their own destinies in life, including their psychological and physical health, and that there is a direct connection between our psychological well-being and physical well-being. Neuroscientist Antonio Damasio affirms this view: "The fact that psychological disturbances, mild or strong, can cause disease of the body proper is finally beginning to be accepted, but the circumstances in which they can, and the degree to which they can, remain unstudied" (Damasio, 1994, p. 256). The National Institutes of Health (NIH) has funded numerous studies more recently to find out the causal relationship between psychological states of mind, such as happiness, and the common cold, as one example.

It is quite telling how even the high achievers in our society do not speak about or understand the cognitive attributes of their experiences. Sadly, many high achievers never cultivate any components of an integrated, healthy self.

Michael Jackson (1958–2009) died from an unusual overdose of physician-injected anesthesia. Using iSelf model as our lens, he did not have an awareness of an inner self, one with a higher purpose in life, or one who had an understanding of integrity, or who was able to experience inner peace. Clearly, the quality of his life was not to his potential, while having reached an extremely high level of potential as an artist but not as a human being. In spite of having all the usual protective factors in place—a close family, a large support system of doctors and mental health professionals, and high socioeconomic status—he was not able to experience restful sleep or inner peace that comes from finding a balance among the numerous iSelf components.

Many other highly successful people are not aware of an inner self or of the importance of finding a healthy balance among the self-attributions, and therefore, and analogously, are no different than average alcohol, food, and drug addicts.

In this celebrity- and reality-show crazed culture, I see a glimmer of hope for self-knowledge in the *Biggest Loser* television show. On the *Biggest Loser*, the show's weight loss participants experience a breakthrough in who they are in relationship to food, achieving a higher level of consciousness of knowing that they have choices in how they relate to food. Most often, what blocks them from seeing that higher view is a limiting belief and emotion; unidentified and not processed emotions block our ability to experience ourselves as separate from our external circumstances. Most often what allows people to place themselves first, to take care of themselves physically and to become physically well, is confronting a deeply embedded or unconscious belief that was formed around a highly emotional incident in their lives or learned through behavior modeling—usually in their families.

For example, growing up, and all through my college years and into early adulthood, I did not know that I was a separate person, separate from my family of five brothers and sisters and parents, separate from my peer groups or particular segments of society. I grew up not having a separation between me as a self and my family; my identity was and my reality was that I *was* my family. Therefore, when someone in my family was having difficulty, most often an emotional difficulty, so too did I. I was also experiencing that emotional situation as my own. As such, and being a family grounded in the Polish food traditions, I ate an abundance of traditional foods that were not healthy for my blood type or physical makeup. When I ate traditional meals with pork I experienced jaundice, and when I ate chicken or poultry products and wheat products such as pasta or breads, I experienced digestive problems, all contributing to weight gain and depressive moods. Yet the concept of making independent food choices was foreign to me.

An additional example is that when I saw people in Heineken beer commercials that were obviously from the upper crust of our society, my belief was that if I drank this beer I too would move higher than my middle-class station in life, simply by drinking and identifying with this brand. Fortunately, never an alcoholic, I certainly drank at the prompting of advertising and at peer and family gatherings, more heavily than I really wanted. Rather than prompting upward mobility, what actually happened was that the more I drank, the more I felt alone, far away from my own values and further away from my own inner connection to my soul, a feeling of emptiness and nothingness.

The wheat products that I ate served to depress my moods and impede my digestion, yet these were considered among the healthier food choices promoted by the U.S. Department of Agriculture (USDA). Therefore, through a combination of not knowing myself, believing in the power of advertising images, and of the importance of family and the knowledge of the USDA, I became caught in a vicious circle of eating what I had thought were the right foods, becoming depressed, drinking to lift my moods, and then becoming unhappy with myself and eating foods that made me feel better. From my transformed mind-set, I know now that it would have been better to clarify my own dreams for a better life, for a better quality of life than my own upbringing, rather than associate any type of beer with success and belonging.

So after becoming 75 pounds overweight, unhealthy physically and emotionally, I was watching marathon runner Joan Benoit competing in the 1980 Olympic games on television while I was eating a big ham-and-cheese sandwich, drinking a beer or two, and saying to myself, *I want to do that*. I immediately put down the food and drink and went running. Within 6 months, I had lost over 75 pounds in preparation for running the Boston Marathon. During this time, I experimented with numerous diets and lifestyle choices to arrive at one that worked for me and continues to this day.

On my long runs, I would think about my own self, purpose in life, and how to matter in this life.

### Is This the Best We Can Do?

We are all attempting to matter in the world, to make our unique differences, to know and manifest our unique purposes for our lives as a contribution to the greater good. What I have discovered through my own experience of transforming my conscious awareness about myself and my relationship to food, alcohol, and the external circumstances, and through my professional counseling and teaching experiences, is that to know your life's purpose is an important protective factor in life, whether child, adolescent, or adult.

In a study published in *Pediatrics*, researchers Goodman and Whitaker found that "depressed adolescents are at increased risk for the development and persistence of obesity" (Goodman & Whitaker, 2002, p. 1). This is just one of numerous studies that point to the causal relationship between inner psychological states, emotional well-being in this particular case, and physical health. In the iSelf model, emotions make up an important positive psychology attribute and component part of the self. Conclusive and compelling studies (Strauss, 2000; Wechsler, et al., 2004) demonstrate the importance of having a sense of purpose in life and strong self-esteem as important protective factors against obesity and other physical illnesses. Taken together, there is a causal relationship between depression and obesity, and self-esteem and obesity, as evidenced by these studies and numerous others.

## Social Construction of Reality

As humankind, we have evolved and developed, we have become who we are, but have we thought or reflected upon the process in the making and the outcome or progress to date? Where in the world do we encourage human beings who are in development to pause and think about our progress, as individuals, groups, societies, or as a human race? How far have we come?

Harvard University Professor Robert Kegan (1994) asserted that we do not have the mental paradigm or way of thinking to be able to handle modern life with its inherent complexities and stressors: "The expectations upon us . . . demand something more than mere behavior, the acquisition of specific skills, or the mastery of particular knowledge. They make demands on our minds, on how we know, on the complexity of our consciousness" (Kegan, 1994, p. 5). Take this assumption and place it in the context of the social construction of reality (Berger & Luckmann, 1966). Having reached this breaking point, we as a society are demanding that we create a new mind, a new model of how to survive and hopefully thrive and contribute to the continued and collective construction of reality. We especially need a new socioconstruction of the reality dynamic between the inner self and culture. This dynamic, between the inner self and culture, is important if we are to teach people to take control over their own destinies and create a better world, more consistent with what we can envision and see that is possible.

The thesis of this book is that we need a new mind to be effective human beings in the 21st century, and schooling is where the new mind can be taught and developed. As part and parcel of discussing a new mind, I am extending the conversation begun with the cognitive revolution in the 1950s with the work of Harvard University psychologist and father of the cognitive revolution, Jerome Bruner (1960; 1990; 1996), and others who at that time determined that our views of the human mind needed to change and broaden to take into consideration the growing role, in dominance and availability, of culture. Part of my theoretical reference is social-learning theory (Bruner, Bandura, et al.), which situates the mind between cultural forces and influences and the brain of the individual. The mind is not simply cognitive processing or our ability to process ever more complex thought processes and increased volumes of information available through ever-expanding technology. The new mind I am discussing is a biological development that involves both ontogenetic and phylogenic perspectives. We cannot escape the powerful influence of culture in modern society when shaping personal meaning.

From sociocultural theory, we know that human development begins at the social level and moves toward individual internalization (Vygotsky, 1987). Further, human beings develop in a variety of contexts or environments that surround the individual in a constant interaction. The aim of the cognitive revolution was "to discover and to describe formally the meanings that human beings created out of their encounters with the world" (Bruner, 1990, p. 2). According to Bruner, "as a species, we adapt to our environment in terms of what things, acts, events, signs are taken to mean. Meanings infuse our perceptions and thought processes in a way not to be found elsewhere in the animal kingdom" (p. 164). I argue that if reality is made not found, and the "reality we impute to the worlds we inhabit is a constructed one" (Bruner, 1990, p. 19), then we *can* create a better world if we more fully realize our collective influence on the culture and society.

## Evolution of Mind

Since the cognitive revolution began in 1956, the new cognitive science was redefined as the interdisciplinary combination of these six disciplines: psychology, linguistics, neuroscience, computer science, anthropology, and philosophy (Miller, 2003). To develop an integrated framework for these six disciplines is a daunting task, indeed. The lack of a common thread or thesis incorporating the disciplines results in the halting progress not only in the field of cognitive science but also in the inclusion and application of the disciplines to education and the development of the next generation of human beings. Therefore, the iSelf model proposes a new and integrated theory around a single learning system, or self-system, which is applicable to K–16 schooling to meet the demands of a changing society and of a changing human species.

The iSelf model draws upon human evolutionary psychology perspectives, which include phylogenic, "of or relating to evolutionary development" (American Heritage Dictionary, 1993), and ontogenic, "of or relating to the development of a single organism" (American Heritage Dictionary, 1993). Princeton University professor Dr. Michael Tomasello distinguishes the two, referencing our uniquely human lineage:

> The development of specific traits, such as the opposable thumb in humans, can be viewed both from the point of view of the development of that trait in individual organisms (ontogeny) and the development of that trait in the human lineage (phylogeny). The development of knowledge and knowing mechanisms exhibits a parallel distinction. Phylogentically, human beings recently arrived at a point in time where we can now manifest more fully the ability to be more fully human. To be more fully human means additional functionality of the mind to further identify with conspecifics, which led to an understanding of them as intentional and mental beings like the self. (Tomasello, 2000, p. 10)

Our new functionality of the mind is knowing about our own and others' selves. The brain has evolved to include new conceptions about the functions of mind, including a socioconstructed meaning (Brzycki, 2009; Damasio, 1994; Immordino-Yang and Fischer, 2009a; 2009b).

For the 21st century, the knowledge that we need and related learning systems to process, understand, and use are changing as well:

> We can consider the growth of an individual's corpus of knowledge and epistemological norms or his or her brain (ontogeny) or the growth of human knowledge and establishment of epistemological norms across generations or the development of brains in the human lineage (phylogeny). (Bradie & Harms, 2012)

Hence we must bring together ontogeny with phylogeny when developing a new kind of mind in order to characterize our present level of consciousness and determine what type of knowledge is critical to developing the species (what Piaget would call *genetic epistemology*). Phylogenic and ontogenic distinctions also help communicate the new theory of mind for impact and understanding throughout society. The adaptability of man is a cultural phenomenon. It is the product of learning and the ability to learn. Hence, to continuously adapt as cultural complexities grow exponentially, we need to place more importance on how we learn and more pointedly, how to enhance learning.

It is helpful to think about the iSelf model on the evolutionary continuum of human psychology. Examples include Freud's psychoanalysis and Piaget's genetic psychology, the personality and humanistic psychology offered by

Maslow and Rogers, the sociocultural model of Vygotsky, the social learning theories of Bandura, and the model of information processing and new perspectives of mind offered by Bruner and Damasio. Within the past 10 years, we have witnessed breakthroughs in our understanding of what it means to be human through positive psychology, created by Seligman, Csikszentmihalyi, Deci and Ryan, Ryff, and so on. All these bodies of knowledge helped integrate the individual with the culture, which makes possible the iSelf model and potentially a new mind that will help us to live more fully in the 21st century.

Phylogenically, education and psychology need to better merge and become the dominant tool for transmission of the culture and species. For most people in the world, and certainly in the United States, education takes place in a school setting, but equally and oftentimes more potently in culture, out in the world. Therefore, learning occurs constantly whether we are aware of it or not. Ontogenically, each individual human being needs a new way to learn that is holistic and provides tools to not merely survive but advance and flourish.

## Teaching and Learning

It is important to ask where the self is formed in modern society and where it should be formed. "Perhaps the single most universal thing about human experience is the phenomenon of 'Self,' and we know that education is crucial to its formation" (Bruner, 1996, p. 35). The inner and external selves interact in a complex dynamic to make meaning and shape our realities. The "Self requires an inner knowing and is shaped through an interaction with our worlds" (Bruner, 1996, p. 35). In schooling, the self too often becomes objectified and subjugated in a lower position to academic knowledge. Only when a student demonstrates academic knowledge is she awarded and honored, as if this is the measure of a good human being, or our humaneness, or our human potentials. In this way, our students are objectified through schooling processes.

We have reached a point in our cognitive development in which we overemphasize the academic and cognitive dimension when teaching our young students, hence limiting them as human beings. Based on our evolutionary development, we no longer need to follow an industry or production model of schooling where the focus is upon narrow, measurable, academic outcomes. We can now consider and teach to each individual child in a classroom setting as human beings with teaching and learning methods that focus on differentiated instruction (Tomlinson, 1999; 2000; 2001). Through schooling, we have the opportunity to see our children as whole people, not merely as intellects that learn about subjects that are too often detached from their own worlds or reality. We can focus upon what makes our children happy people through schooling.

What is needed, and what the iSelf model provides, is integration of pedagogy with a psychology of the self in order to produce human outcomes, more fully and holistically, and not merely academic or achievement outcomes. After all, it is noted philosopher and psychologist William James (1900; 1992) who commented about educating young people, saying that "the absolute, uncriticised reality of the self is the root of the whole matter" (James, 1992, p. 1055). By combining pedagogy of self with psychology of self, we can produce minds that are more able to handle the stresses, complexities, and psychological and physical well-being issues of our time.

To shift the focus to helping children and adolescents learn about themselves and all associated developmental attributions would bring into balance, a healthy balance, the role that academics play in a young person's life and contribute to a future life-course trajectory of success that includes health and well-being. Imparting attributes of human development should be the new focus of teachers and the purpose of schooling, rather than academic achievement—but certainly not at the expense of academic learning. Indeed, this shift does not lessen the importance of academic learning; it actually enhances it! Academic learning is one way to impart developmental attributes, and learning developmental attributes strengthens academic learning. However, we should not use the promise of these attributes primarily for academic achievement gains to satisfy administrative and education system needs for accountability.

Human developmental attributions are critical to children in all socioeconomic levels, where the inner life of children should be taught to them so that they may learn to transfer knowledge more effectively—that is, "far transfer" and make productive use of that self-knowledge in multiple contexts and situations. Therefore, self-knowledge learned through schooling would transfer to greater effectiveness when confronting, for example, highly emotional relationship issues. With the ability to transfer self-knowledge, self-directed learning and critical thinking attributions are also taught. To promise that academic learning and the development of purely cognitive capabilities through schooling will propel students on a positive life-course trajectory is false. In fact, it objectifies young people when we make it a higher priority to learn curriculum standards than self-knowledge—it is immoral to do so.

We teach teachers how to bridge the achievement gap by focusing upon rationales for failure and intervening. We also teach teachers how to rationalize failure—that is, socioeconomic levels contribute to learning achievement gaps. But I would suggest that the iSelf model and the learning of self-knowledge is the key strategy to implement to bridge this gap. This is precisely because all children need special attention, to their minds, hearts, and souls, their total self, to help them overcome common and prevalent life stressors where the risk factors are high for all children in the 21st century, and a little higher in certain communities. We can counteract the risk factors inherent in these inner-city environments by teaching the number-one protective factor: self-knowledge.

Students from all cultures, socioeconomic backgrounds, political views, and multicultural backgrounds have dreams of success and know themselves to be unique human beings on a special life course fulfilling their own purpose. As Vice President Joe Biden said in a speech in May 2012, "poor people have just as big dreams as rich people!" They want a system of education that helps them flourish and manifest their unique dreams and life purpose, not one that interprets their failures to differences in race or wealth or gender (McCarty, Hadley, Wallace, & Benally, 1991), to reinforce the inner view, or inner self of each student, versus the usual focus upon the external and circumstantial. We too often site economic status and say children from poorer neighborhoods are not able to achieve academically equal to their wealthier counterparts. The view is that poorer children have too many deficits for which to compensate, such as a troubled home life, parents not having attended college, and gangs and street crime, among others. Given this argument, as a society, we would have to wait until all poor children's societal and economic circumstances improved to see academic achievement gains from schooling. Certainly, the ideal is societal and economic fairness and equity. However, the transformed view, using the iSelf model as our lens, wouldn't wait, but rather highlight the unique interests and strengths of each person, regardless of socioeconomic status, and develop self-knowledge focused schooling processes, such as personalized lesson plans to meet each person's needs. This could be the great equalizer—the focus upon the person's mind and inner life—versus the economic status and external life, which is beyond the young person's or parents' control.

## Positive Psychology

The iSelf model integrates positive psychology to represent a new view of the human mind and a psychological paradigm that considers individual happiness, purpose in life, and intrinsic motivations to succeed in life.

Positive psychology represents an evolution in psychology and a significant contribution to our definition of mind in the iSelf paradigm. In fact, it represents one of the three legs of the original mission of psychology as it emerged in the United States at the beginning of the 20th century. In addition to "curing" mental illness and understanding how to develop superior intelligence, the third mission for American psychology was to bring about the enhancement of everyday living through increased individual happiness, noble purpose in life, and intrinsic motivations to succeed in life.

A contemporary of humanistic psychologists Maslow (1954; 1968) and Rogers (1961; 1989) is Marie Jahoda (1958), whose foundational work has helped us make a paradigm shift from *mental illness* to *mental health*, which is the focus of positive psychology and of this study. Her work provides a framework for understanding the conceptual distinctions of mental health applied to education. The six processes that contribute to mental health are (1) acceptance of oneself, (2) growth/development/becoming, (3) integration of personality, (4) autonomy, (5) accurate perception of reality, (6) and environmental mastery. All six of these processes are developed and learned through schooling and are critical success factors for a positive life-course trajectory. In a similar manner to Jahoda's influence, I hope to inform the new role of positive psychology in education and a new paradigm.

Schooling and our growth in psychological thinking has elevated our conscious awareness that there is a "self" to consider and that people can and should be happy. It has just been since the annual report of the American Psychological Association in 1998 that the newest branch of psychology, whose concepts include happiness, well-being, purpose in life, emotional intelligence, among other distinctly human traits, was introduced. This insight offers educators multiple pathways to develop the personalized human goodness that lies within each of us regardless of race, socioeconomic background, intellectual DNA, emotional and psychological capabilities, or gender. The iSelf model forms the foundation for personalized learning; it enhances and strengthens a teaching and learning model emerging in K–12 schooling precisely because it includes positive psychology concepts and attributions such as happiness and well-being.

Past American Psychological Association President and Professor Martin Seligman (2000; 2005; 2011) asserts that the goal of traditional psychology "was to bring patients from a negative, ailing state to a neutral normal state—from a minus five to a zero" (Seligman in Wallis, 2005). The vision of positive psychology is to bring human beings from zero to plus five and answer the question, "what are the enabling conditions that make human beings flourish" (Seligman, 2000)? This is an important question for educators, counselors, and medical professionals to consider when empowering the full and unique potentials of all children from all cultures and backgrounds. Therefore, the view of the human mind and a psychological paradigm that considers individual differences and how we construct our unique realities as part of an enabling condition should guide educators, especially in light of the increased stressors embedded in the 21st-century world we have created.

As our society becomes more and more complex (with growing multiculturalism with individual difference characterized by community and culture, two-income families striving to make ends meet and meet retirement and college expenditures among other financial stressors, and communication tools such as social media), our outdated, 19th-century education system increasingly does not deliver but still promises a better life through doing well in school. These stressors multiply to force children into a "minuses" psychological state. Children and adolescents therefore will require additional cognitive and socioemotional (Cohen, 2006; Duckworth, Steen, & Seligman, 2005) tools, processes, and supports to maximize learning and development outcomes in terms of not only academic achievement but also health and well-being. "Happy people are healthier, more successful, and more socially engaged" (Cohen, 2006, p. 203); therefore we should develop models of understanding children's happiness and what teachers can do to impart our children's health and well-being (Deci, Nezlak, & Sheinman, 1981; Deci & Ryan, 1985; 1995; Glas, 2006; Murphy & Mason, 2006).

The fact that children's health and well-being and their full and unique potentials are not being maximized using all the pedagogical, psychological, and medical methods available, demands that we study teaching, counseling, and medical best practices that impart a healthy self through schooling. Therefore, educators should consider the view of the human mind and a psychological paradigm that addresses individual differences and how we construct our unique realities as part of an enabling condition. I argue that teachers can do so much more to impact the human development of students as well as academic achievement, and given that schools are in the *people* business, they have the responsibility to do so.

## Academic and Well-Being Outcomes

The changing course of curriculum requires that it reflect societal changes toward self-awareness and well-being, or a whole-child perspective. Unfortunately, societal changes have brought about current child well-being and school performance statistics that are tragic and unconscionable.

These statistics require a change in our curriculum and education, as well as in health policies, toward a focus upon the mental and physical health and well-being of our children. Children are experiencing many problems in and out of schools. It is critical for educators to shift their focus to imparting the integrated self-system and positive psychology attributes in order to teach children how to flourish in life through schooling.

To impact child well-being statistics requires rethinking our curriculum and other schooling processes, to establish a more balanced view, where well-being is valued along with academics and elevated to a higher priority when considering the purpose of education in the 21st century.

Examples of tragic child well-being and school performance statistics include school dropout rates of approximately 25% for all students in the United States, according to the National Center for Education Statistics (NCES, 2005a; 2005b; 2011). Most recent statistics found that graduation rates for the largest 50 cities are 51.8% (EPE Research Center, 2008). Our K–12 system of education does not work for over a quarter of students going through this system—certainly not creating conditions for our students to flourish academically through schooling. Our system of education is intended to provide school-aged children with the tools to succeed in life, but a large percentage are not taking advantage of this system of education. For example, in 17 of the 50 largest U.S. cities, fewer than half of the students who entered high school in 2003 ended up graduating. In Detroit, not even one in four students finished high school (*Chronicle of Higher Education*, April 11, 2008).

We are also failing our children who stay in school. In Pennsylvania, less than 50% of 11th graders are proficient in math, 20% are not proficient in reading, just 44% of students attend college, only 28% receive college degrees, and only 44% of high school graduates possess a college-ready transcript (Pennsylvania Department of Education, 2005). Therefore, school-aged children are not engaged in their schooling and are not learning the essential academic tools to succeed in life in the 21st century.

According to the Centers for Disease Control (CDC), approximately 60% of our children are overweight, and 20% obese (CDC, 2011), with approximately 70% of adults overweight or obese. In 2003–2004 there was an increase of teen suicide of +76% among 10- to 14-year-old girls over the previous year, a +32% increase among 15- to 19-year-old girls, and a +9% increase among 15- to 19-year-old males (CDC, 2007). If teachers are imparting self-knowledge and positive psychology attributes through the iSelf model, then they will be contributing to the well-being of children—a critical indicator of success across the life-span. If our system of education is producing more happy children, then these statistics on obesity and suicide would not be so pronounced.

Whichever manner you use to assess student outcomes from K–16 schooling, well-being or academic, we are not meeting even minimum standards, let alone a higher vision for what is possible for each student. The vision of the iSelf model is to empower young people to a higher vision and a better quality of life, or a "plus 5." As educators, counselors, and mental and physical health practitioners, we know something is not quite right with well-being outcomes, and we want to do more to empower our young people, yet we are not certain what to do or how to do it. We do not have a paradigm for thinking through these integrated, complex problems or to effectively combine education and psychology.

We are starting to notice the negative well-being outcomes because they are having an economic impact. Children that are products of schooling processes become working, productive citizens, making our society a better place or not. Many have speculated that with the growing body of evidence of a myriad of mental and physical health problems (whether via the decreasing ability of schooling to provide a high-quality work force or a mind-set that does not provide for more creative thinking to solve the problems of the 21st century), the quality of our children's lives in future generations will be poorer, for the first time in American history.

Additional evidence of the financial impact includes the fact that approximately 75% of all health care expenditures go toward behavior-based illnesses (Borysenko, 1987), so if we provide early and preventative interventions, we could potentially save billions of dollars in direct costs. For example, in 2010, the United States spent more than $2.6 trillion on health care (Centers for Medicare and Medicaid Services, 2010), including almost $71 billion on treating mental illnesses, and the total expenditure for treatment of substance abuse in the United States was $600 billion in 2012 (National Institute on Drug Abuse, 2012). To underscore the economic argument for early interventions into child and adolescent well-being through schooling, "the estimated annual cost of treating obesity in the U.S. adult non-institutionalized population is $164 billion or 16.5% of national spending on medical care" (Cawley & Meyerhoefer, 2012), and has steadily increased over the years with no end in sight. Indeed, according to a recent study given present trends, in 13 states, 60% of adults will be obese by 2030, adding an additional $66 billion annually to our health care costs (Levi et al., 2012).

More than half of Americans are either overweight or obese. Moreover, the prevalence of overweight and obesity has increased by 12% and 70%, respectively, over the past decade. This trend is alarming, given the association between obesity and many chronic diseases, including type 2 diabetes, cardiovascular disease, several types of cancer (endometrial, postmenopausal breast, kidney, and colon), musculoskeletal disorders, sleep apnea, and gallbladder disease (Finkelstein, Fiebelkorn, & Wang, 2003). I argue if we took merely a portion of these expenditures and invested in the well-being of young people, this investment would provide a substantial return to the quality of people's lives and to the fabric of our society. We are operating in a paradigm of crisis instead of a paradigm of prevention in health care and in education.

It is our paradigm, including our inherent guiding beliefs, that structures our activities and the specific problems upon which we choose to focus. It is our paradigm that makes sense of the facts or the circumstances we are now experiencing. Kuhn (1962) identifies a "crisis phase" in the changing of paradigms. He defines it as "when significant anomalies, inelegances, challenges, and the like accumulate to the point where the reigning paradigm is increasingly felt to be failing or discredited in the eyes of a significant proportion of the relevant community" (Kuhn, 1962, p. 184). As a counselor and a teacher working with people, I believe we are in need of a new paradigm for understanding and impacting people. If we shift our paradigm to prevention and to health and well-being, that would help children and adolescents learn about themselves and all associated attributions, bringing into balance, a healthy balance, the role that academics plays in a young person's life through schooling experiences and contributing to a future life-course trajectory of success and well-being.

**CHAPTER 3**

# A New Kind of Mind

What kind of minds are we creating through schooling and cultural media, and does this serve humankind? Mind, brain, and education (MBE) researcher and pioneer, Antonio Damasio, weighs in on this debate:

> The truly embodied mind I envision, however, does not relinquish its most refined levels of operation, those constituting its soul and spirit. From my perspective, it is just that soul and spirit, with all their dignity and human scale, are now complex and unique states of an organism. Perhaps the most indispensible thing we can do as human beings, every day of our lives, is remind ourselves and others of our complexity, fragility, finiteness, and uniqueness. (Damasio, 1994, p. 252)

Further, Csikszentmihalyi said:

> Our minds, in reflecting on what we see, endow these images with separate identities, identities they have only in our imagination. This is the process of reification, by which we attribute reality to mental constructions. The self is such a reification, and certainly one of the most significant ones. We usually think of it as a force, a spark, an inner flame with an indivisible integrity. Yet, from what we know now, the self is more in the nature of a figment of the imagination, something we create to account for the multiplicity of impressions, emotions, thoughts, and feelings that the brain records in consciousness. (Csikszentmihalyi, 1993, p. 216)

Does schooling encourage the process "reflecting on what we see . . . to endow these images . . . in our imaginations" and the "uniqueness of our souls and spirits?" Which reality are our children learning through schooling, and are we teaching children how to construct reality or just take what is taught as their reality? Do we teach children that their emotions are important in the growth of their consciousness? Do we need a new view of schooling in modernity in terms of the type of minds we are creating and producing? Criticisms of schooling and of our system of education have always existed. This is largely due to the importance placed upon receiving a good education and its value to empower a positive life-course trajectory, including obtaining a means to a higher standard of living. John Dewey's (1859–1952) progressive education hoped to place the child at the center of schooling and of pedagogy to counter the prevailing view that schooling was harsh, harsher than working in the factories of the day. Public schooling had emerged at this time as a preferred alternative to keep youth busy and productive. However, Dewey's child-centered model relied too much upon the teacher for learning, and hence it was not sustainable when implemented on a broad scale. Compulsory schooling was enacted on a state-by-state basis and finally completed in the United States nationwide in 1917. At this time, schooling consisted of rote learning, concentrating on basic skills of reading and arithmetic. So we can see that to shift the education debate to incorporate the child's interests was certainly a breath of fresh air and welcomed by numerous educators and parents alike; although, because the child-centered approach was so new, some parents and educators were concerned that children would not receive a good education, like the type that they received. Anytime a dramatic change is introduced into our system of education, people resist it. This is because they are taught to believe that "the system" that they were taught in worked for them and provided basic skills necessary to survive economically in the world. What is missing is a paradigm that the system can change to empower people to thrive, flourish, and achieve their full and unique potentials, and not merely survive—a new paradigm to consider.

Since the early part of the 1900s, there has been a battle for the hearts and minds of children occurring on the battlefield of schooling. Various groups attempt to influence the nature of the education received by young people realizing the close connection between society's needs and the mechanism for satisfying these needs—schooling. We have a view of the purpose of education based on what we feel society needs. In today's educational paradigm, it is to supply quality employees to meet 21st-century demands in the workplace. At the heart of the debate is the type of knowledge that is important, given changes in society and modern life.

## Creativity

There is a loud call and need for schooling to produce more creative people at a time when schooling has reached the end of one paradigm and needs to create the next. Sir Ken Robinson's (2001) breakthrough work advocates for a new purpose of education, to empower the creativity of people, which is a key 21st-century skill required by employers. While a noble purpose, I sense Robinsons struggle with internal versus external motivations. On the one hand, he indicates that creativity is a 21st-century skill required by employers. On the other hand, he asserts:

> Education has an economic function; this does not mean that the functions of education are wholly economic. Education has many social, personal and community purposes that have to be balanced with broader economic functions. Human intelligence includes the capacity for academic activity; this does not mean that academic activity is the whole of intelligence. (Robinson, 2001, p. 93)

Robinson argues the need for creativity is driven by the global economy. He comes from the old paradigm of why education is important—to supply companies with workers. Hence his argument and numerous creativity studies come from the external view, externally driven, by corporate America, versus internally, out of an innate desire, talent, or inspiration. Within this paradigm, we will get more of what we already have, not a transformation of the entire system of education, which I am arguing is needed and called for by humankind.

A transformed mind-set and paradigm, and the one called for by society today, would be one based on our human potential and our abilities not only to be creative but to literally create who we are and a new reality for human being and our society. If individual well-being or a whole person's happiness is the foci, then productive, creative, emotionally competent people will emerge from our system of education—the type of attributes we want to make our society and companies better. To create a better society and better workers, we need to create better people first. iSelf demonstrates that we can and should teach children what is inside themselves as the most direct pathway to building a better society and work force through better people. We are increasing the social and human capital through education in a very direct manner: Each person can improve our society and has a special and unique role and responsibility to do so. We are being called to change society for the better, and if we teach children what is inside them, which is the real driver of economic and cultural change and achievement, we will change the paradigm to meet the human needs of our time.

The study of creativity is also grounded in the positive psychology (Csikszentmihalyi, 1997; Rogers, 1954; Sternberg, 1999; Sternberg & Lubart, 1995) branch of psychology and finds its home in the humanistic curriculum philosophy. The work of Mihaly Csikszentmihalyi (1997), in particular the concept of "flow," points us in the most appropriate direction for both psychologists and educators who are attempting to impart this important attribute. *Flow* occurs when one's being is totally engaged in an activity, so much so that it is described as being physically aware and totally present. One example from sports is the experience of skiing, when you are carving up the slopes with ease and grace with perfect S curves on newly fallen snow. You are totally present to each snowflake—temperature, bodily movements, your experience. Thoughts are few if at all. You are in a state of being, suspended from the circumstances yet totally aware of them—almost a state of nirvana. In this state of being, all is possible, a feeling of hope and possibility overcomes, and you can see goodness in everything and in all.

This state of being, or flow, is also possible in any domain, in school, in relationships, while driving along a country road, among others. The key to creating flow and this state of being where creativity is possible is to suspend the cognitive thoughts around survival, financial worries, relationship problems, or those daily problems we face, and think about what is possible for yourself, significant others, and for all—what is known as the "self–other–all" method of teaching and learning—and transform consciousness through therapeutic contexts. I have had numerous experiences of this when drawing and painting, teaching, or running—these are deeply personal experiences. These are the environments where I most often find myself able to lose myself in the moment and have these deeply personal experiences. The settings for these moments will vary from person to person, but every individual is capable of achieving this state of flow—each just needs to seek out the places where it is more likely to happen. Teachers and counselors can teach students and clients how to create these experiences for themselves.

## Pedagogy That Empowers

Paulo Freire (1921–1997), pioneer in humanistic schooling and a pedagogy that empowers everyday human beings to change society, whose work is known as *critical pedagogy*, has inspired generations and millions of like-minded educators to teach and learn in ways that will create social change and make conditions better for the oppressed and for all.

In today's world, as we witness the "occupy Wall Street movement," the 99% feel oppressed and therefore are candidates for this type of learning—pedagogy to free humankind. Haven't we as an advanced democracy moved beyond the oppressor–oppressed dynamic? People still, today, "have adapted to the structure of domination in which they are immersed, and have become resigned to it, are inhibited from waging the struggle for freedom so long as they feel incapable of running the risks it requires" (Freire, 2000, p. 47). This characterizes the plight of most of us: We are resigned to exploring what is possible for each of us, to free our souls and spirits from our narrow education received from schooling and in culture through the media. Unconsciously we make the decision to conform and resign ourselves to the power structures in place, and this is just what those in power, the "1%," want. The paradigm that is emerging is one where our spirits and our souls want to be free—free from the narrow mind-set, from the belief systems and behaviors of the present paradigm we are experiencing in our society.

According to Freire, critical pedagogy is designed for the purpose of enabling the learner to become aware of and conscious of the conditions in his life, in society, and to have the necessary skills, knowledge, and resources to be able to plan and create change. It is consciousness-raising. Critical pedagogy empowers the learner to discover new possibilities and then act on them. As our society is constantly changing more and more rapidly, so too should schooling and the purpose of education change to reflect the new realities and inherent challenges. Critical pedagogy is as relevant today as it was when it was first introduced in 1970.

Freire began to focus upon the importance of self-knowledge, self-reflection, and interpsychological relationship between the self and others: "Humans, however, because they are aware of themselves and thus of the world—because they are conscious beings—exist in a dialectical relationship between the determination of limits and their own freedom" (Freire, 2000, p. 99). I go further. It is my hope that the iSelf model will help us engage that *dialectical relationship* to create the need for and the framework for the transformation of the self and of schooling—one that frees our individual and collective souls and spirits to manifest our unique purposes in life as our destinies. I have discovered that this creates inner peace within oneself and the expression of unconditional love to others.

## Education Aligned With Psychology

As we situate new theories of psychology and education within paradigms or ways of thinking about situations or problems (whether or not our present paradigm is working), it is appropriate to go deeper into the important work of Thomas Kuhn (1962), who introduced us to the ideas of paradigms and paradigm shifts and causes of revolutions. Kuhn suggested that, in modern culture, explanations are the foundation stones for imaginative conceptual schemes that define not only the pursuit of knowledge but the very way people perceive and experience reality. He claimed that ultimately these schemes stand or fall not on logical criteria but on the basis of (1) their adequacy as efficient devices for summarizing bits of information, (2) their ability to provide emotional satisfaction and thus to inspire commitment, and (3) their fruitfulness for generating predictions of additional observations—that is, "their effectiveness as guides to research, and as frameworks for the organization of knowledge" (Kuhn, 1962, p. 40).

Within the industrial schooling paradigm, the way we perceive and experience reality in modernity, the methods and processes used in both education and psychology fit; they are adequate for explaining why education works or not and why people thrive or not. Our usual explanations have provided emotional satisfaction, inspired commitment, and helped organize how we perceive two bodies of knowledge (education and psychology). However, we have not explored a new paradigm for human being and for education and psychology that would empower what is possible for human beings by *combining* both fields—education with psychology.

Our emotional responses to the critical educational issues of our time—ensuring the health and well-being of our youth, living a life of fulfillment and satisfaction, and seeing and achieving our unique potentials life—have been numbed. Schooling has successfully dissociated our conscious selves from our abilities to feel and take action to rectify our situation. The term *dissociation* is a clinical term to describe the separation of our psychological processes from our feelings and experiences. Dissociation often occurs following a trauma, such as childhood abuse, family divorce, and violent events, among others, and in this way it is a natural defense mechanism. Related disorders also help to explain why our youth are in such a critical state in terms of their health and well-being, and include depersonalization and dissociative identity disorder, to name a few (American Psychiatric Association, 2000). If the reader construes that schooling itself can be abusive in shutting out and denying emotions, and therefore enabling these disorders, the reader would be correct.

There are schools that do many things well, but within a paradigm and context that is both outdated and narrow, not the new and needed context of potential and possibilities and of mental and physical well-being. Our ability to produce a better society through better people depends on this new contextual view. We need a system of education that will produce a breakthrough in what is possible for our society, to see and achieve our innate potentials in life. When we do this, we can resolve anger, political positioning and vitriol, bullying and man's inhumanity to man, and emotional confusion at key transitions in life-course development.

## The Standards Based Paradigm Is Ineffective

The purpose of education since the release of *A Nation at Risk* (1983) and the No Child Left Behind 2001 (NCLB) era is to train workers for industry, manufacturing, and service-sector jobs that require a baseline of basic skills. This purpose has not changed since the beginning of the 1900s and continues today with the call to train students with those 21st-century skills required for newer technical and collaborative requirements. However, the call for higher and higher standards in K–12 schooling has not materialized, meaning standardized test scores that measure basic reading, math, and science skills are dismal at best. So what do educational policy makers call for? New Common Core standards that are considered more difficult and rigorous and include higher-order thinking skills that better prepare students for college and 21st-century careers. This may sound reasonable within the present paradigm, but it is not.

Originally NCLB 2001 called for 100% of all students to be at the basic level by 2014; however, the current consensus view is that this goal is unattainable. So when leaders call for even higher standards, it does not make sense. The alternative is to make certain that we train students in self-knowledge, tap into their inner motivations to succeed, teach them to dream of the type of life they want, and teach socioemotional, whole child well-being strategies that produce healthier, happier people. Then students will succeed at standards that are even higher than those called for by policy makers through the Elementary and Secondary Education Act (ESEA) reauthorization or Race to the Top funding criteria.

In the face of financial constraints, NCLB is becoming obsolete, in that more than half of the U.S. states have applied for and received waivers from the law's requirements. A new understanding is emerging that NCLB subject content standards are too narrow and do not impart higher-order cognitive, creativity, and communication skills called for by industry. The Common Core standards have been developed to answer this call for college and career readiness. Note that these standards hold the promise of better preparing adolescent learners for college and career readiness within the standards based paradigm, not the self-based or well-being-based paradigm discussed in this text. Once again, this is a new attempt to sell the old promise that these new standards will deliver on the promise of a better quality of life; all the while, over 50% of college students drop out.

The Common Core standards aim to further develop critical cognitive skills needed for 21st-century jobs; they still promise a better life through learning basic skills. What policy makers are essentially doing is promising a positive 21st-century life and career with adherence to the basic skills mindset taught through the old paradigm.

Our paradigm of understanding human beings and our system of education can either constrain or limit what is possible or provide freedom and new possibilities. As we collectively discuss which paradigm of education is appropriate for the 21st century, it is my hope that our discussion is around education for the future of human beings, which will require a new focus upon teaching what it means to be truly human.

Do we as a society want to reinforce those attitudes, beliefs, and behaviors from our past, or do we want to transform these to a more enlightened and transformed view of human being? The purpose of education in modern society, in the face of our tragic outcomes, should be to teach self-knowledge in service to the health and well-being of all humankind.

A new kind of mind is one where we are self-aware, able to process the vast amounts of information and stimuli received through everyday living, constructing ourselves and our realities based on both the internal and external integration. A new kind of mind is engaged in a continual inquiry into one's life purpose, dreams, and happiness, referenced by which results or evidence exist in one's life that demonstrates these attributes, effectively combining iSelf model attributes for service to a greater good and the ability to experience inner peace, love, understanding, and kindness, and then express these fully.

**CHAPTER 4**

# THE INTEGRATED SELF-MODEL DESCRIPTION

The integrated self-model (iSelf) is the lens to understand both the theory and practice of empowering the inner life of people, including their motivation, emotions, purpose, cognition, schema, character, personality, self-esteem, and locus of control, among others discussed in this chapter. As we are theorizing that we need a new kind of mind for the 21st century, it is also essential to include the external to the inner self influences, or the social construction of reality, to arrive at a complete and whole picture of the self of a person, and then include this view in our iSelf model.

When the iSelf model is taught through schooling, we will empower the mental and physical well-being of children and adolescents. Teachers, counselors, and parents will help students achieve extraordinary academic and well-being results. These results will be due to the context from which we come—that of seeing the unique potential of each person and not the deficit of what needs to be taught to bring a student to basic or proficient levels of content knowledge.

Academic content knowledge is not enough. Full human potential and excellence are not possible until we teach self-knowledge through the socioconstructivism of well-being and the use of language to create our frame of reality.

All iSelf model distinctions are meant for healthy, normal, functioning, nonpathological people, as well as those with more acute psychological needs. In addition, the iSelf model is meant for all developmental stages, although it is best when used with children who are at least 8 years old, following Piaget's (1936; 1957) concrete operational stage of development, when the abilities to classify, seriate, and understand reversibility are functioning.

Underlying the iSelf model is a fundamental belief that we—parents, teachers, counselors—can turn over more to the child. In this way we are teaching self-responsibility, including how to construct a self that represents a child's higher purpose and greater vision for what is possible, without the limitations, oftentimes unconsciously communicated to the child by the parent, teacher, or counselor.

Elementary and secondary education teachers are deeply concerned about student academic achievement and the effectiveness of their teaching styles. Recent research demonstrates the direct connection between good teaching and student results and between good curricula and student outcomes. Teachers are also deeply concerned about the well-being of their students. In my experience and research studies, teachers often ask, are my students better people *and* better students as a result of my influence upon them in the short time that I have them in class (Brzycki, 2009)?

## Why Teach Self-Knowledge in Schooling?

The self is the number one protective factor for schools and parents to impart. We know that young people today are feeling many stresses associated with modern life. Research has shown that these stressors lead to drug and alcohol use, depression, obesity and other eating disorders, suicide, bullying, and cutting, among others. Young people need new strategies to deal with these concerns as they go through them and for the rest of their lives. When we help our students handle these everyday stressors and manifestations by teaching self-knowledge in schooling, they are intrinsically motivated to learn and, in my experience, perform way beyond our highest expectations.

Children are experiencing many problems in and out of schools. It is critical for educators to shift their focus to imparting self-system and positive psychology attributes in order to teach children how to flourish in life through schooling. Further, there is no one model of self or theory of self in schooling or counseling psychology or health that allows for both assessment and interventions. If we utilized a common model of self, then we would have better results across professional service providers in education, psychology, and health. If we want to see both academic and well-being outcomes from schooling processes, then we need to utilize a uniform, well-structured concept or model of self, as in the iSelf model presented. When we understand that the learning that occurs in schooling and counseling is the same and that the learning pathway is the self and one or more components of the iSelf model, service providers will utilize the well-structured and well-researched iSelf model.

## iSelf Model Attributions

I situate my definition and use of self in a postmodern, socioconstructivist view where the self is socially constructed through a dynamic interaction between interpsychological and intrapsychological processes. The iSelf model incorporates self-system and positive psychology attributes that reinforce one another through development across the life-span and mostly through K–16 formal schooling experiences. An analogy would be a mobile, where one element, when moved, impacts all other component parts to varying degrees. By way of example, if a student is clear about her unique purpose in life (one attribute), this may impact her motivation to succeed (another attribute) by making larger contributions to the greater good envisioned.

Previous research conducted on self-system and positive psychology attributes typically isolates one of many attributes or at most looks at the relationship between only one attribute and school achievement. That view minimizes the holistic nature and dynamic that exists among all component parts of the self.

The iSelf model incorporates self-attributes identified by numerous progressive educators and humanistic psychologists. William James (1900) offered a view of a self in the early 1890s: "A man's self is the sum of all that he can call his" (p. 291). According to James, this includes the inner dimensions of self, such as feelings, thoughts, and spiritual understandings, and the outer dimensions of self, such as physical and social interactions. The inward life is the central nucleus of the self. Dewey (1916) extended key distinctions of the self and their application to education to include moral development, interests, conscious purpose, desire, and reflection, among others. He also placed these distinctions at the center of teaching and learning, with what is known to educators as "child-centered pedagogy," which characterized the progressive movement throughout the 1920s and into the early 1950s (Cremin, 1964). Dewey (1916) encouraged educators to never see the self as complete—that it is always "becoming," which I take to mean always changing, growing, and developing.

Founder of humanistic psychology, Carl Rogers (1961; 1980), placed our experiences at the center of the process of constructing or coming to know ourselves. He founded "client-centered therapy," widely used today, in which the discovery of the self of the client is at the heart of well-being and success pathways. Humanistic psychology scholars regard self-actualization, discovery of self, and self-understanding as important to learn through life's experiences. Rogers (1961; 1980) theorized that education requires a "whole person" focus, which he defined as the bringing together of the affective with the cognitive mind and the body. He asserted that the whole person goes to school, not just the intellect.

When a person's self—mind, body, and soul—are in a state of balance, when there is a clear understanding of each of the iSelf components, many positive qualities come into being. One such quality, for example, is character.

## Character

Character is formed or shaped through life experiences that both create and inform each of the self-distinctions and dimensions. Said another way, character is achieved when there is integrity or an alignment among one's purpose in life, dreams, and commitments, and one's approaches to achieving these are aligned with the results that show up in one's day-to-day reality. Erikson (1963; 1968; 1980) offers a complementary view: The most important event at this stage (stage 8—ego integrity versus despair) is coming to accept one's life and reflecting on that life in a positive manner. According to Erikson, achieving a sense of integrity means fully accepting oneself, the good and the not so good. Accepting responsibility for one's life and being able to correct mistakes from the past and achieve satisfaction with the self is essential. The inability to do this results in a feeling of despair. In today's world, too many of us feel despair and we lack integrity because we do not have a model to know ourselves well enough to reflect upon our lives and to know right from wrong.

There are many good descriptions of character traits from the character education literature, listed as follows:

- *Responsibility.* Doing what you say you will do; being accountable and dependable
- *Perseverance.* Pursing goals with determination and resilience
- *Caring.* Demonstrating kindness through feeling empathetic toward another
- *Self-discipline.* Demonstrating a focus toward controlling emotions, impulses, and desires; giving your best in all situations
- *Citizenship.* Being involved in service to school, community, and country from a desire to make things better for all
- *Honesty.* Telling the truth, admitting wrongdoing, being trustworthy, and acting with integrity
- *Courage.* Doing the right thing in the face of difficulty and following your conscience instead of groupthink or pressures from peers

- *Respect.* Showing high regard for an authority figure, peers, and self; treating others as you would want to be treated and valuing people for their unique qualities
- *Fairness.* Practicing justice, equity, and equality; treating others with value
- *Integrity.* Adhering to a moral code, aligning purpose, dreams, commitments, and results that reflect your best self, the best person you can be
- *Purpose.* Higher understanding of why you are here and taking actions to manifest it in all that you do

Adapted from Character Education Net, http://www.charactered.net/main/traits.asp.

Character is broadly conceived to encompass the cognitive, emotional, and behavioral aspects of the moral life (Lickona, Schaps, & Lewis, 2003). The development of character requires that we have central guiding principles that lie deep within our inner being, such as caring, honesty, fairness, responsibility, and respect for self and others. Archetypal psychologist James Hillman (1996) uses the analogy of a person living with a "soul's code," meaning that every individual has a unique essence and innate calling in life, which (if we were aware) could guide us in the numerous and often difficult choices we are required to make in a life.

Educational psychologist Thomas Lickona (1991) asserts that two great moral values, respect and responsibility, are important to consider in K–16 schooling because "they are necessary for healthy personal development, caring interpersonal relationships, a humane and democratic society, and a just and peaceful world" (p. 43). Young people today want to know right from wrong, and they want to learn how to access their own conscience, but "the conscience does not descend upon us from on high" (Coles, 1997b, p. 58). Rather, students learn right and wrong from parents, teaches, and counselors who guide them to a growing awareness of inner qualities and callings and their inner soul's code.

I recall a very difficult situation from my early career as a new teacher in one of Massachusetts's largest cities, which tested my own character. My recollection of this situation is particularly acute at this time as the nation follows the events of the Jerry Sandusky child-abuse trial with revelations of the lack of character of four Penn State leaders who actively covered up the sexual abuse of children. Character is important especially in the face of its absence in this case and others like it.

I was a new teacher teaching social studies and remedial reading at the high school level. I was popular with the students, who knew they could come to me for honest, sincere, and empowering guidance on all the issues that adolescents address. I represented an outsider's view: someone who was not a part of the ingrained working-class community power structure or part and parcel to intergenerational secrets.

One day after one of my classes, a student who had grown to trust me confided that her best friend was being sexually abused by a longtime, very popular, third-generation social studies teacher. After numerous conversations with her and then her friend to verify the accuracy and obtain relevant facts, I went immediately to both the district superintendent and the police department to report this abuse. Having counseled youth for years, I knew of the emotional and psychological damage of abuse. I drew upon my own deep sense of a deep "soul's code" to empower all children to a better quality of life, which in this case meant alleviating emotional pain and suffering and beginning the healing process. My dream at that time was to be the source of empowerment for young people in a school system that more often than not disempowered their spirits, hopes, and dreams.

It was very gut wrenching to know that my report could destroy a beloved teacher's career, reputation, marriage, and family, while damaging my own career prospects in that school district. I knew that as the bearer of bad news, and one who upset the community's power structure by telling a long-held secret, I would never be considered a part of this closed community.

I did it anyway. The teacher did not lose his job, nor were there any legal actions taken, so one can only wonder whether justice was served. However, the girl who was being abused received professional mental health services through extensive counseling, and she was removed from any contact with the teacher. I understand that she went on to college and to live a great life.

Since that time I have held my head high. This has served as a source of pride for me in my career and a reminder to always do the right thing regardless of the consequences. The four key leaders at Penn State who allegedly covered up the child abuse did not draw upon their soul's code and moral compass. The consequence is a great university and wonderful community in turmoil and upset.

## A Model of Self Developed From the Research Data

Presently, there is no unifying theory of the self for educators or counselors to consider in theory or practice, nor a working model of how to utilize positive psychology and an integrative psychology approach in education or schooling.

With the iSelf model, I'd like to see educators acknowledge, once and for all, that in addition to a brain there is a mind and a soul, that we do have emotions and varying cognitive capabilities, and that all these make up the self of an individual—most important, they are not separate, but integrated. Too often researchers and academics isolate one or two of these attributes in an attempt to study them; this may make sense from a pure researcher's perspective, but it does not make any sense whatsoever to advancing our understanding and transformation of human beings. We are not that simple. Teachers and counselors need to operate across the integrated self of children and adolescents, not single out one or two variables to observe and develop.

The iSelf model represents what is going on inside a person. It is a way to conceptualize all the components of the self. When we discuss the self of a person, we speak in terms of attributions, or an attribute that is a functioning mechanism of the self that includes an understanding of internal mind with what is represented externally as an expression. Each attribute influences the dynamic equilibrium of the whole self.

In Figure 2, I group the iSelf attributes in order to provide the reader with an entry point, but the organization and interplay of the attributes constantly changes. The mind, body, and soul enhance the attributes, and the attributes enhance the mind, body, and soul. It is helpful to keep in mind the workings of a mobile to simulate the constant dynamic at work.

## Self-System Attributes Defined

Developmental psychologist Susan Harter offers an integrated construct of the self she calls the "self-system" (Harter, 1999). By "system" she does not mean to establish a predictable view of how component parts of the self operate. Rather, Harter means to offer a holistic view that is consistent with that of Dewey (1900; 1902; 1916) and James (1900; 1992), where a self is the sum of all dynamic component parts.

Building upon Harter's (1999) concepts and conceptualization, I define the self-system and self-system attributes to consist of self-concept, self-esteem, self-efficacy, self-understanding, identity, locus of control, self-affects, and self-schemas.

### Self-Concept

This refers to how you view yourself; your frame made up of important references. *Self-image* and *self-perception* are synonymous terms. Important references can be what you are most interested in participating in—your interests and activities. These interests are usual grouped or categorized (e.g., academic

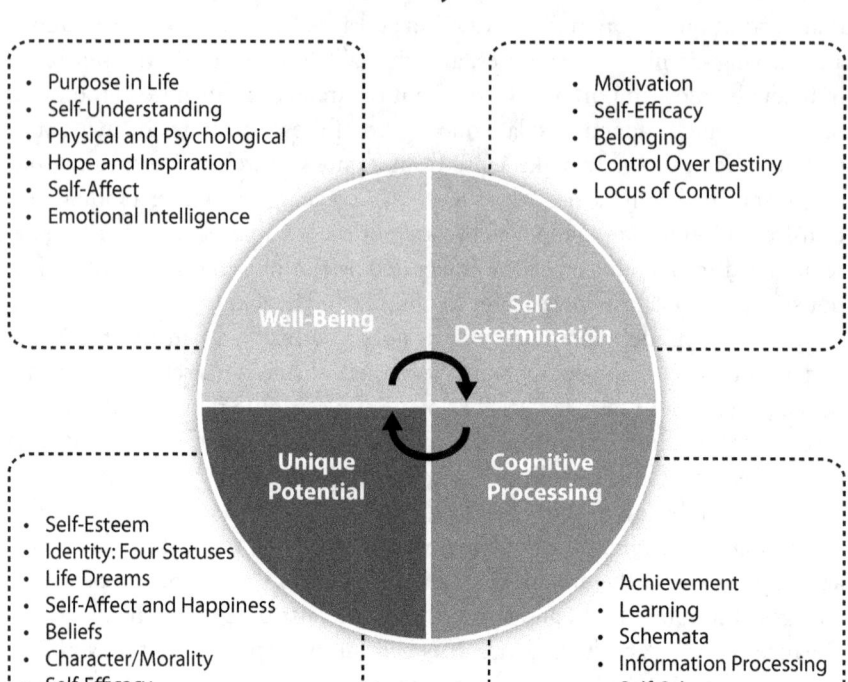

**Figure 2.** The iSelf Model: Component Parts That Include Self-System and Positive Psychology Attributes

and nonacademic, peer group, intellectual and nonintellectual, physical and nonphysical, athletic and nonathletic, artistic and nonartistic, among others). Self-concept most often develops through becoming aware of innate strengths and developing qualities and characteristics and the quality of the experience of performance when exercising these. It develops through a process of attempting to express an innate desire or interest combined with the messages received through the experience. An individual's innate cognitive strengths are commonly organized along the lines of Gardner's (1983) theory of multiple intelligences (MI), which include strengths defined as interpersonal and intrapersonal, naturalistic and spiritual, logical and linguistic, kinesthetic and spatial, and musical and artistic.

## Self-Esteem

This refers to the value that you place upon those strengths, characteristics, and activities that make up your self-concept—values such as feeling good or bad about your abilities in math, sports, or music. Numerous scholars and researchers have found a direct correlation between self-esteem and performance. The following quote underscores the important connection between negative self-esteem and therefore negative self-system constructs and well-being outcomes: "a child who experiences attachment figures as rejecting or emotionally unavailable and non supportive will construct a working model of the self as unlovable, incompetent, and generally unworthy" (Harter, 1999, p. 13). Thus "the most common affective correlate of negative self-perceptions is depression. In the extreme, depressive reactions associated with negative self-perceptions will lead to suicidal behaviors" (Harter & Marold, 1992, p. 13; Locker & Cropley, 2004).

## Self-Efficacy

This refers to your beliefs about your potentialities and about your capacity to grow and learn to become the person you want to become. Efficacy is the belief that you can accomplish a goal. Bandura (1997; Pintrich & Schunk, 2002) conceptualized four sources of self-efficacy that are relevant to our discussion: The first source is mastery experiences, which are our direct experiences of success or failure. Successes raise our efficacy beliefs and failures lower our efficacy beliefs. The second is physiological and emotional arousal, which impacts efficacy beliefs depending on whether we are anxious or worried (low efficacy) or excited or happy (high efficacy). The third is vicarious experience, which ties our efficacy beliefs to someone who models accomplishments and the degree to which we identify with the model. When the model performs well, our efficacy increases, but when the model performs poorly, our efficacy expectations decrease. The fourth, social persuasion, uses the power of performance feedback to boost efficacy expectations, but efficacy will only be enhanced if the persuader is credible, trustworthy, and an expert.

## Self-Understanding

This refers to the conscious knowing that you are a separate self from your circumstances, family, society, culture, media, and peers. It is the knowing that you have a separate way of feeling, experiencing events, and interpreting the world, and a personal understanding of your uniqueness vis-à-vis others. Self-understanding is sometimes used synonymously with self-knowledge. This attribute is important in that often we do not have healthy boundaries between ourselves and others, or between ourselves and our control over substances such as foods, drugs, and alcohol. Expressions of self-understanding include higher and higher levels of consciousness, more and more aware that there are higher states and that they contribute to enlightened views.

### Identity

This refers to your distinct personality. Erik Erikson (1963; 1968; 1980) posited that we form and reform our identities over the course of a lifetime and at different and distinct stages of development. His idea of developing and changing mental schemas inform the iSelf model:

> An increasing sense of identity is experienced preconsciously as a sense of psychosocial well-being. Its most obvious concomitants are feeling of being at home in one's body, a sense of "knowing where one is going," and an inner assuredness of anticipated recognition from those who count. Such a sense of identity, however, is never gained nor maintained once and for all. Like a "good conscience" it is constantly lost and regained. (Erikson, 1980, p. 128)

Building upon Erikson's work, James Marcia asserts that there are four identity statuses, depending on whether people have explored options and made commitments (Marcia, 1991; 1994; 2002). The first is identity achievement, which requires the exploration of both realistic and unrealistic options and commits to pursuing a choice or choices made. The second is identity foreclosure, which is a commitment made without exploration (no experimentation with a range of options) but simply commits based on the goals, values, and lifestyle of others. The third is identity diffusion, when individuals do not explore or commit, but rather reach no conclusions about who they are, what they want to do with their lives, or who they want to become as a person—no direction. Adolescents who experience diffusion may be apathetic and withdrawn, with little hope for the future, or they may be openly rebellious (Berger & Thompson, 1995; Kroger, 1996). The fourth is identity moratorium, when the individual is in the midst of struggling with choices, still exploring options, but delaying committing to personal and or professional growth or direction (Woolfolk, 2004). In this fourth status, an individual is apt to suffer from an identity crisis, common among young adults in college or recently postcollege.

### Locus of Control

This refers to your belief system regarding the causes of experiences and the factors to which you attribute success or failure (Rotter, 1966). There is a critical distinction between internal and external locus of control in assessing beliefs about who has influence over one's life course. A healthy internal locus of control suggests that an individual attributes success to his own efforts and abilities. A person who expects to succeed will be more internally motivated and more likely to want to learn, take full responsibility for the circumstances in her life, and know she can change them to manifest her own destiny in life. External locus of control suggests that a person attributes success to luck or fate or to circumstances outside of one's self and control. People with external locus of control are more likely to experience anxiety, resignation, depression, and withdrawal from fully experiencing life—to be a victim of their circumstances.

### Self-Schema

This refers to a mental model made up of bits of information that are representations of both your internal beliefs and external cultural beliefs known as *schemata*. The schema organizes the schemata, for example, into beliefs learned from life's experiences. The schema is where meaning is made or processed between one's internal and external worlds to create one's reality. Our schemas are mental structures that influence our perception of reality, interpretation of experiences, and then how we plan and take action. Using the language of paradigm previously discussed, a self-schema is one's personal paradigm of reality. The self-schema takes incoming information and uses it to create the additional self-attributes, such as self-concept, self-efficacy, identity, meaning, and affect/emotions; it is critical in making us uniquely who we are.

Personal as well as cultural beliefs make up an individual's paradigm of reality and how one sees oneself and one's world. Schema theory provides the critical link between the internal and external self and provides the space for the creation of mind. Cognitive sociologist and Princeton Professor Paul DiMaggio (1997) focuses upon "schema theory as especially relevant to the representation of social phenomena" (DiMaggio, 1997, p. 283), and "the ways in which social identities enter into the constitution of individual selves" (DiMaggio, 1997, p. 275). Cultural beliefs are integrated into the self as schemata, which are acquired "by individuals during development" (DiMaggio, 1997, p. 280). Reflecting the socioconstruction of the mind, and the inescapable influence of peer groups in schools, family, and the culture at large, Harvard University educational philosopher Israel Scheffler asserts, "development of self-knowledge grows out of the social process" (Scheffler, 1985, p. 25).

### Self-Affect

This refers to a personal feeling or emotion that is sometimes difficult to use language to describe because it is an experience. It involves multiple sensations to varying degrees. "Without affect, feelings do not feel because they have no intensity, and without feelings, rational decision-making becomes problematic" (Damasio, 1994, p. 22). Also, "affect plays an important role in determining the relationship between our bodies, our environment, and others, and the subjective experience that we feel/think as affect dissolves into experience" (Shouse, 2005). In short, self-affect is the ability to feel and to know that you are feeling emotions.

## Positive Psychology Attributes

The iSelf model also incorporates attributes from positive psychology. Positive psychology is an evolution of the cognitive developmental and humanistic views of the self. I define positive psychology attributes (Csikszentmihalyi, 1993; Seligman & Csikszentmihalyi, 2000; Snyder & Lopez, 2002) to consist of such commonly understood concepts as life purpose, life satisfaction, life meaning, happiness, intrinsic motivation, inspiration, and possible selves, where these contribute to psychological and subjective well-being outcomes (Ryan & Deci, 2001; Lent, Singley, Sheu, & Gainor, 2005) and therefore are important protective factors for educators, counselors, and health professionals to consider. Positive psychology introduces more existential perspectives to embrace spirituality, happiness, hope, and dreams.

### Life Purpose and Spirituality

This refers to the reason you are here, for your existence (*raison d'être*), and describes or includes your basic nature or being: the essence of a human being, the totality of all things that exist, the qualities that constitute existence or essence, and one's basic nature. It includes your mission in life as an avenue or pathway to manifest your purpose—an inner calling to pursue an activity or perform a service, a vocation, the area of life where you will manifest your life's purpose. This calling is spiritual in nature and involves a connection with a higher power, an uplifting and transcending force, or feeling of need: to feel the calling to contribute to the human condition in some way, unique to you and your life experiences and views of a better world or greater good. It is what we commit our lives to, bigger than ourselves, using our unique talents, values, and vision in the service of creating a better world. It is part of the underlying motivation and driving force that guides our actions and brings us fulfillment. Our purpose is bigger than we are; it is a lifelong process that we can continuously discover and improve upon and compels us to make a difference in our lives, the lives of others, and the condition of the world. This George Bernard Shaw quote characterizes the spirit of a person's purpose:

This is the true joy in life, the being used for a purpose recognized by yourself as a mighty one; the being a force of nature instead of a feverish selfish little clod of ailments and grievances complaining that the world will not devote itself to making you happy. I want to be thoroughly used up when I die, for the harder I work the more I live. I rejoice in life for its own sake. Life is no "brief candle" to me. It is a sort of splendid torch which I have got hold of for the moment, and I want to make it burn as brightly as possible before handing it on to future generations. (*Man and Superman*, 1973)

## Life Meaning

This involves being able to process the vast amounts of information that you take in constantly and create meaning, a deeper understanding, connecting with an attribute of the self. This is the process of interpreting information as relevant to some aspect of yourself or your life, special to you and the way you interpret life events. Taking information and consciously placing meaning on it can be self-referential or other-referential. Self-referential involves connecting or encoding with an internal self-attribute, where other-referential involves connecting with external context, such as relationships or renewable energy, usually categorized as "other" or "all."

## Intrinsic Motivation

This is your inner drive to achieve to accomplish or reach a desired state. This inner drive may come from instinct, a deep subconsciousness, or a conscious want, and is usually juxtaposed with extrinsic motivation, which refers to the external forces that move you to act. Learning adds to and changes our internal motivations to manifest that which we desire for our best self-interest. When you learn that you have a new belief about the importance of relationships and you define yourself by this belief, then you are internally motivated to develop meaningful relationships that reinforce your belief system. "Learners who are intrinsically motivated may engage in an activity because it gives them pleasure, helps them develop a skill they think is important, or is the ethically and morally right thing to do" (Ormrod, 2006, p. 181).

## Happiness

This is an emotion of elation, of joy, of feeling that all is well. An experience that is interpreted as a state of being happy, happiness is an interpretation or a conscious thought. The term *subjective happiness* is often used because there is no absolute state; it is an interpretation of an experience that makes you happy. The experience reflects a deeper want has been realized. This deeper want may be a conscious or intuitive desire. Satisfaction is an example of a feeling of happiness—evidence that a want or desire or intended result has been realized or manifest. Happiness occurs when the resulting circumstances in your life match your dreams, commitments, and goals for your life, after taking action or implementing a strategy to produce results. There is a balance or a dynamic equilibrium between wants and desires and evidence or circumstances of having the "wants."

### Inspiration, Hope, and Dreams

These all involve a vision of a future state, including all circumstances and emotions: what you can see that you want in your mind's eye. This involves being inspired to dream, to spark the insight or seed of a desired future state through another person within one's inner consciousness or life experience, and to hope that you can manifest that dream. It is what you see in the future, like a dream of what is possible, and a mental image produced by the imagination to see in your mind's eye, unusual competence or perception, and intelligent foresight. "Hopeful thought reflects the belief that one can find pathways to desired goals [and envisioned dreams] and then become motivated to use those pathways" (Snyder, Rand, Sigmon, 2005, p. 257).

### Possible Selves

This is a conception that you can become what you see is possible. It is a thought process where you inquire into "what if" questions and possible scenarios for who you can become and your life direction. You believe either that you are locked into a single way of being or becoming or that you can exercise freedom to change who you are and your life. The possible selves attribute represents your ideas of what you might become, what you would like to become, and what you are afraid of becoming, and thus provide a conceptual link between cognition and motivation. Possible selves are the cognitive components of hopes, fears, goals, and threats; they give the specific self-relevant form, meaning, organization, and direction to these dynamics. It is suggested that possible selves function as incentives for future behavior and provide an evaluative and interpretive context for the current view of self (Markus & Nurious, 1986, p. 1).

### Self-Determination

Self-determination is defined by three needs: the need to control the course of your life (autonomy), the need to be effective in dealing with your environment (competence), and the need to have close, affectionate relationships (relatedness). "To be self determined is to endorse one's actions at the highest level of reflection [and] when self determined people experience a sense of freedom to do what is interesting, personally important, and revitalizing" (Deci & Ryan, 1985).

## Emotional Intelligence and Positive Emotions

This is your ability to discern numerous subtle distinctions of a wide range of emotions, such as sadness and depression, happiness and elation, anger and rage. This involves the ability to manage the emotions with thought and to express them effectively and appropriately within a context. To recognize emotions in others is a quality of empathy or the ability to empathize. According to Goleman (1995), emotional intelligence consists of the capacity for each or all these ingredients: confidence, curiosity, intentionality, self-control, relatedness, capacity to communicate, and cooperativeness (p. 194). Positive emotions consist of episodes of pleasure, happiness, energy, confidence, positive mood, enthusiasm, love and caring, and so on.

## Well-Being

This refers to your psychological and physical health, where health is not simply the absence of illness, as in mental illness, but the more positive connotation how well your life is going; your well-being is what is good for you. Well-being includes emotional health, vitality and satisfaction, life direction and ability to make a difference, physical health and energy to function fully, healthy behaviors such as diet and exercise, quality of relationships, financial wealth, experiencing a high quality of life, and living a good life.

## Creativity

This involves making connections between ideas or experiences that were previously unconnected (Robinson, 2001, p. 11). Creative people are those who express unusual thoughts, who are interesting and stimulating—in short, people who appear to be unusually bright. They are people who experience the world in novel and original ways. These are (personally creative) individuals whose perceptions are fresh, whose judgments are insightful, who may make important discoveries that only they know about. These individuals often change our culture in some important way (e.g., Da Vinci, Edison, Picasso, Einstein; Csikszentmihalyi, 1996, pp. 25–26). Being creative involves coming up with something new—for example, a new idea out of nothing that is worthwhile and useful and a unique expression of you.

## An Expanded Definition of Well-Being

The iSelf model, when applied to schooling and counseling practices and methods, leads to students' psychological and physical well-being. According to Seligman, "well-being" is a construct within the branch of psychology known as *positive psychology*. Well-being comes from our personal experiences in life—meaning we can and do experience well-being in numerous ways. We construct our meaning of well-being made up of these component parts:

- Positive emotion (of which happiness and life satisfaction are elements)
- Engagement (of which motivation, both intrinsic and extrinsic, are elements)
- Relationships (empowering others while empowering self)
- Meaning (life purpose and the ability to create meaning)
- Achievement (accomplishing results that indicate whether or not one's life purpose is manifest)

Adapted from Seligman, 2001, p. 24.

Positive psychologist and University of Wisconsin professor and researcher Dr. Carol Ryff (1985; 1998; 2003) has another, compatible view and has developed psychological well-being scales consisting of these dimensions:

- *Autonomy.* A person who would score high is self-determining and independent, able to resist social pressures to think and act in certain ways, regulates behavior from within, and evaluates one's self by personal standards. Someone who would score low is concerned about the expectations and evaluations of others, relies on judgments of others to make important decisions, and conforms to social pressures to think and act in certain ways.
- *Environmental mastery.* A high scorer has a sense of mastery and competence in managing the environment, controls a complex array of external activities, makes effective use of surrounding opportunities, and is able to choose or create contexts suitable to personal needs and values. A low scorer has difficulty managing everyday affairs, feels unable to change or improve surrounding contexts, is unaware of surrounding opportunities, and lacks sense of control over the external world.
- *Personal growth.* A high scorer has a feeling of continued development, sees the self as growing and expanding, is open to new experiences, has a sense of realizing his or her potential, sees improvement in self and behavior over time, and is changing in ways that reflect more self-knowledge and effectiveness. A low scorer has a sense of personal stagnation, lacks sense of improvement or expansion over time, feels bored and uninterested with life, and feels unable to develop new attitudes or behaviors.

- *Positive relations with others.* A high scorer has warm, satisfying, trusting relationships with others; is concerned about the welfare of others; is capable of strong empathy, affection, and intimacy; and understands the give and take of human relationships. A low scorer has few close, trusting relationships with others; finds it difficult to be warm, open, and concerned about others; is isolated and frustrated in interpersonal relationships; and is unwilling to make compromises to sustain important ties with others.
- *Purpose in life.* A high scorer has goals in life and a sense of directedness, feels there is meaning to present and past life, holds beliefs that give life purpose, and has aims and objectives for living. A low scorer lacks a sense of meaning in life, has few goals or aims, lacks a sense of direction, does not see the purpose of previous life experiences, and has no outlook or beliefs that give life meaning.
- *Self-acceptance.* A high scorer possesses a positive attitude toward the self, acknowledges and accepts multiple aspects of self including good and bad qualities, and feels positive about previous life experiences. A low scorer feels dissatisfied with self, is disappointed with what has occurred in past life, is troubled about certain personal qualities, and wishes to be different than what he or she is.

High scorers using the Ryff scale of psychological well-being have a lower risk of mental health disorders or physical health diagnosis such as obesity, cutting, and substance abuse, among others. As such, well-being is an important protective factor to impart in a child's life.

I agree with both Seligman and Ryff, and from psychotherapeutic concepts and my own classroom and clinical experiences, I would also frame the components of a healthy self as follows:

- *Living consciously.* Attempting to transform oneself to higher and higher levels of consciousness
- *Self-acceptance.* Understanding personal strengths and weaknesses
- *Self-assertiveness.* Having confidence to express personal ideas and feelings, and having the experience of self-efficacy
- *Self-responsibility.* Not being dependent upon others for one's own joyous sense of greatness and relying on one's own internal resources and strengths
- *Living purposely.* Knowing who one is as a human being and why one is here on earth contributing to the quality of life of humankind
- *Living with integrity.* Living consistent with one's own moral compass and moral code and manifesting one's own unique purpose, dreams, and goals for a good life

- *Experiencing one's experiences.* Being aware of what is real and authentic, not limited by preconceptions or dissociation

Adapted from *The Six Pillars of Self-Esteem*, 1994.

## Revisiting the Nature Versus Nurture Debate

The iSelf model also embraces recent developments in brain science, but I caution against accepting blindly that "you are your synapses" (LeDoux, 2002, p. ix). Neuroscientist Joseph LeDoux's (2002) main point is that "you are your synapses," which to a developmental cognitive psychologist, especially one who understands and practices socioconstructivist psychology, is a troubling statement in that it disregards our basic humanity or humanness for creating one's self and our realities. LeDoux argues that cognitive science was successful because it figured out how to study the mind without getting bogged down in questions about "subjective experience" (2002, p. 205). But socioconstructivists such as Bruner, Vygotsky, and others would say that it is precisely in the context of these "subjective experiences" that personal meaning is made and thus a personality and a person with a mind is created or constructed.

LeDoux states that "information received by sensory systems activate emotional-processing circuits, which evaluate the meaning of the stimulus input and initiate specific emotional responses by triggering output circuits" (2002, p. 206). His thesis would add more to the study of cognitive psychology and our understanding of self-construction if he referenced the role of schema and, in particular, how each human being brings his or her own unique self-schema to everyday lived experiences, and this part of the human mind is what mediates the external environment with inner personal meaning. I would argue that we are not so computerlike.

The self-schema is the mechanism that takes our natural brain processes and manages our interpretations from the external experiences in everyday living. We can change our brains and brain chemistry, literally, through how we interpret our world using our self-schema.

LeDoux accurately discusses the roles of the executive functioning with the amygdala with that of the hippocampus and working memory and seems to assert that these drive human beings' lives through their synaptic connections and circuitry. What about the role of self-knowledge or consciousness or motivation or higher-order thinking processes in understanding creating meaning in one's life—more of an active participant when shaping a life? I would underscore this LeDoux point: "Because therapy is itself a learning experience, it, too, involves changes in synaptic connections. Brain circuits and psychological experiences are not different things, but rather, different ways of describing the same thing" (2002, p. 262). LeDoux goes on to underscore my problem with his overemphasis upon the brain for understanding the self: "The problem is that it is not clear how the changes at the neural level relate to those at the psychological level" (2002, p. 94). I would add, then, why study these as a basis for understanding the self? Both sides of the nature–nurture debate are important and included in the iSelf model.

LeDoux gets it right with his definition of the self: "The self is the totality of what an organism is physically, biologically, psychologically, socially, and culturally" (2002, p. 31). This serves to place the self at the heart of the new kind of mind and informs our iSelf model. Even LeDoux sees that many would have difficulty with his overemphasis on brain science to tell us who we are:

> Many will surely counter that the self is psychological, social, moral, aesthetic, or spiritual, rather than neural, in nature. My synaptic theory of the self is not proposed as an alternative to these views. It is, rather, an attempt to portray the way the psychological, social, moral, aesthetic or spiritual self is realized. (p. 3)

Rather than becoming overly concerned with a decision on the nature versus nurture debate, or the specifics of neural firings, the iSelf model asks that we simply concede that the brain is malleable and that our choices can change our psychological makeups.

The iSelf model offers a view that includes the roles both of the synapses and of culture and mind when shaping a human being, while offering a pathway of empowering both to higher levels through counseling and in the classroom.

## iSelf Model and Information Processing

The dynamic among the component parts of the iSelf model emerges upon contact with the external world and our everyday lives and lived experiences. Here, it is important to describe the conceptual model of how the mind works together with the brain's information processing model (Figure 3), which is the generally accepted view used by cognitive developmental psychologists and educational psychologists to describe mental activity. The information processing model (Anderson, 1995; Schunk, 2000) attempts to model human mental activity: perception, short-term memory, long-term memory, executive control processes, decision making, and so on.

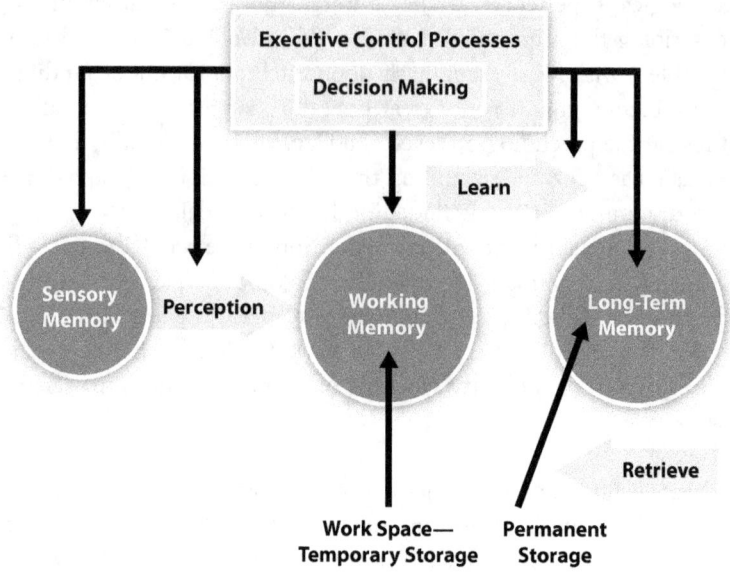

**Figure 3.** Information Processing Model (Adapted from Atkinson and Shiffrin, 1968)

Let's explore the critical interaction between the mind and the brain through an example that is common to most. A person puts herself in a situation where she will learn about who she is—for example, in a movie theatre. Watching a movie is seemingly a passive learning situation. This person may not have an intention to learn about herself; nevertheless, learning is automatic and always occurring. We never stop learning because, as the information processing model helps to conceptualize, through our sensory memory and perception we are actively doing something with external stimuli. We use our sensory memory to take in certain images and sound and then retrieve or recall memories in working memory—a very short-term process, usually 3–5 seconds. This entire process is being managed by the executive control processes, among which is the metacognitive process, which helps make connections between the activity in working memory and future decisions. The moviegoer, hence, may formulate future dreams based on the movie plot or character, for example, and feel inspired in some way that is personally meaningful.

As the individual placed herself in this movie's story, depending on her existing sense of purpose, developmental needs, emotional desires, and dreams for her life, she will learn something about herself. All her self-attributes, her whole self, are situated at the center of this process. Emotions of excitement may arise suggesting a new possibility for her life-course trajectory, whereupon she will leave the movie theatre move motivated to pursue and manifest her newly discovered dreams. Her integrated self, situated between her internal state of mind and the cultural influence, has changed. But she in turn can change the culture; through the deepened self-knowledge and ability to create a new reality about who she is and the difference she is called to make in the world, resulting in a better world through her actions and impact.

### Emotions and Learning: I Feel, Therefore I Learn!

Emotions impact our understanding of ourselves and our growth and development. The integrated self incorporates emotions into our mental processing and creation of the mind.

If our synapses and the external culture act on each other, and if we are in a constant state of learning in numerous environments, then our feelings or emotions target what we learn and our motivations to learn. In recent mind, brain, and education (MBE) research, we have discovered that the mind actually grows and changes with and within each new learning experience (Fischer & Giedd, in Sparks, 2012). Dr. Giedd at the National Institute of Mental Health has pierced our commonly held misconceptions that the brain is somehow a hardwired computer or that learning paths are hardwired, singular, and cognitive (Sparks, 2012). I believe that our system of education is built upon these misconceptions.

Harvard's Dr. Fischer underscores this point with, "what we find is people really do change their brain" (Fischer, in Sparks, 2012, p. 1). The implication is that anyone can learn anything at anytime: during therapy sessions, in math classes, or conducting Google searches. Everyone learns if provided with the best, right approach for that particular person's brain and mind; then the person can literally change her brain functioning. If we create teaching methods and learning experiences that harness the motivations or emotional need to learn, then we will have more direct pathways to learning. When viewed through the iSelf lens, that method is teaching self-knowledge so that natural internal self-motivations are engaged toward personal dreams and the manifestation of life's purpose. In both school and counseling settings, the student or client works in partnership with the teacher or counselor to create those learning activities that best suit and change the brain functioning to meet the mind's purpose and dreams and the emotional responses to these.

Emotions impact and interact with the brain's prefrontal cortex, where executive functioning resides, and the hippocampus, where memory lives.

These interactions impact the mind's ability to be active or quiet. Young people are fascinated by the brain and mind and self-concepts and, in my experience, eat these up more readily than any academic subject content.

The iSelf model, when applied through schooling, helps effective teachers teach young students important self-distinctions *using* subject content in their classrooms. What then occurs is deeper learning, in that there is a more of a direct transfer of knowledge. The self is the context that makes the academic content meaningful and therefore creates a deeper understanding.

Emotions tell each of us what is important to learn, know, and be able to do. It is tragic that our schools have ignored this critical dimension of the self and of learning. It is tragic because teachers are searching for ways to not only engage their students in learning academic content but also make learning more meaningful and purposeful for each student. We need to impart emotional intelligence, self-awareness, and health through schooling so that we can create a more thoughtful and civil society with honest debate about how to solve the real and deep problems we confront.

A recent story from the headlines underscores the need to teach emotional well-being. When asked about the reasons why a group of 15–20 teenagers stood by and watched a 15-year-old girl gang raped and beaten as their classmates filed into the school auditorium for the annual homecoming dance, mind-body healing pioneer and expert Dr. Deepak Chopra declared in a CNN interview that "there is an epidemic of emotional retardation," underscoring the need to teach what healthy emotions are and provide a method of emotional healing for our children through schooling. If viewing the rape through the iSelf lens, at least one of these 15–20 bystanders would have seen the immorality of this event and intervened in a number of possible ways. They would have empathized with the girl and taken some appropriate action. Further, the adolescents gang raping and beating the girl would have been able to better process their emotions and not taken out their frustrations and anger on the girl. Thus the event would not have occurred in the first place.

Here is a case in point where a teacher and a parent did not know the importance of emotions and the inner life of a young student: The young daughter of one of my graduate students wrote this poem in a bell-ringer exercise (a beginning class exercise that focuses students upon entering a class), as assigned by her homeroom teacher (used with permission by the parent):

> Depression overcomes my body,
> suffocating the joys of life.
> Adding on more childish fears.
> My hopes are beginning to flow

> Under the surface of my knowing,
> that usually makes me feel better.
> But not this time.
> I can't function correctly in this life.
> Will someone please tell me what I've messed up on this time?
> Won't someone notice the pain I'm experiencing?
> Please, somebody out there must save me before I drown
> in my own sorrow.
> Please—anyone!!!

The teacher—under pressure to improve standardized tests scores in language arts and having received her teacher training in a traditional teacher education program where the current and dominant policies and best practices are taught—instead of approaching the girl privately to inquire into her state of mind, graded the poem using state language arts standards as her reference. The teacher, though skilled at teaching curriculum standards and teaching to the test, failed to even notice the state of mind of an 11-year-old girl.

This girl's mother requested my consultation, and together we put into place a way to think about this girl's inner state, along with her family environment. The mother and daughter worked on their purposes in life and then took actions to manifest these. They both were sexually abused as children by family members, and so, armed with new iSelf distinctions, they went on to develop a sexual-abuse prevention program that was eventually proposed for statewide adoption. The mother, who was diagnosed with bipolar affective disorder, with the approval of her medical doctor, went off of her medications after reshaping her entire paradigm of self and her reality and becoming whole again with herself, which created a healthy balance in her brain chemistry.

The girl, with the genetic factor associated with bipolar affective disorder, could have easily fallen into this family diagnosis, instead of gaining a new level of emotional intelligence through her learning. Her learning took the form of writing the poem, diagnosing it from a self-lens, and subsequent short mother-daughter meetings to discuss purpose in life and motivations to take action, demonstrating the effectiveness of using iSelf distinctions when learning about academics and personal knowledge, resulting in enhanced poetry writing and personal well-being.

If we had taken a brain scan of the daughter, we most likely would seen her left amygdala, which is the fear hub, highly active, because of her fears about her life, her self, and her future. Using her sentiments, her hopes were flowing but, unlike in her previous experiences, these were not making her feel better. She needed a pathway for these hopes to take action and begin to manifest them. In her case, and in this situation, this restored equilibrium among her many mind, brain, and self functions.

Through our work together, in both the mother and the daughter, we would have seen changes in the brain gray matter, both in the prefrontal cortex (where, psychologically, executive functioning resides) and in the left amygdala (the brain's emotional center). Therefore, the mother healed through learning about herself and becoming more highly emotional, passionate really, about her purpose in life. Bipolar disorder can be treated through changes in the brain chemistry and functioning, and learning about one's higher purpose in life can literally change brain functioning.

Recent mind, brain, and education (MBE) research supports these interconnections and results:

> Advances in neuroscience have been increasingly used to inform educational theory and practice. However, while the most successful strides forward have been made in the areas of academic disciplinary skills such as reading and mathematical processing, a great deal of new evidence from social and affective neuroscience is prime for application to education . . . In particular, social and affective neuroscience are revealing more clearly than ever before the interdependence of cognition and emotion in the brain, the importance of emotion in guiding successful learning, and the critical role of teachers in managing the social environment of the classroom so that optimal emotional and cognitive learning can take place. (Immordino-Yang & Faeth, 2010, p. 67)

I have found that emotional well-being can be achieved if any individual—child, adolescent or adult—is taught that he has a unique self with specific attributions such as unique purpose. This alone shifts his way of being to more of an ontological inquiry, with a newfound inner peace, and leads to subsequent changes in behavior and experiences of emotional well-being characterized as less anxiety and stress.

## Evolution of the Mind

Educators, counselors, and medical professionals need to better understand the centrality of "emotional thought" in learning, especially when considering a new normal in modern society where we are disconnected from our emotions. Figure 4 depicts this dynamic relationship among emotions and cognition, highlighting the important role of both emotional thought and high reason or higher consciousness and its conscious or unconscious impact upon the body:

# The Integrated Self-Model Description

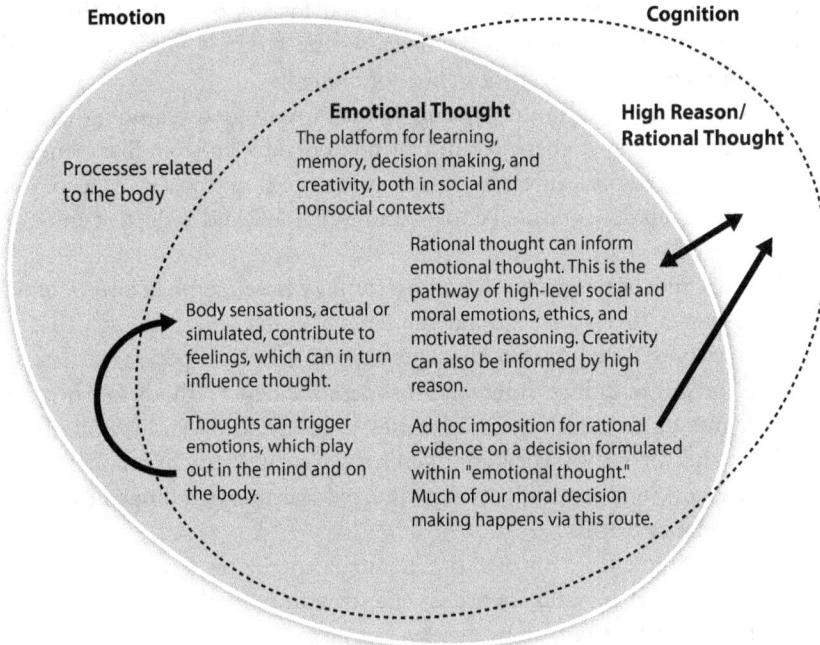

**Figure 4.** Emotions and Cognition Evolution (Reproduced with permission from John Wiley and Sons)

The evolutionary shadow cast by emotion over cognition influences the modern mind. In the diagram, the solid ellipse represents emotion; the dashed ellipse represents cognition. The extensive overlap between the two ellipses represents the domain of emotional thought. Emotional thought can be conscious or nonconscious and is the means by which bodily sensations come into our conscious awareness. High reason is a small section of the diagram and requires consciousness. (Immordino-Yang & Damasio, 2007, p. 8)

Prior to the mid-20th century and the cognitive revolution, psychology did not involve the study or the influence of emotions and motivations on learning. More recently, when describing human behavior, psychologists now talk about "cold" and "hot" cognition. "Cold cognition" describes our thoughts as information to be processed or problems to be rationally solved. "Hot cognition" describes the influence of motivation and emotion on our thoughts and decisions. Additionally, neuroscientists would concur that the brain has changed to meet the challenges of modern life; so, too, must our conception of the self and hence the importance of iSelf model in schooling, counseling, and medicine. However, as our education model is still from the 19th century and using mid-20th-century psychology, we are teaching students that cold cognition takes priority over those hot components.

Hot cognition is also understood to mean motivated reasoning (Kunda, 1990) and consists of these additional components and familiar concepts: motivation, emotions, interests, goals, intentions, purposes, expectations, needs, self-regulation, personal choice, and individual and collective emotions and motivations.

The disciplines of education and psychology have merged closer together over the past 5 to 7 years, around the language and concepts used that are common to both. In education, concepts such as "clinical experiences" describe teacher-student teaching; "interventions" describe new methods to work with students one on one, such as in responses to intervention and reading interventions; and the use of "coaching" describes the latest teacher model, which allows teachers to coach students' self-directed learning in a flipped classroom or to personalize learning.

As an example from my own professional experiences, I have taught reading in a school setting and counseled clients with borderline personality disorder in a clinical setting, using the exact same intervention method, applying the iSelf model.

As emotions are critical to consider and encourage in classroom learning and therapeutic settings to achieve breakthroughs in healing, I provide a list of possible methods, applicable to both classrooms and counseling, to draw on when working with children. There is no difference when using "person-centered" methods in teaching social studies or when healing emotionally unstable personality disorder, as the pathway in, to the inner self, is one of the attributes of the iSelf model.

Hot cognitive components determine the *effectiveness* of psychological and learning interventions. Clinical psychologists have designed psychological intervention strategies (methods) or approaches centered on a person's emotions and cognitive changes, including beliefs and thinking patterns, which can be utilized in K–16 classrooms. These counseling methods are as follows.

## Person Centered

Client-centered therapy, also known as person-centered therapy, is a nondirective form of talk therapy that was developed by humanist psychologist Carl Rogers during the 1940s and 1950s. Today, it is one of the most widely used approaches in psychotherapy.

Carl Rogers was one of the most influential psychologists of the 20th century. He was a humanist thinker and believed that people are fundamentally good. He also believed that people have an actualizing tendency, or a desire to fulfill their potential and become the best people they can be. Rogers initially started out calling his technique *nondirective therapy*. While his goal was to be as nondirective as possible, he eventually realized that therapists guide clients even in subtle ways. He also found that clients often do look to their therapists for some type of guidance or direction. Eventually, the technique came to be known as *client-centered therapy*. Today, Rogers's approach to therapy is often referred to by either of these two names, but it is also frequently known simply as *Rogerian therapy*.

It is also important to note that Rogers was deliberate in his use of the term *client* rather than *patient*. He believed that the term *patient* implied that the individual was sick and seeking a cure from a therapist. By using the term *client* instead, Rogers emphasized the importance of individuals in seeking assistance, controlling their destiny, and overcoming their difficulties. Self-direction plays a vital part of client-centered therapy. (See http://psychology.about.com/od/typesofpsychotherapy/a/client-centered-therapy.htm.)

## Coaching

The coaching method is intended to empower the future personal and professional potentials of clients. It is becoming the most effective method for shifting responsibility for a positive life direction because the counselor works closely with the client to define problems and creative solutions. The analogy often used is that from the sport of football, where the quarterback is on the field taking positive actions to win, while the coach is on the sidelines observing and advising. Coaching works because it assumes that people are good and want to manifest their full and unique potentials in life. Additionally, it works because the coach trusts the client's spirit, talents, and motivations to create positive changes toward a future of her choosing. The coaching process places the client and her whole person needs at the center of counseling sessions and uses personalized and person-centered methods.

## Strengths Based

Strengths-based counseling represents a paradigm shift in counseling methods associated with the similar shift that positive psychology represents. It focuses upon what is working in life, in various domains, and how to leverage those positive attributes. For example, a client may have a strong sense of life purpose, a strength, but not be aware of his emotions and how these emotions play out in his relationships. A counselor will focus upon his life's purpose and inquire or facilitate a discussion about additional self-attributes or levels of conscious awareness to propel desired life directions. The base assumption is that all healthy, functioning individuals do indeed have positive attributions of which they may not be aware, where having this awareness would empower motivation and energy toward the fulfillment of desired goals and dreams. Strengths-based counseling is focused upon future states of mind, reality, and success, versus processing past experiences in order to heal these. A common reference is that clients start their therapy from "0" on a scale of "–5 to 0 to +5" in terms of their well-being, with the goal being to achieve in the positive range. The iSelf model attributions serve as an effective framework to assess well-being, guide discussions, and measure results or effectiveness of the intervention.

### Transpersonal

Here is a definition of transpersonal psychology:

> Transpersonal psychologists attempt to integrate timeless wisdom with modern Western psychology and translate spiritual principles into scientifically grounded, contemporary language. Transpersonal psychology addresses the full spectrum of human psycho-spiritual development—from our deepest wounds and needs, to the existential crisis of the human being, to the most transcendent capacities of our consciousness. (Caplan, 2009)

Our self-definition includes the whole self and mind, body and spirit dimensions, and therefore provides another effective method to intervene:

> The development of the self from a sense of identity which is exclusively individual to one that is deeper, broader, more inclusive, and more unified with the whole. The core concept in transpersonal psychology is non-duality, the recognition that each part or person is fundamentally and ultimately a part of a larger, more comprehensive whole. From this insight come two other central insights: the intrinsic health and basic goodness of the whole and each of its parts. (Davis, 2003)

### Cognitive Behavioral Therapy

Cognitive behavioral therapy (CBT) is a common type of mental health counseling (psychotherapy). With cognitive behavioral therapy, you work with a mental health counselor (psychotherapist) in a structured way, attending a limited number of sessions. By helping you become aware of inaccurate or negative thinking, cognitive behavioral therapy allows you to view challenging situations more clearly and respond to them in a more effective way. Cognitive behavioral therapy can be a very helpful tool in treating mental illnesses such as anxiety or depression, but not everyone who benefits from cognitive behavioral therapy has a mental health condition. It can be a very effective tool to help anyone learn how to better manage stressful life situations (Mayo Clinic Staff, 2012). It works by examining self-destructive beliefs and belief systems and then changing these to address specific self-destructive behaviors:

> Scientific studies of CBT have demonstrated its usefulness for a wide variety of mental illnesses including mood disorders, anxiety disorders, personality disorders, eating disorders, substance abuse disorders, sleep disorders and psychotic disorders. Studies have shown that CBT actually changes brain activity in people with mental illnesses who receive this treatment, suggesting that the brain is actually improving its functioning as a result of engaging in this form of therapy. (National Alliance on Mental Illness, http://www.nami.org)

### Existential

Existential therapy was introduced by Victor Frankl and Rollo May. Existentialism is an area of philosophy concerned with the meaning of human existence. It looks at issues such as love, death, and the meaning of life—and how one deals with the sense of value and meanings in one's own life. In an existentialist approach to therapy, there are basic dimensions of the human condition. These are the capacity for self-awareness, the tension between freedom and responsibility, the creation of an identity and the establishment of meaningful relationships, the search for meaning, the acceptance of anxiety as a condition of living, and the awareness of death and nonbeing.

Existentialists believe that our human capacity for self-awareness gives us possibilities for freedom—as we realize that we are finite and time is limited, we have the potential and the choice to act or not to act. Meaning is not automatic, and we must seek it, and we are subject to loneliness, meaninglessness, guilt, and isolation. Therefore, people are free to choose among alternatives available to them in living and have a large role in shaping their own personal destinies. The manner in which we live and what we become are results of our choices, and people must take responsibility for directing their own lives:

> The aim of existential therapy is to encourage clients to reflect on life, recognize their range of alternatives and decide among them. The goal is to make people realize the ways they passively accepted circumstances and surrender control in order for them to start consciously shaping their own lives by exploring options for creating a meaningful existence. The therapies central tasks are to invite the client to recognize how they have allowed others to

decide for them, and to encourage clients to take steps towards autonomy (independence). (Psychology Campus, 2011)

All these counseling methods focus upon personal change in an environment that facilitates growth and development. If these counseling methods work, are approved, and endorsed, why not make them or adapt them to education where children are in need of these methods?

Emotions are important because they motivate us to grow and develop and make a difference in the world—the real world. Without emotions and motivated reasoning, change is not possible. When a client or student knows what she wants, and she is passionate about it for whatever reason, structural tension is created. *Structural tension* is a clinical term to describe the energy created when an individual concurrently envisions a desired future state, while being completely aware of the limitations of present or current reality. The difference between the desired future state and current reality creates a tension that seeks resolution toward one or the other. The idea of structural tension applies the first axiom of structural dynamics (Odum, 1988) to individual change. In any counseling or teaching relationship, it is critical to establish this structural tension in order to empower positive change. When this tension is created, emotional thought drives the change process. As educators and counselors, it is our responsibility to guide positive changes.

The iSelf model uses the first axiom of structural dynamics (Odum, 1988) that tension seeks resolution (Figure 5). This initiates the change process—the emotional desire to attain a future state, a goal, a dream. This axiom is essential for educators, counselors, and medical professionals to understand and apply to schooling-based curricula, counseling methods, and mental and physical health programs.

In Figure 5, three levels of tension between the left-hand side, current reality, and the degree to which a future state is desired are presented. The first level is "No Tension," which indicates that a person is just going through the motions, floating in his life, allowing circumstances to dictate direction and feelings, and self, with very little commitment toward anyone or anything, including himself and his own growth and development. Additionally, he does not have a clear picture of his present reality, either emotional state or physical situation. The second level, "Moderate Tension," indicates a modest commitment to a desired future state, most often with the ability to envision general circumstances such as amount of money needed, new car, or girlfriend. Most likely this person is not able to envision a future state that includes emotions or how he wants to feel as an important part of the quality of his life dream. This person is also not very clear about his present emotional state. The

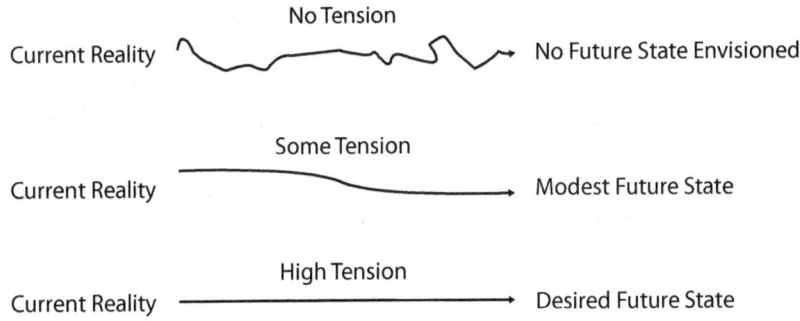

**Figure 5.** Structural Tension in Counseling and Teaching

third level, "High Tension," indicates the ability to dream about a complete and whole picture that includes emotional states of being, who one wants to become (e.g., a good person who makes a difference), and numerous and clear distinctions about both emotional and circumstantial future realities. This person also clearly identifies his current emotional state, even if it includes sadness or frustration that the future state is yet to be realized. This person also is clearer about his unique potential in life—something special that he has to give or contribute to others.

Effective counseling and teaching changes minds and brains in the same way and through the same pathway—the integrated self of the person in our care. In both settings, we are changing behaviors through changing thoughts and feelings that impact the neural networks in our brains. When a student or patient is learning, all these are at work; all are changing simultaneously. As such, as counselors and teachers, we need to be aware of and responsible for our interventions, as they are impacting the self of the students or patients at very deep and fundamental levels. Neurological research confirms what psychologists and educational psychologists already know empirically through observing mind and body connections in action. Brain science is adding to the understanding of these connections by mapping them using brain scans.

In education, mental health, or physical health policy discussions, when we concentrate our research or methods only on cognition or cognitive skills, we decontextualize thinking from the emotional self and the consciousness of the whole being. When we feel emotions, it signals an actual physiological state in body and brain, triggering a pattern of behavior that literally shifts blood flow, which is measurable, underscoring that learning is a whole-being process. When children go to school, they come with a predisposition based on their experiences, where all children have both good and bad experiences to draw upon. One of our jobs as educators and counselors is to teach children how to create new experiences through new frames of cognitive thought (which is the basis behind cognitive behavioral therapy and other counseling methods). If we can teach how to literally change children's mind-sets, we can teach them how to enjoy and look forward to the next new experience. They are engaged in life and learning.

Relevant to this discussion, Dr. Mary Helen Immordino-Yang and Dr. Antonio Damasio conduct neuroscience research on affective and social dimensions of human development in education. Their work informs my thesis that we need a new kind of mind, which the integrated self-model represents as follows:

> The processes of recognizing and responding to complex situations, which we suggest hold the origins of creativity, are fundamentally emotional and social. As such, they are shaped by and evaluated within a cultural context and are based upon emotional processing. No matter how complex and esoteric they become, our repertoire of behavioral and cognitive options continues to exist in the service of emotional goals. (Immordino-Yang & Damasio, 2007, p. 7)

In sum, everything we do for ourselves or for others serves the self at some or many levels. In a presentation made at the University of Southern California's Rossier School of Education (viewed at http://www.youtube.com/watch?v=KyjatC2MCYY), Dr. Immordino-Yang showed through brain scans that the insula or insula cortex works with the medial prefrontal cortex, which serves as an important "convergence zone" for episodic memory, perception, planning, and the subjective experience of the self. The functions of the insula include perception, motor control, self-awareness, cognitive functioning, emotional awareness, desire, moral reasoning, cognitive control, self-recognition, body movement, interoception (sensing state of gut, heart, pain, and so on), and interpersonal experience, and it is interconnected with emotions. The medial prefrontal cortex is important because it is the social-cognitive processing center that allows us to identify, categorize, and experience feelings for those we care about. Understanding the insular cortex with its relationship to emotional desires is an important protective factor for preventing depressive disorders, obesity, and obesity-related illnesses, and encouraging overall well-being.

Immordino-Yang's and Damasio's work demonstrates once and for all that there is a center for the conscious self located in the brain and refutes any suggestion among scientists that the self is only a phenomenon, a construct that has no basis in fact or reality. There is a science to the study of and knowing about the self. The self is not a phenomenon. We now have a construct, the iSelf model, and fMRIs can identify areas of the brain where consciousness, emotions, and so on function, where the unique mapping of all iSelf attributions are as unique as our DNA and our bodies. Therefore, the iSelf is the DNA of each person's self.

Immordino-Yang's and Damasio's work underscores this point: "Recent advances in neuroscience are highlighting the connections between emotion, social functioning and decision making that have the potential to revolutionize our understanding of the role of affect in education" (Immordino-Yang & Damasio, 2007, p. 3). Neuroscience may be highlighting the connections, but we certainly already knew about them through the work of psychologists Bandura, Bruner, Vygotsky, Seligman, Goleman, and so on. It is the inability of current educators and educational psychologists to translate this knowledge into methods that can be readily implemented in school and counseling settings that has limited the impact and possibility to revolutionize education.

What is needed to transform teaching and learning and education is a model that creates a compelling context that could make the work of these theorists impactful and useful. The application of the iSelf model delivers on this promise.

## The Self and Neurological Research

Research findings on neural connections strengthen the argument against the conventional separation between cognition and emotions. Neurologist Antonio Damasio (1994) argues that there are no "higher" and "lower" brain centers:

> The apparatus of rationality, traditionally presumed to be neocortical, does not seem to work without that of biological regulation, traditionally presumed to be subcortical. Rationality results from the combined activity of the neocortex and the older brain core. In short, there appears to be a collection of systems in the human brain consistently dedicated to the goal-oriented thinking process we call reasoning, and to the response selection we call decision making, with a special emphasis on the personal and social domain. This same collection of systems is also involved in emotion and feeling, and is partly dedicated to processing body signals. (p. xiii)

It is the self of the individual that places himself in learning experiences that marry emotions with thinking to arrive at an outcome, a result from the learning experience. All learning is dedicated toward achieving goals that emphasize the personal and social domains. The self mediates between the social and the personal, and the external with the internal. We make conscious decisions to place ourselves in particular situations where we are called upon to learn, to express, and to add to the interactive dynamics of the interpsychological and intrapsychological processes required to succeed or manifest our goal. Damasio's "collection of systems dedicated to goal-oriented thinking" reinforces the view that reasoning toward the manifestation of a dream considers both personal and social interests, not an either/or perspective. Said another way, inherently, at the being level as human beings, we do not do anything that does not produce positive outcomes for both ourselves and others.

What are the implications of these connections among the mind and brain, physiologically? Through time and placement in subsequent learning experiences, emotions and thinking and actual physical responses activate or trigger the endocrine systems, the heart, blood pressure, and others that affect cognition and emotion. This integrated and dynamic relationship among brain functioning, including emotions, with bodily systems, confirms support for making the teaching of the self a priority if we desire health and well-being outcomes. Understanding how to use emotions proactively and purposely, toward that which is important to the individual, promotes motivated learning and hence deeper learning. The learning of the components of the self and their interactions in various learning situations contributes to a whole person who develops completely and with conscious intention to grow and develop. The whole person learns that she has control over her own destiny in life and is responsible for putting together her own mind. Personal growth becomes an enduring goal. Recall that when using the Ryff scale, personal growth is one of the dimensions of well-being. Therefore teaching well-being strategies results in an individual who feels good about who she is and her place in the world. This self-knowledge and understanding forms an important protective factor against depression, alcohol and drug abuse, smoking, obesity, and other addictive behaviors.

## The Self and Emotions

LeDoux identified brain pathways that carry sensory signals to sites of emotion and of cognition. He found that the thalamus (an area that relays sensory information) conveys sensory stimuli to the amygdala (the site of basic emotional memory) and to the cortex (where cognition occurs). From the cortex, the stimuli go on to the hippocampus, a site involved in memory and also linked to the amygdala. Simply put, there is more than one route to emotional learning, and an emotional response can precede a cognitive perception and response:

> Placing a basic emotional memory process in the amygdalic pathway yields obvious benefits. The amygdala is a critical site of learning because of its central location between input and output stations. Each route that leads to the

amygdala—sensory thalamus, sensory cortex, and hippocampus—delivers unique information to the organ . . . The thalamus activates the amygdala at about the same time as it activates the cortex. The arrangement may enable emotional responses to begin in the amygdala before we completely recognize what it is we are reacting to or what we are feeling. (LeDoux, 1994, pp. 55–56)

Further, "because the neural emotional system can act independently of the neocortex, some emotional reactions and emotional memories can be formed without any conscious, cognitive participation at all" (LeDoux, quoted in Goleman, 1995, p. 18). There are numerous implications of these findings, including our emotional reactions to food or experiences that remind us of emotional memories where the response is to eat. Think about your emotional responses to food around your family Thanksgiving table or other holiday gathering as evidence.

As LeDoux (1994) explains, we form emotional memories from emotional events, and the emotional memory can be elicited through an event similar to the initial event. Emotional memory is not "declarative" memory—which is memory of explicit, consciously accessible information such as prime numbers or names of U.S. states. Rather, it most likely operates independently of our conscious awareness. Nonetheless, and most important, "emotional and declarative memories are stored and retrieved in parallel, and their activities are joined seamlessly in our conscious experience." Thus emotions "exert a powerful influence on declarative memory and other thought processes." The amygdala "plays an essential part in modulating the storage and strength of memories" (p. 5).

The implications of these findings for "memory" problems and for education are clear. We begin to see how, at the neural level, an emotional response can enhance or impair cognition and learning. Input from the thalamus to the amygdala, based on prior positive or negative experiences, may impede or foster declarative memory—our ability to retrieve and consciously use information for decoding and comprehending. Additionally, if declarative information is referenced to the integrated self of the learner and to something deemed important by the learner, then an automatic emotional response enhances learning.

Emotions also affect working memory, the active memory used for a current task (LeDoux, 1994; 1996). Negative emotions (conveyed from the amygdala and parts of the limbic system) can impair the activity of the prefrontal cortex, an area of the brain involved in working memory and executive functioning: "That is why when we are emotionally upset we say we just can't think straight—and why continual emotional distress can create deficits in a child's intellectual abilities, crippling the capacity to learn" (Goleman, 1995, p. 27). Of course, it follows that positive emotion can facilitate working memory.

Many significant neurological studies have been conducted (Christianson, 1992; Dolcos et al., 2004; Dolcos & McCarthy, 2006; Kensinger & Corkin, 2004; etc.). These utilize functional magnetic resonance imaging (fMRI) to investigate the effect of emotions and provide neuroimaging evidence. I would hope that educators, medical professionals, and counselors alike would see the importance and value in teaching young people about their emotional self, especially in light of Dr. Chopra's views about the emotional well-being of youth today.

The significance for using the iSelf model as a framework for teaching about self-knowledge and a new kind of mind through schooling is that it effectively integrates the cognitive with the emotional with the mind, acknowledging that these are not separate when confronting real-world situations. These real-world situations require a framework and approaches grounded in the most recent cognitive science breakthroughs. Here, the enhancing effects of emotion on cognitive functions can inform our framework, as we are proposing to empower paradigm changes in thinking, feeling, and behavior, requiring all the parts of an individual.

## Emotions and Health Research

We need to create an intervention prevention model that works through teaching traditional schooling subjects to enhance health and well-being. Emotions are an important variable to convey when changing behaviors systemically, preventing illness and risky behavior through enhanced cognitive capacity. A recent National Institutes of Health (NIH) sponsored Carnegie-Mellon study shows that a "positive emotional style" impacts well-being outcomes, including the common cold. Additionally, "a positive emotional style also was associated with less smoking, more exercise, better sleep, and lower levels of the stress hormone's epinephrine, norepinephrine, and cortisol" (Cohen et al., 2006).

Teaching in schools about the distinctions of the integrated self, including the attributions of affect and emotional intelligence, could help prevent numerous illnesses and behaviors that lead to obesity, depression, and abuse, among others. If this type of research is sponsored by the NIH, with proven correlations between the mind and health, then why aren't we teaching this important connection to youth through schooling? Wouldn't it make good economic, health, social, and education policy, with inherent strategies and best practices that could begin to impact the acute well-being needs of our society? If we find it important to research the correlations between emotional styles and the common cold, can't we at least encourage children to learn about their own emotional styles and their correlations with a positive life-course trajectory? And further, shouldn't we?

## Mind-Body Connections and the NIH

We have come a long way in our understanding of the human mind through the cognitive sciences to where we now understand that there is an inseparable link among emotions, cognition, and motivation that is global in nature, impacting all areas of a person's life. This mind-body connection is so widely understood to be important that the NIH has devoted significant resources to related research.

NIH's work has found that many of the leading causes of morbidity and mortality in the United States are attributable to social, behavioral, and lifestyle factors (e.g., tobacco use, lack of exercise, poor diet, and drug and alcohol abuse). In addition, numerous studies have documented that psychological stress is linked to a variety of health outcomes, and researchers and public health officials are becoming increasingly interested in understanding the nature of this relationship. Research has shown, for example, that psychological stress can contribute to increased rates of heart disease, decreased immune system functioning, and premature aging. Other research has demonstrated that cognitions, attitudes, beliefs, values, social support, prayer, and meditation can reduce psychological stress and contribute to positive health outcomes. Consequently, over the past decade, NIH has increased its efforts to encourage and support health and behavior research, of which mind-body research is one component.

If the NIH has funded these studies exploring the mental and behavioral causes of well-being, with such positive outcomes, then why have educators and the medical practitioners ignored these? To protect their viability—their usefulness, their client base—is one likely explanation. Another and equally plausible explanation is that the study of human emotions does not fit their existing paradigms. Since 1999, numerous mind-body centers and research programs have been funded by the NIH, Office of Behavioral and Social Sciences Research (OBSSR):

- Columbia University: Mind-Body-Behavioral Medicine Clinical Trials Infrastructure
- Johns Hopkins University: Center for Mind-Body Research
- New York University School of Medicine: Development of a Mind-Body Center at NYUSOM

- Ohio State University: Center for Stress and Wound Healing
- Rutgers University: The State University of New Jersey Center for the Study of Health Beliefs and Behavior
- University of California–Berkeley: Social Disparities in the Early Neurobiology of Stress
- University of California–Los Angeles: Mind/Brain/Body Interactions in Stress-Related Disorders
- University of Miami: Center for Psycho-Oncology Research
- University of Michigan: Michigan Interdisciplinary Center on Social Inequality, Mind, and Body
- University of North Carolina–Chapel Hill: Gastrointestinal Biopsychosocial Research Center
- University of Pittsburgh Medical Center and Carnegie Mellon University: Understanding Shared Psychobiological Pathways
- University of Pittsburgh/Carnegie Mellon University: Pittsburgh Mind-Body Center II
- University of Rochester: Rochester Center for Mind-Body Research
- University of Texas: Medical Branch of Psychoneuroimmunology, Stress, and Healthy Aging in Hispanics
- University of Utah: Utah Center for Exploring Mind-Body Interactions
- University of Wisconsin: Mechanisms of Mind-Body Interaction: Emotion Interface

## Education Research

As we make the case for a new education system—one that prevents mental and physical health disorders, while simultaneously enhances academic performance, with a neuropsychological foundation—we must consider how a set of interrelated psychological processes may inform our intervention and prevention model.

Further adding to the iSelf model, German psychologist and University of Munich Professor Pekrun and others (2002) affirm that emotions are to be viewed as involving sets of interrelated psychological processes (affective, cognitive, motivational, and physiological component processes). Pekrun's model of cognitive and motivational mediators (Pekrun, 1992) asserts that the influence of learning emotions on achievement is mediated by cognitive and motivational mechanisms (cognitive resources, learning motivation, and learning strategies). This model of cognitive and motivational mediators between emotions and academic achievement is embedded in our comprehensive iSelf model that shows not only the effect of emotions on learning and achievement but also the antecedents of emotions such as internal self-appraisals, self-interest and degree to which learning enhances one's potential, and external, environmental factors such as situations that encourage self-expression and efficacy.

University of Michigan researcher Paul Pintrich has added to our understanding of hot and cold components and their interactions. In one Pintrich (1990) study of 173 adolescent girls and boys, he found a significant correlation between students' motivation and deeper cognitive engagement in academic material:

> The motivational components were linked in important ways to student cognitive engagement and academic performance in the classroom. Self-efficacy was positively related to student cognitive engagement and performance. Students who believed they were capable were more likely to report use of cognitive strategies, to be more self-regulating in terms of reporting more use of metacognitive strategies, and to persist more often at difficult or uninteresting academic tasks. (p. 38)

The importance of these results for our purposes in creating new schooling processes is that higher levels of self-efficacy and intrinsic value were correlated with higher levels of self-regulation. If we want to increase academic and well-being outcomes through schooling, we need to place intrinsic motivations of our students at the center of our teaching and counseling intervention program. Pintrich states: "However, knowledge of cognitive and metacognitive strategies is usually not enough to promote student achievement; students also must be motivated to use the strategies as well as regulate their cognition and effort" (Pintrich, 1990, p. 1).

Underscoring the need to make "hot cognition" variables the center of our prevention model, studies on emotions and learning show that poor learning outcomes can produce negative emotions, and in turn, negative emotions can impair learning. Induced negative emotions have been shown to hamper performance on cognitive tasks, whereas positive emotions have an opposite effect (Izard, 1984; Masters, Barden, & Ford, 1979).

## Self-Schema and Learning

The self-schema, an important component of the iSelf model, is a rather complex concept, yet critical to teaching and learning and therapeutic processes because it represents how people become aware of, structure, and create their own realities. Psychologist and Tufts University Professor Robert Sternberg (2007) affirms the importance of developing a child's self-schema as a pathway to helping children become aware that they are unique and are actively creating their lives: "The children have the abilities, but they are not brought out by the ways in which they are taught, which divorce academic content from the children's realities" (p. 152). We can and should use academic content to help children define their own realities of who they are and are going to be, to foster self-awareness and understanding separate from external circumstances, such as family or peers.

DiMaggio (1997) deepens our view of this dynamic in that "individuals experience culture as disparate bits of information and as schematic structures that organize information" (p. 263). *Schemata* are beliefs learned from life experiences, and they shape our views of reality. Therefore, schemata are important to include in our broader construct of self in education. Teachers and counselors in particular shape the beliefs of their students and clients through their methods, yet most often neither we nor our students are aware of this influence. In order to teach the integrated self, we should help students identify and discern the cultural beliefs that shape our realities—and we should do so as a moral responsibility and as a prevention method. This is an opportunity to fundamentally, and at the being level, prevent mental and physical illness, among other desirable outcomes.

According to DiMaggio, "culture is stored in memory" and the individual "organizes the information in the form of schemata" (DiMaggio, 1997, p. 268), where "schemata are both representations of knowledge and information processing mechanisms" (DiMaggio, 1997, p. 269). This view marries the cognitive with the philosophical understandings of knowledge: "in schematic cognition we find the mechanisms by which culture shapes and biases thought" (DiMaggio, 1997, p. 269). Individuals, every day, in all classroom lessons, bring "mental structures that influence perception, interpretation, planning and action" (DiMaggio, 1997, p. 270). In classrooms and in counseling sessions, personal improvement and achievement cannot occur without a well-formed self-schema.

Reality gets constructed through the self in everyday teaching and learning processes that occur in the classroom and in counseling and therapeutic processes. As teachers and counselors, when we present a new piece of information, it requires our students or clients to either assimilate that information into their existing paradigm of reality or create a new paradigm of reality in order to accommodate it. We need to teach our students the mental processes at work when constructing a self with schematic representations of one's identity (Markus, 1977):

> Work on identity suggests the possibility that the self may be an emotionally supersaturated cluster of schemata tending toward consistency and stability

over time. Schemata that are embedded in the self-schemata, then, are more closely articulated with other schemata than those that are not incorporated into the self. (DiMaggio, 1997, p. 279)

This means that teaching and learning effectiveness is dependent upon "schemata embedded in the self-schemata." In Section 2, we discuss the use of and effectiveness of using the *self-referential* method for deepening the connection between academic concepts and information to the self-schema.

As we have discussed, the learning system that is used by students and patients is identical. Therefore, schemata are important in both settings. Educational psychologist, philosopher, and theorist Pajares (1992) discusses the important role of schemata in the teaching and learning of the self: "knowledge is fluid and evolves as new experiences are interpreted and integrated into existing schemata" (Pajares, 1992, p. 312). Further, "Sigel (1985) defined beliefs as mental constructions of experience—often condensed and integrated into schemata or concepts, whereas Harvey (1986) defined belief as an individual's representation of reality" (Pajares, 1992, p. 313). For our purposes as classroom teachers and counselors, the shaping of a student's self is the process of constructing reality out of experiences in the form of beliefs and knowledge. I would suggest that this learning how to construct a self is paramount in our system of education, especially a construct of the self with positive psychology attributes. If our students know that they are in charge of creating their own destinies in life through their construction of reality and of their selves, they will more readily want to learn academic content. There is natural self-interest.

## Self-Knowledge and Schooling

Schooling, as the most dominant force in the social construction of the selves of children, adolescents, and young adults in grades K–16, demands that we teach a new tool for thriving in the 21st century.

Thought leader David P. Baker underscores the transformative effect of schooling: "Formal education on such a vast scale in the world and in the United States culture does more than socializing children, it constructs and transforms society" (Baker, 2010, p. 1). But the cognitive demand of schooling imparts the value that "students are students more than they are children" (p. 13) as opposed to people with good moral character, well-balanced personalities, and unique ways of interpreting life experiences creating a personal purpose, among other attributes essential for a fulfilling and successful life. This focus on "academic intelligence" through increased cognitive abilities is called "an objectified good" by educational theorists (Baker & LeTendre, 2005).

There is recognition that children and adolescents who possess self-understanding grow up to be more accomplished in the domain of school and later in life as healthier adults (Hawkins et al., 2008). Additionally, self-efficacy is the leading antecedent to children's aspirations and career trajectories (Bandura et al., 2001) and performance in the classroom (Pajares, 1996). Indeed, a strong self-system enables individuals to exercise a measure of control over their thoughts, feelings, and actions (Bandura, 1986). There are clearly important attributes for children and adolescents to learn through their development through schooling, and this is where the self-system and positive psychology come together for me in the way I conceptualize teaching and learning, the self of the learner, and the iSelf model.

In the Lent et al. (2005) study, the researchers proposed an integrative model or a unifying theory of well-being and psychosocial adjustment. Their model includes personality traits and affective dispositions, life satisfaction, self-efficacy expectations and environmental supports and resources. They found that the most direct path to life satisfaction was through domain satisfaction—the experience of success in an area of life, such as school. "Domain satisfaction was found to be the single most consistent predictor of overall life satisfaction" (Lent et al., 2005, p. 439), demonstrating the importance of developing a positive self-system through the domain of schooling in the life of an adolescent as a protective factor to a positive life-course trajectory (Patrick et al., 2007; Shannahan, 2000).

The self is a social construction; at the same time, it is the mediator of the social construction of reality (Berger & Luckmann, 1966). The self mediates the cognitive with the environment—it is the self of the learner that is the context of all personal meaning, *a priori*, where reality gets created in one's life. For children and adolescents, this occurs most readily in their schooling environment. Educational psychologist Pajares (1992; 1996) underscores the need for educators to take an integrated view to completely understand key components of the self:

> Self efficacy is considered an important component of an individual's self concept. The literature on self-schemas and possible selves provides a concept of self with four dimensions, one of which, the efficacy dimension, is characterized by individuals' beliefs about their potentialities. (Pajares, 1996, p. 557)

It is important for teachers to impart "beliefs" about their students "potentialities" frequently through the teaching and learning process. Thus, when combined with imparting a self-efficacy attribution, a teacher is making a difference in the life of a student who may not believe that she can manifest her own unique potential in life.

## Empowering Adolescent Well-Being and Academic Performance Through Schooling

In order to describe how teaching self-knowledge through schooling will empower the potentials of K–16 students, we must take the iSelf model and demonstrate the processes that work to apply it in counseling and schooling environments.

Teachers are important in the life of a child not only for imparting academic content knowledge but also, and more directly than is known, for aiding cognitive and human development in terms of an integrated, whole view of children. There is a dynamic and integrated network between academic outcomes and the self-system and positive psychology attributes. If teachers better understand and focus upon these attributes as outcomes through curricula, then their students will be more successful in academic schooling outcomes *and* well-being outcomes. In this process, a teacher is teaching a whole person, not merely the intellect. Therefore, academic outcomes are no more important to well-being outcomes when empowering the full potential of children, and they are not mutually exclusive.

# CHAPTER 5

# THE PURPOSE OF EDUCATION IN THE 21ST CENTURY

Promoting well-being is the ultimate objective of our policy decisions.

—Dr. Ben Bernanke, chairman of the Federal Reserve, 2012

Our system of education, our society, and all of humanity are at a critical crossroad and struggle, deciding which is more important to the quality of life: economic needs or human needs. Education can be a social vaccine to prevent negative outcomes and create a society we envision. We design our education system to achieve our vision for the greatest good for all and to meet our changing needs, both societal and human: "Educational aims always reflect the aims—explicit or implicit—of the societal needs" (Noddings, 2003, p. 88).

I believe the purpose of education in the 21st century is to empower the health and well-being of people. When we do this—satisfying our human needs for belonging, self-actualization, self-understanding, happiness, love, and aesthetics—economic needs will be met. People spend so much of their time and energy merely attempting to survive financially without realizing that we have all that we need. There is an abundance of wealth, enough wealth in the world to go around; no one should feel that they will not get their share at the level of survival. The real issue economically is whether or not people have enough financial resources to manifest their higher purpose in service to humanity and the greater good.

I am not advocating total elimination of our present standards-based education characterized by No Child Left Behind (NCLB) 2001 (which began with *A Nation at Risk* in 1983) in favor of a singular focus upon well-being. I am advocating that well-being be the context that is larger than standards. The 21st century, modern era needs a different type of person produced from our system of education. But the newest innovation within the standards-based model, the Common Core standards, do very little to enhance the type of person needed. The iSelf model, however, is an entirely new approach that helps produces the type of person we need and wish to cultivate in the 21st century: one who is self-directed, whole, healthy, and intrinsically motivated to serve others (whether family, company, community, the world). The iSelf model will enhance educators' ability to produce 21st-century people.

Modern schooling currently reflects 19th-century methods and processes that reinforce the old paradigm of producing unhealthy people who are becoming more limited in their competencies. Within a total quality management (TQM) business model imposed on education, our habit is to make more things more scientific, to work harder at being able to measure our learning or measure our production using scientific metrics. Instead of expanding our view of what needs to be taught and why, we narrow our view to a few content standards and basically transfer information dissociated from students' needs and understanding; this is too much of a transfer for students to connect with or use the information in multiple contexts or real-world applications. The model does not meet the need.

Using Toffler's (1970) waves of change as a template to understand paradigms, we should see we are getting to the end of the "information age." The impending new age or wave that is emerging has not yet been labeled or identified.

Life for humans is changing, with social, economic, cultural, and political domains increasing in their complexities. As our population grows, so too our tools or means of communication to serve our need to relate more thoroughly. We want and need to understand our selves and each other so as to gain a measure of efficacy in addressing everyday concerns and responsibilities. But, more to the point, we need to understand ourselves to gain greater intimacy and depth of experiences. Within the span of the third wave (the information age) from 1950 to 2000, we witnessed how the Internet was invented in 1968 and created new opportunities for productivity, new technologies (such as nanotechnology and biotechnology), and virtual worlds for people to experience. In some ways, information technology has created new opportunities for personal or self-expression. However, our society's mental and physical illnesses point to the need to usher in a new age, one that furthers our expression in healthier ways.

## Beyond the Information Age

All aspects of human life—social, economic, cultural, and political—are rapidly changing as we move forward in the 21st century. Every wave of change in history was expected to meet certain changing demands of human society (Jalai & Mahmoodi, 2009). The duration of each age depended on its ability to satisfy those new demands and needs. As society reaches its goals or realizes that it cannot under the present paradigm, society replaces the previous age with a new one.

The agricultural age provided food for a growing population within a relatively simplistic culture and lasted for about 1,000 years. The industrial age, with its rapidly growing culture, complexities, and increased capacities to develop and produce materials and goods, lasted only about 300 years. In the latter half of the 20th century, the information age emerged with the societal goal to increase the availability of information and knowledge. During the past 60 years, we have created a knowledge-based society, with unimaginable complexities in terms of human relations, global society interdependence, and even basic communication.

Each wave of change brought about new systems and institutional relationships in the settings of business, education, transportation, communication, and family. Each wave has been of successively shorter duration due to growing populations, increased cultural complexities, and humanity's ability to change through adaptation. Each age has also enhanced social and human capital through new institutions and social policies that value empowering those most needy in our society.

For example, let's consider how the family has changed within the information age. As a society, we evolved from the traditional nuclear family structure in which one parent worked outside the home while the other concentrated on raising children and maintaining the home. Over time, this model was replaced by one in which both parents worked outside of the home, or divorce forced single parents to go to work while leaving children to fend for themselves emotionally. This model has left children often bereft of mentorship and guidance. Schools and schooling processes have been asked to fill the void more often than not during this period.

Let's also consider how extensively business has changed throughout the information age. We went from an economy of family-oriented businesses during the agrarian age to new bureaucratic structures of the industrial age that encouraged mass production and an adversarial view of competitors. The information age transformed this perspective toward customized production and a team approach, operating under the view that we can all win through increased cooperation, even with our competitors. Each age required a different human mind and mind-set to manifest the goals and aspirations of the age. During the industrial age, we needed a compliant person who conformed to the norms, accepted top-down communication and commands and the division of labor, and had the ability to compartmentalize his tasks and functions. With the information age, we have needed people who can take personal initiative, deviate from the norm, think in new and creative ways, communicate through numerous networks, and think beyond their own function to see the entire process as a way to add value to the business organization.

Although the world of business has progressed in the information age, the values, practices, and perceived needs of the educational system are still stuck in another age—the industrial age. Our education paradigm has a "sorting focus," borrowing from business language and concepts and an industrial model of manufacturing. Sorting means that you categorize your product and then batch processes based on the categorization. In education, this translates into either a time-based or seat-time-based system (in which classes are groups of students with equal academic capabilities) or a teacher-based system (where a student's ability to learn is predicated on whether the teacher can teach in the way those students learn best). Rather than create a new paradigm, schooling in the information age has, for the most part, used the computer and Internet to further standardize and measure learning, further entrenching industrial age values and practices.

Doesn't it make sense to create a system that is learning based, giving priority to the person's individual needs instead of the standardized scale of learning? Shouldn't we be imparting competencies that develop the strengths of each person and dedicate resources to make certain that students are learning in accordance with *their* personalized learning plan? All this and more *is* possible, yet the current paradigm of education does not allow for us to create new methods that place students and their potential at the center of schooling.

Recently, as the information age comes under pressure to evolve, there have been exciting new developments that promise to transform our system of education. One example, an offshoot of the success of the online, open-source learning materials from Khan Academy, flips the classroom: Teachers oversee and coach their students on academic material (primarily math and science). Students view short videos at home on the Internet on course concepts, and then teachers act as mentors and coaches as students work on problem solving together in the classroom. Both teachers and students are accepting this model as it relates to academic content, so it now makes sense to provide these teachers with the tools to help students construct a self and utilize the same tools to better understand their students' personalized learning needs.

However, in spite of all our technological advances, human biological DNA remains the same. Educators, counselors, and medical doctors have not advanced their understanding of the human mind to keep pace with recent psychological research. Students need the new ability to think in a new way, with a new mind to meet the demands of the 21st century. The growing field of mind, brain, and education (MBE) substantiates proof of previously unseen neurological pathways and the integrated nature of the brain, offering hope for possibilities of a unique self. New psychological paradigms elevate the integrated mind over the synaptic brain and acknowledge the socioconstruction of each mind, setting the stage for the next wave of change. As counselors and as teachers, we have methods, media, and new understandings of the integrated self that we are not utilizing. Students have access to mass amounts of information in multiple formats that can be delivered in a customized format based on interests, but they are not being taught anywhere—neither through schooling nor media—how to reflect on this information, conceptualize new possibilities, develop relationships, and formulate new ideas from the information provided; they are also not taught how to harness emotional and metacognitive capabilities.

We are ready for the next wave, age, or paradigm to meet the new set of human needs in our society. I am calling the emerging next wave the "integration age" because society is calling for two kinds of integration. First, the individual needs to better integrate her self's components to address personal issues, hopes, and dreams. Second, the individual must also integrate with the Internet-fueled global society in which problems are solved collectively. If we don't integrate, then the current culture will continue to be overwhelmed with negative outcomes.

The goal of the integrated age will be to create a whole human being who is capable of experiencing an alignment among all component parts of the self—the physical, spiritual, psychological, and emotional. Humanity is demanding more. The next educational paradigm will teach people to take charge of their futures through self-determination and to change through their increased cognitive capabilities to dream or envision. Change is inevitable and constant and takes one of three forms: crisis, adaptation, or vision. What is required in society is a person-centric view to address the personal issues and concerns and hopes and dreams of each individual in our global society.

## Paradigm Crisis or Not?

Modern society has given us more than we can handle, and we need to focus on developing the mental models or paradigms of self-understanding, with which to handle growing complexities. In short, "we cannot meet the challenges of the 21st century with the educational ideologies of the 19th" (Robinson, 2001, p. 201). I argue that our present paradigm of education is not adequate, given the complexity of modern life; in fact, it contributes to the myriad well-being problems throughout our society. This view (that our present paradigm of education and NCLB policies, methods, practices, and goals were developed for another time and for the purpose of producing docile workers) is supported by education professor Sir Ken Robinson's research: "The economic and intellectual assumptions on which our systems of education have been built originated in another time and for other purposes" (Robinson, 2001, p. 198). I would add that these assumptions and systems of education also originated in another paradigm.

Theoretical scientist and Harvard University professor Thomas Kuhn (1962) describes four distinct phases through which paradigms pass. I present these stages here to assist in evaluating whether we are indeed in the midst of a paradigm crisis:

1. During the "preparadigmatic phase," a number of theoretical approaches or schools, often fused with much broader philosophical concerns, are in competition with each other, with none of them commanding the respect and allegiance of the relevant (educational) community.
2. When some paradigm develops sufficient sophistication and support to be widely recognized and used as the principal framework, then the field has emerged into a "paradigmatic phase." In this stage, educators engage in activities deemed to be normal or the norm, largely employing the reigning paradigm to conceptualize and solve problems, develop instruments, and make theoretical specifications. The paradigm is relatively safe, and educators proceed to solve problems and continue using it rather than challenge assumptions or develop fundamental revisions. This phase currently shapes the NCLB research, policy formulation, administrative procedures, and teaching and learning practices.
3. A "crisis phase" is entered when significant anomalies and challenges accumulate to the point where the reigning paradigm is increasingly felt to be failing or discredited in the eyes of a significant proportion of the relevant (educational) community. New paradigms may be developed or revived, and there is likely to be a period of competition among the various perspectives—perhaps comparable to the preparadigmatic phase. Recent data on poor academic and well-being outcomes demonstrate we are currently experiencing this phase.
4. A "revolution" or "transformation" is likely to occur—a relatively discontinuous leap or shift to a significantly different paradigm that usually involves a radical reconstruction of the field's basic criteria and conceptualizations. My proposal for a more humanistic pathway using the iSelf model would be considered an "education revolution" if it were to shape

policies, research, institutionalization of its curriculum, and teaching and learning practices.

Adapted from Effrat, 1972, p. 9–10.

I argue that our existing standards-based paradigm of education does not (but should) have as its purpose to impart the understanding of one's unique potential in life and how to manifest it. The basic assumptions of the reigning paradigm are approaching a "paradigm crisis" (Kuhn, 1962), as evidenced by the growing myriad of problems in our society that can be directly related to a lack of an understanding of one's unique self and potential and the model that is used to teach people what is important in life.

Paradigms of education have different purposes and therefore different curricular emphases. Presently, one underlying purpose of the schools standards-based system is to transmit the dominant culture. This philosophy is situated in Bourdieu's (1977; 1986) social reproduction theory, which espouses "the educational system fulfills a function of legitimation which is more and more necessary to the perpetuation of the social order" (1977, p. 60). Do we want to perpetuate the embedded social beliefs about health and well-being?

The paradigm we use produces the outcomes or results, but which results serve our young people and our society more thoroughly in the 21st century: good grades or good human beings?

## NCLB: Cognitive Focus and Results

The overemphasis upon standards characterizes the current educational paradigm that shaped school reform known as No Child Left Behind (NCLB), which offers a relatively formed and safe haven to educators, who proceed to solve puzzles and problems within its confines rather than challenge overall assumptions or develop fundamental revisions. The policies, programs, methods, and theories within this paradigm are well formed; it is understood that educators focus singularly on helping students achieve *academic* success to the level of a common measure of proficiency, not to each student's potential.

In a review of the literature on "potential," there appear to be few references to approaches to helping young people learn how to achieve academic or other potentials in life. The idea of potential is addressed neither within our existing educational system nor in our human psychological paradigm. With academic proficiency as the goal, we are not teaching young people how to see or achieve their full potentials in life. Further, the intersection between humanistic education and standards-based curricula has not been researched by education researchers, indicating that an approach that offers promise for empowering self over academics, and one to replace the outdated NCLB, is not even on the radar screen.

Even though NCLB attempts to represent the needs of business and social economics, ironically a chorus of complaints can be heard from business leaders that our system of education is not producing enough qualified workers with 21st-century skills: "We now have a school curriculum that teaches [four] subjects but only limited ways of thinking" (Robinson, 2001, p. 201). To further demonstrate the point that our standards-based model is failing to empower the full academic and personal potentials of our young people, the "skills that business leaders are requesting from the system of education are: problem solving, creativity, imagination, being original, the meaning of life, speaking your mind, thinking differently, freedom to create, able to understand at different levels of conscious awareness" (Robinson, 2001, pp. 112–122). Achievement outcomes confirm that students are not manifesting their academic potentials, let alone their overall personal potentials, nor are they developing those skills that will empower their professional success.

The paradigm of the standards-based model overemphasizes, misunderstands, and misapplies cognitive psychology to the teaching and assessing of outcomes in the four core subject areas (i.e., reading, writing, math, and science). Improved cognitive development and associated, measurable academic variables are seen as the pathway to improved student achievement outcomes. I am asserting that within this view, you cannot teach young people to see and achieve their unique potentials in life. Educators have used the "cognitive revolution" in psychology, and in particular, its application to mathematics and science education (Anderson, Reder, & Simon, 2000), as a foundation to emphasize learning strategies and outcomes that are included in the new generation of standards, the Common Core standards. Yet cognition cannot fully explain human potential in that the self involves levels of consciousness, inner emotions, character, a sense of purpose and calling (Hillman, 1996) that cannot be measured as cognitive scientists would like us to be able to do.

When educational researchers attempt to quantify cognition in learning, they decontextualize the information from the learner; however, learning occurs in a broader context or environment that cannot always be measured (Simon, 1981; Card, Moran, & Newell, 1983; Resnick & Resnick, 1992). Classroom teaching practices that focus solely on developing improved cognitive functioning actually decontextualize the information from the learner, making learning personally meaningless. The most effective teaching method for contextualizing the learning of academic content and making it personally meaningful is the self-referential method (Rogers, 1981), which is discussed in Section 2.

Most often, the study of theories and practices from the standards-based paradigm focus on NCLB measurable student achievement. Reform advocates focus on the measurement of standards and skills learned, representing a technical quality view. Quality is measured by math and reading test scores for which students are products. The one constant focus is to improve students' intellectual functioning. The U.S. Department of Education has sponsored research to support its "reforms," with researchers providing leadership in using scientific methods (Reyna, 2002; Feuer & Towne, 2002) and studies in math and reading (Gersten et al., 2002; Greer, 2002). In a study conducted by the Northwest Evaluation Association (2005), researchers made a connection between student achievement and growth—but here "growth" means the number of students increasing their test scores. The focus, clearly, is on measurable academic achievements and levels of cognition needed to perform well with no regard to the "growth" of the person who is learning. The Department of Education is willing to sponsor research into the causes for growth of academic achievement but not in the growth of people.

## NCLB and Business Models

Educational policy makers and experts in support of the current, standards-based paradigm contend that the best way to help people reach their full potential is to focus upon cognitive, intellectual development. Stanford University educators and researchers David Tyack and Larry Cuban have studied education reform in the United States and concluded that our present system of education, our present paradigm, is dominated by the "cult of efficiency" (1995). Certainly, since the 1983 publication of *A Nation at Risk,* our education paradigm has been informed by business total quality management models (Deming, 1986); educators have adopted business processes and are "coldly scientific" (Senge et al., 2000) in their educational goals, styles, methods, and policies.

The more businesslike and scientific pursuit of system efficiencies means that "quantitative targets, measures of performance relative to targets are driven throughout the system" (Senge et al., 2000, p. 44), dominate our standards-based system of education. Deming himself finds fault with the overuse and overreliance upon this quantitative management approach, acknowledging that this system has "'destroyed our people,' because of its [negative] impacts on intrinsic motivation, curiosity, risk taking and innovation, and personal responsibility" (Senge et al., 2000, p. 45). Interestingly, these are the very personal traits now called for by the business community and the 21st-century skills model.

Senge (2000) argued that misusing Deming's approaches in our system of education creates a "machine world of teachers in control, students dependent on teachers' approval, and learning defined as getting an A on the test":

> Most of us developed our survival skills for industrial-age institutions in first and second grade. We learned how to please the teacher, as we would later try to please our boss. We learned how to be quiet when we felt lost, how to avoid wrong answers, and to avoid blame. (p. 34)

I agree with Senge, Cuban, and Tyack that schools can be a "generative" institution for creating a more humanistic society, "just as school has been the generative institution for machine-age thinking" (p. 34). Our schools are cold, inhuman places, precisely because we focus upon measuring academic learning outcomes only. An alternative would be to require students to demonstrate humane competencies, such as service to others, kindness to classmates, and personal well-being and personal growth.

The tragic well-being statistics and state of the human condition underscores my thesis that the present paradigm is producing people whose intrinsic motivations are deadened, whose sense of possibilities in their lives and for a better world are absent, and whose whole-person well-being is neither valued nor encouraged in our schools or society.

After pouring billions of taxpayer dollars and foundation funding into standards-based education since 1983 (with accelerated spending since NCLB in 2001), test scores reflecting literacy and math achievement remain relatively flat. Schools are not on target to be able to achieve 2014 minimum proficiency standards established in 2001, and the United States' ranking among the countries of the world is weak and sinking. According to a Harvard University study (Hanuschek, Peterson, & Woessmann, 2012) the United States ranks 25th in math, 17th in science, and 14th in reading. When we cannot achieve the very goals upon which we focus, does it make sense to continue to solve academic achievement problems from our present mind-set?

There are implications for *not* making the shift in our mind-sets that I am calling for, that of continuing down our current path: further division and vitriol and deterioration of our quality of life; a continued inability to reach compromise on important legislation in Congress; the continued downward spiral of children's well-being; more prevalent dependency upon prescription drugs; increased incidences of bullying and suicide; and increased stressors of making a living and attempting to offset the powerful, unforeseen, and unconscious forces against families, children, and all people in our society. Analogously, we are the fish swimming in the fish tank, and we do not know what we have allowed to pollute our water—and if we do, we have no way to clean up the mess. We cannot afford to perpetuate our society's problems, and we need our schools to create another paradigm to enable societal change through changes in our educational system.

### Forces for Change

When I speak of a new mind, I do not mean a common mind-set in which we are taught through our education to think alike, with common values and norms and expectations. Closer to the heart and spirit of our American society, individuals should have a set of educational rights that allow for the freedom of thought and expression, a diversity of views, and ways of thinking about the world and its issues and solutions. But the present paradigm encourages black-and-white, simplistic, either-or thinking, a confrontational style in which one side is bullied or forced to conform to the majority. The iSelf model will teach self-awareness that also informs awareness of others, where all sides and views are heard and understood, and then a new contextual view or perspective is taken that incorporates them—enabling all to have a voice in creating a better world, for all.

One example of the growing force that is attempting to influence (if not outright dominate) our thinking, values, and reality is the growth of television news agencies as a force in shaping the discourse and views and realities of their viewers. The attitude is not merely to minimize the views of others by touting alternatives, but rather to openly criticize others for not agreeing or conforming. The mission seems to be to find a way, by persuasion or force, to get everyone to agree on one common set of values. This force is not healthy for our society or for empowering individual self-expression. We shrink our understanding of what is possible and therefore overlook creative solutions to problems faced in our society. Consider the growing corporate influence in our political and judicial processes by allowing unlimited political action committees (PAC) money to influence the democratic process. This can be considered further reinforcement of the use of force and domination to shape laws, policies, and people's attitudes, ultimately limiting freedom. While I support open and free communication regardless of political leanings, we lack the societal and educational structures to enable people to think for themselves and assess the very views being espoused—making today's media output paramount to propaganda at a minimum and brainwashing at worst.

In a similar manner, the city of New York used law and policy to guide the consumption of soft drinks to deter obesity rates. The city would be better served to address the issue more fundamentally and teach children how to place self-knowledge at the center of their education to make choices that serve their health and well-being. Admittedly, this systemic approach would require a longer time frame to achieve because we live in a society that values immediate gratification and quantity over quality; large soft drinks are what we have taught people to want, therefore more is good. This present paradigm permeates our schools and cultural media.

Additionally, when we allow the media, with its corporate ownership and influence, to be the predominate force shaping children's belief systems about themselves and their worlds, then we have not placed the power to shape our realities in the correct place: in the minds of children. Individuals have their set of beliefs that are learned somewhere: through time spent with family and peers, in school, and absorbing culture and media. Of these, culture and media have come to take precedence in forming our belief systems. Students have gone online, out of reach of parents and other key guides in creating good people.

Further, we have taken out of the teachers' hands the ability to shape the hearts and minds of children beyond imparting simplistic information, due to the narrow focus required by NCLB and the standards-based paradigm this policy represents. What is missing is a dialogue about a new educational theory that shifts the power to create a better world by linking the body to the mind, self to other, and emotions and emotional responses to issues that are real and troubling. Ask parents and they will likely agree—once their child reaches school age, schooling becomes the second most dominant force in shaping children's beliefs. Beliefs, however, are acquired either consciously or subconsciously through everyday life *experiences*, not through academic lectures. If we are able to make this shift in our thinking, to place *people* and *experiences* at the center of our thinking, then we can help others better understand how we arrived at our beliefs and how our experiences have either supported or inhibited the manifestation of our full potential.

## Humanistic Education

Currently, the primary school-based model to impart potential in life is through the NCLB standards-based model and its narrow testing of knowledge and skills. The iSelf model is a pathway to full potential—academic and personal—that will help schools focus upon whole child well-being. In the words of psychologist James Hillman,

> I want us to envision that what children go through has to do with finding a place in the world for their specific calling [purpose and potential in life]. They are trying to live two lives at once, the one they were born with and

the one of the place and among the people they were born into. (Hillman, 1996, p. 13)

I invite the reader to determine which pathway to potential better provides young people with a theoretical foundation for understanding their lives; as educators, isn't this our mission?

The broader, more holistic view of potential includes teaching young people to expand their capabilities, capacities, and propensities in self-understanding, healthy self-esteem, personal agency, self-expression, and intrinsic motivation. Going a step further, children should be encouraged to explore their ability to interact socially and given guidance in understanding their emotional, spiritual, physical, and psychological health. An educational paradigm that focuses upon understanding the self is a more effective way to help young people reach all their potentials in life.

Educational philosopher and Columbia University professor Maxine Greene informs the alternative humanistic paradigm by advocating a "curriculum for human beings" in which educators "create possibilities for human empowerment" (1995). This is what I mean when I describe a system of education that creates a pathway for learning about human potential, where "individual and social development [are] processes that are 'always in the making'" (Greene, 1995). Further, we need this kind of learning in the 21st-century classroom.

A central guiding principle to helping young people learn how to achieve their academic potentials, *and* their human potentials, is the focus upon the self. To this end, psychiatrist and Harvard University professor Jerome Bruner suggests rethinking the aims of education to focus upon the "phenomenon of 'Self' which is the single most universal thing about human experience" (Bruner, 1996, p. 35). Renowned child development researcher and author Robert Coles, who has spent his life researching the inner life of children, suggests that we need to teach children "how to be good people whose moral character sustains them as adults" (Coles, 1997a). He expresses disappointment over how our schools pay so little attention to the inner life of children, "to affirming their humanity" (Coles, 1997b, p. 4).

Schools and policy makers continue their march on the standards-based path to develop the intellectual cognitive abilities in four core subject areas. Yet some educational psychologists and philosophers are calling for schools to take a humanistic view and address the whole child, where "whole" is understood as a child's sense of self, self-esteem, agency, motivation, emotional well-being, psycho-emotional and social-emotional development, spiritual and character development, and cognitive/intellectual development, beyond their academic abilities.

The humanistic pathway can take two forms (McNeil, 2005, p. 5), using human attributes to help young people be better students (what is known as *confluent*) and using human attributes to help young people be better people (what is known as *consciousness*). Educational philosopher Nel Noddings (2003; 2005; 2006) provides a powerful understanding of the need to educate the whole child when she argues that children are whole people, individuals with widely ranging interests and aptitudes, and as such all parts of the whole should be considered.

Educational psychologist and researcher Barbara McCombs (2003) details the American Psychological Association's learner-centered psychological principles (LCPs) that have been successfully implemented and researched and have contributed to our understanding of the value of shifting the teaching and learning process from a teacher-centered to student-centered learning process. An important advance in humanistic education, LCP emphasizes that cognitive and metacognitive factors, motivational and affective factors, developmental and social factors, and individual differences factors guide the teaching and learning practices in schools. These principles even highlight some of the distinctions of the inner self that are included in the iSelf model. However, one of the limitations of the LCP is its focus on motivational and affective factors that primarily pertain to a student's academic performance, not their self-knowledge or future interests.

One must wonder whether the use of psychology in education has, in many ways, taken the form of manipulating young people to learn their academic lessons at higher levels, not to inform or empower who they are. Sadly, students know this. In my research and experience, this approach accounts for much of the disengagement witnessed in schooling and contributes to persistent academic achievement problems, such as flat test scores, year after year, high dropout rates in high school and college, and poor psychological and physical well-being problems so acute in our society today.

Having established that our society's needs are changing, and that phylogenetically and ontogenetically we have evolved to a point in time where we are ready for a new human mind, paradigm shift, and transformative approach, I will now present a way to think about where we are in creating new educational practices that will serve and empower our evolution and development.

# Section 2

# PRACTICE

# CHAPTER 6

# CURRICULUM

In the ongoing battle to reform education to adhere and conform more precisely to the standards-based philosophy, we have lost sight that "curriculum can be interpreted as a vision of the educated adult, a plan for a pedagogical journey toward the good life, or students' actual classroom engagements with ideas and ways of knowing" (Henderson & Hawthorne, 2000, p. 3). "School curricula can also be viewed as a social and political representation of the accumulation of our society's value and knowledge traditions, representing particular social-political conceptions of a society" (Henderson & Hawthorne, 2000, p. 3). How do we move beyond a purely standards-based model to satisfy our vision of the educated person? How do we convey that education is a journey about how to achieve the good life, with mental and physical well-being flourishing?

In order to demonstrate what a new curriculum that focuses upon the whole child would look like, I present one example of what *not* to do. Much is at stake when policy makers influence curricula. When we adhere too strongly to a single belief system in education, we further deepen our adherence to a standards-based system that objectifies the learner by eliminating critical thinking skills from schooling. In 2012, a proposed Texas policy stated formal opposition to "the teaching of Higher Order Thinking Skills, (HOTS) (values clarification), . . . critical thinking skills and similar programs that are simply a relabeling of Outcome-Based Education (OBE) (mastery learning) which focus on behavior modification and have the purpose of challenging the students' fixed beliefs and undermining parental authority" (Republican Party of Texas, 2012, p. 20). Although this statement was later denounced as an unintended addition to the document following an overwhelming outcry from across the country, this assault on critical-thinking skills is rather chilling, especially when the 21st century requires advancing such skills, which also contribute to the well-being of Texas youth.

The current paradigm of education creates an environment in which students have "fixed beliefs" that should not be challenged, questioned or changed, implying that children should believe what their parents believe. This notion places a limitation on what is possible for each child, preventing her from becoming who she is, uniquely, and surpassing her parents—or, as they say in Texas, "to 'rise above your raisin'."

What is needed is a path or a curriculum that helps people to take responsibility for creating their own paradigm of self, including their own beliefs. I will discuss a curriculum known as the Self Across the Curriculum (SAC) that was developed to impart iSelf model attributions. It has been taught at the university level to preservice and in-service master teachers through undergraduate and graduate coursework. These teachers have taken the SAC and developed lesson plans and learning activities for their high school social studies, middle school science, elementary literacy, and college educational psychology classes.

The SAC teaches students how to first understand themselves, *a priori*, and how to process and understand the content information that is taught through traditional subjects (e.g., math and social studies). What results is deeper learning and understanding of both the self and the subject content. The deeper learning occurs because of the direct transfer or near transfer of knowledge and far transfer or high-road transfer.

Let's define these terms. *Direct transfer* of knowledge is synonymous with *near transfer* and represents the influence of previously learned material on new material. It represents the ease or automaticity of which someone can take a concept or piece of information or skills learned in a particular context. The direct or near transfer of knowledge is considered unconscious or automatic. This is what educators and counselors would hope to be able to teach: that learning about how to reach higher states of consciousness and to change one's self to create a better life characterized by mental and physical well-being could be an automatic process.

When learning is self-referential and the self is used as a prism or the lens through which to view all subjects, then the information learned relates more directly to other situations and uses higher cognitive and metacognitive functions. This is an example of *far transfer*, or the ability to utilize the information learned in multiple contexts given changing conditions and circumstances. This too is what educators and counselors would hope to teach through attainment of higher states of self-awareness.

In contrast, the way students in the United States learn algebra (and, for that matter, all subjects) in the NCLB era has proven to be problematic. The rote knowledge requirement that serves as learning in today's classroom actually increases the level of resistance to the transferability of that knowledge—or what is known as *transfer resistance* or *inflexibility* (Anderson & Lebiere, 1998). Rote knowledge has direct correlations to low academic achievement in mathematics because students with rote knowledge have great difficulty on both near- and far-transfer problems (Hiebert & Carpenter, 1992), particularly in the domain of algebra (Blume & Heckman, 1997). If students first apply rote knowledge to an iSelf attribution, then greater high-road transfer and flexibility result.

High-road transfer involves cognitive understanding, purposeful and conscious analysis, mindfulness, and application of strategies that cut across disciplines. In high-road transfer, there is a deliberate mindful abstraction of an idea that can transfer, and then conscious and intentional application of a concept when faced by a problem for which the concept may be useful. For example, one of my counseling clients reported that she was feeling too much pressure, emotional stress, and anxiety from her parents and school officials, who were pushing her to perform at high levels in terms of grades. She would turn this pressure into self-defeating conversations in her thought processes as a defense mechanism to block out the emotional discomfort. She learned that she had a dream of helping people to feel better about themselves and be better able to handle family dynamics. With high-road transfer, she realized she wanted to do well in high school so that she could attend college and study human development and family studies. She learned the concept of structural tension (discussed in Section 1) and better understood her own situation of being able to handle life's pressures within her family. She then purposely created structural tension for her future career and academic life-course trajectory.

Just as the popular K–16 Writing Across the Curriculum (WAC) has two simultaneous goals, to teach writing skills through content and to use writing to teach subject content, the SAC also has two goals: to teach self-knowledge through content and to use self-knowledge to connect with the content more thoroughly and deeply. This type of teaching and learning requires a different focus, an internal focus versus an external one; it drives the learner to look inward first, to know one's self and attain a sense of purpose, dreams, moral center, and personal strengths, so as to literally create or construct one's self using the iSelf model as a framework. The advantage of learning about the self, *a priori*, is that when it is time to develop a strategy to learn about and apply subject content, students demonstrate dramatically increased efficacy and creativity when problem solving.

The SAC utilizes a *contextual teaching and learning* method, which connects the content that students are learning (e.g., environmental science) with the context in which that content can be used (e.g., designing a city park and planting trees) and also with attributions of the self in real-world situations. Connecting content with context is an important component part of bringing meaning to the learning process and making learning more personalized. Further, SAC's intent is to access the natural learning system that all students possess—learning about one's self—as this is our first interest.

The SAC also utilizes the *self-referential teaching and learning method*, in which teachers help each learner personalize the subject content so as to deepen the encoding of that information. Numerous studies demonstrate this deeper learning. Rogers, Kuiper, and Kirker (1977) write:

> The degree to which the self is implicated in processing personal information was investigated. Subjects rated adjectives on four tasks designed to force varying kinds of encoding: structural, phonemic, semantic, and self-reference. In two experiments, incidental recall of the rated words indicated that adjectives rated under the self-reference task were recalled the best. These results indicate that self-reference is a rich and powerful encoding process. As an aspect of the human information-processing system, the self appears to function as a superordinate schema that is deeply involved in the processing, interpretation, and memory of personal information. (Rogers, Kuiper, & Kirker, 1977, p. 677)

The self-schema component of the iSelf model is critical to learning and growing and developing as a person through schooling and all learning environments, and it is important for educators and mental and physical health service providers to use it in their work.

Leading self-referential scholars underscore this view: "In order for self-reference to be such a useful encoding process, the self must be a uniform, well-structured concept. During the recall phase of the study, subjects probably use the self as a retrieval cue" (Moscovitch & Craik, 1976). "In order for [self reference] to be functional, the self must be a consistent and uniform schema" (Rogers, Kuiper, & Kirker, 1977, p. 686).

## Connecting Academic Subjects to the Self

Upon visiting the idea of integrating distinctions of self into lesson planning, a teacher could easily become overwhelmed, given all the other day-to-day responsibilities to align lessons with curricula and Common Core standards, as well as prepare students for standardized testing. Many would go as far as to say that this is not the job of a teacher—to empower students' well-being—that it is beyond the mission of schools to develop students along these dimensions.

However, my research into the core beliefs of teachers demonstrates that, typically, this is why they got into teaching in the first place. They believe their mission is to empower the self of their students and impart a significant protective factor of high self-esteem (Brzycki, 2009). What I have found is that teachers become overwhelmed when they see they see the disconnect between their innate missions as educators and the school and district policies that require adherence to standardized testing guidelines and procedures as the primary functional responsibilities. In other cases, they become overwhelmed because they do not have a method of how to impart self-attributions through their day-to-day schooling processes.

Far more easily than they realize, teachers can readily integrate the self of their students in teaching and learning through everyday classroom lessons. Further, when they integrate the self through academic content, using the self-referential method of teaching and learning, they create a more effective transfer of the knowledge, thereby making the learning more meaningful and lasting, across numerous contexts experienced in life.

For one teacher I interviewed, the process of imparting self-knowledge through academic lessons was transformative:

> I was a language arts teacher, and we did poetry in there, and they jumped on the poetry thing just to kind of release, just to kind of get in touch with themselves and at the beginning of the year. I don't think I would have seen that, so it was kind of like that was like an outlet for a lot of them, and they started entering poetry contests, and they wanted to share with the class, and I thought that was kind of neat. (Brzycki, 2009)

What is being demonstrated in this example is that the teacher saw a number of integrated self-attributes emerge as the students constructed their selves. The students exhibited increased motivation ("jumped on the poetry thing"), self-understanding ("get in touch with themselves"), achievement ("started entering poetry contests"), and self-efficacy ("they wanted to share [more expressively] with the class").

Learning about the integrated self even works in a math classroom. Of all academic content areas that are typically taught in school, math is seen perhaps as the most challenging for imparting self-system and positive psychology attributes. The components of the self are explained with language rather than numbers, which makes contextual teaching critical. One of the high school students I taught was not motivated to learn algebra because he was more interested in maintaining his popular status among his classmates. He was very bright intellectually, emotionally aware (of his own and others emotions), socially talented, gifted physically, and in touch with the modern culture. When asked why he did not do well in school and was not living up to his potential, including in math, he said that he did not know why he should bother; similar responses and associated attitudes are often heard by teachers in all subject areas. I told him a story about Buckminster Fuller's life that would hopefully inspire him and engage his self, including such components as his sense of higher purpose for his life and his own dreams; his self concept and identity; his mathematical, interpersonal, and intrapersonal intelligences; his feelings for helping others; and his desire to make a positive difference in the world.

Buckminster Fuller (1895–1983) was an MIT-trained mechanical engineer who invented the geodesic dome. Variations on this design are often used in large athletic arenas, such as the Superdome in New Orleans, and in freestanding camping tents. The key mathematical and physics concept of the dome is that each piece of the structure reinforces the other, which creates exceptional overall structural strength. If any one piece is weak or structurally unsound, the entire structure is weakened or could collapse. Metaphorically, if each person understands his purpose in life and is actively manifesting that unique purpose, thus reinforcing each other's purposes, then the structure of humankind would work better, or even optimally. If any one of us is not in touch with this component of self-understanding, or actively manifesting it in the world, then the structure of humanity is weakened and could collapse.

At one level, the intellectual level, Fuller's creation was wonderfully inventive and very useful. Yet, at a deeper level, Buckminster Fuller's intention or his guiding purpose was critical to this math student's transformation from a weak student with no direction in life to one who was motivated to learn about his self—as well as math and physics—through schooling. The geodesic dome represents a model for the way human beings can live that would make the world a better place.

This story helped this student realize that he too had a higher and unique purpose for his own life, and maybe he could study architecture as a way to utilize his math skills and make a difference in the world using these skills. From this point on, he had a stronger sense of self-efficacy in school, and the motivation to excel was no longer an issue for him. His life-course trajectory soared.

In a 2012 research study examining the keys to producing academic results in the classroom, Chingos and Whitehurst found curriculum to be equally if not more important than teacher quality. The prevailing view that it is certainly the teacher, but as this study concluded, curriculum is just as important. Chingos and Whitehurst take the view that curricula is equally if not more important than teacher quality when impacting student achievement. With academic content knowledge such an ineffective transfer for most students,

I would concur that if teachers were able to enter the "black box" of teaching and learning to use the iSelf model to deepen learning of the self and academic content, then curriculum could be changed for the better. I use the term black box because, much like a plane's flight recorder, it provides answers to long-held questions about what happens between the teacher and the students when learning happens. That strategy has not been on the radar of researchers, policy makers, or practitioners, but the new pedagogy known as the Self Across the Curriculum (SAC) will hopefully change that. Using the iSelf attributions, SAC is the breakthrough needed to produce young people who are both academically and emotionally prepared to meet 21st-century demands.

## The Self Across the Curriculum

The SAC is a system of pedagogy of the self at the intersection of education and adolescent development. Educators and psychologists realize that an understanding of the self must take on heightened importance due to the increasing awareness of the central, functional role that the self plays in development across the life-span.

The SAC implements teacher beliefs and practices for imparting self-system and positive psychology attributes because of the critical link between the construction of the self and the outcome of happier, healthier, more successful children. This pedagogy considers the beliefs that teachers hold about the importance of their role in the development of the selves of their students, as well as beliefs about classroom practices used to impart self-system and positive psychology attributes. The SAC helps heal emotional wounds experienced from previous stages in childhood and build resiliency as a protective factor. This pedagogy also teaches children, adolescents, and young adults how to achieve psychological and physical well-being—critical knowledge for the 21st-century world citizen.

Representing best teacher practices among K–16 schooling, the SAC incorporates subjective happiness, satisfaction with life, and psychological well-being lesson activities and attributes that have been researched by the Positive Psychology Center at the University of Pennsylvania. I argue that teachers can do much more to positively influence the human development of students; SAC includes the differing teacher intervention and instructional strategies used to impart happy, healthy, and whole children.

This educational approach is applicable for a wide spectrum of professionals: K–16 educators, administrators, policy makers, counselors, and health professionals. Through the curriculum, participants learn how to develop their own paradigm of self and which iSelf attributions are most important to impart to their students (e.g., self-understanding, self-esteem, and character) to dramatically impact their students' academic achievement and overall quality of life by focusing upon psychological and physical well-being. Once teachers or other direct service providers understand these ideas and approaches, they can use them in the classroom or health care and other professional settings. Teachers incorporate them into the development and delivery of personalized learning plans, subject lesson plans, and across all academic subjects, helping students to be better, more engaged learners.

The SAC is solidly grounded in the principles of human development, educational psychology, and educational philosophy. The theoretical basis of SAC is that students will be better learners in their academic subjects if they know themselves better. The focus is on constructing a self that includes self-system and positive psychology attributes, such as self-concept, epistemology, life purpose and dreams, locus of control, self-determination, motivation, and identity and character. Each young person is on a unique path of personal discovery to create his or her own destiny and to live a life of health, wholeness, and accomplishment.

The SAC offers a process for applying the iSelf model as the lens through which to teach subjects and for referring subject content back to the iSelf attributes. Applicable from elementary school through college, the SAC can guide students of all ages in transforming experience into meaning. They are empowered to take their experience of school subjects and academic content to make personal meaning of this content toward their own life purpose, dreams for their lives, and career aspirations. Students transform the experience of who they are in all domains of life—in family and peer relationships, in their community, and in classroom and extracurricular activities; they recognize they can reflect upon whether their choices are driving them toward the place in life they want to go.

The SAC teaches self-reflection about students' own paradigm and mental model of self. Students ask, "Is my paradigm of self working for me? Or do I need to change?" The ability of "freeing oneself from repetitive patterns of old learnings" (Mink, Owen, & Mink, 1993, p. 3) is a critical skill that is necessary for thriving in a constantly changing world. We can teach young people the process to determine for themselves their limiting mental structures and to literally create themselves.

Once teachers and other professionals understand the ideas behind this approach, they can use the strategy in the classroom, the counselor's office, or the health care setting. The ideas can be incorporated into the development and delivery of personalized learning plans across all academic subjects, helping students to become more engaged learners. By using this approach to focus on the balance of psychological and physical well-being, students' academic achievement and overall quality of life are destined to improve.

## Using SAC to Learn About Potential

Monitoring your potential is a challenging, lifelong task but is critical for well-being, so we should not wait until adulthood to acquire this skill. Educational philosopher and former Harvard University professor Israel Scheffler (1985) wrote a seminal book on the idea of human potential throughout human history called *Of Human Potential*. When I had the good fortune of meeting Dr. Scheffler, I was captivated by his way of being. My experience of him was that of a truly kind human being, with an inner peace that comes from knowing his own purpose in life was aligned with the commitments he had made, with his dreams for the difference that he wanted to make in the world, and with his chosen mission as an educator to manifest these. His work has demonstrated that we have the power to teach people to see and achieve their own unique potentials in their lives, and to literally change who they are at a fundamental core, being level: "Human beings formulate rules or laws for themselves by which they monitor their own conduct, and create ideals to which they try to conform" (Scheffler, 1985, p. 24).

If we can teach people that they have constructed these mental rules, they will recognize that they have the power to determine if these continue to represent who they are and want to be. When taught how to reflect upon the iSelf model distinctions, people can uncover their own operating rules and determine if they need to be changed to better reflect their beliefs and life purpose, commitments in life, and dreams, or whether these rules are limiting their self-expression and manifestation of their own sense of their unique purpose and mission in life.

Scheffler (1985) supported the idea that people create their own mental structures that either expand or limit their inherent potentials: "potential reflects both the subject and his social environment, and, moreover, [is] open to considerable change . . . [and] the belief system of the subject must therefore always be taken into account in assessing his potentials" (Scheffler, 1985, pp. 63–66).

We can teach people to be the stewards of their own belief systems. They learn to observe whether these beliefs limit or expand their own view of their own potentials, which then becomes an important preventative method to ensure their lifelong focus is on total well-being—mind, body, and soul.

The idea that people create their own paradigms of reality, and that we need to know how to do this in order to live a good quality of life in modern times, has been researched thoroughly by numerous scholars (Borysenko,

1999; Gardner, 2000; Glasersfeld, 1995; Kegan, 1994; Scheffler, 1995; etc.) but is not making its way into schools to create new pathways of learning. Kegan (1994) underscores the important subject–object dynamic that shapes our views in philosophy, psychology, and education:

> Subject–object theory brings together two powerful lines of intellectual discourse that have influenced not only the field of psychology but nearly every corner of intellectual life in the West in this century. These two lines of thought are constructivism, the idea that people or systems constitute or construct reality; and developmentalism, the idea that people or organic systems evolve through qualitatively different eras of increasing complexity according to regular principles of stability and change. Subject-object theory is a 'constructive-developmental' approach to human experience. It looks at the growth or transformation of how we construct meaning. (Kegan, 1994, pp. 198–199)

Psychologist and former Wellesley College professor Jean Baker Miller (1976) expresses this idea most directly:

> Psychological problems are not so much caused by the unconscious as by deprivations of full consciousness. If we had paths to more valid consciousness all along through life, if we had more accurate terms in which to conceptualize what was happening, if we had more access to the emotions produced, and if we had ways of knowing our true options—we could make better programs for action. Lacking full consciousness, we create out of what is available. (Miller, 1976, p. 94)

Without full consciousness or awareness, people do not have all the tools necessary to understand themselves or each other or to create a better world for themselves and all; therefore, they create out of what is available. If what is available is small and getting smaller (since excess anxiety about surviving modern society decreases full consciousness), then the knowledge that is produced is severely limited. Consequently, the possibility of human flourishing and understanding our full potential is also diminished.

Knowing themselves epistemologically will give students access to their full consciousness and a way to understand the world and reality. *Epistemology* encompasses "the nature, status, and production of knowledge" (Stauss & Corbin, 1998, p. 304). Former psychologist and University of Massachusetts professor Ernst von Glasersfeld (1995) determined human beings construct everything, including knowledge and ourselves and our reality. As educators and counselors, we must be concerned with epistemology because we are in the profession of imparting human knowledge to students and clients so as to learn how to transform their experiences, and the information they are taking in and processing, into personal meaning and relevancy. To know yourself epistemologically means to know that *you* are the subject of your life and that your experiences and the information you take in and process are all objects in the subject–object dynamic in the construction of reality in all dimensions of the self. As human beings who are constructing ourselves through our experiences, our human epistemology addresses experiences that are intertwined with issues of spirituality, emotions, psychology, the physical, and the intellect (Silko, 1996).

Schools are limited by the belief that schooling should be only or primarily about teaching basic subjects and basic knowledge. Unfortunately, basic subject knowledge is only giving people a portion of the total knowledge needed to thrive in modern society. Through implementation of the SAC in the schools, we can teach what is central to know for a successful and satisfying life and provide a prism through which to acquire basic subject knowledge in a way that is personally meaningful. We would hope to raise the conscious awareness of our young people so as to prepare them for a happy life filled with flourishing futures.

## Levels of Consciousness Through Schooling

Consciousness is not a landing place; it is an entry point from which one can cast an eye toward a future desired state. As teachers, counselors, and medical professionals, we know the importance of students achieving higher levels of consciousness. As students reach higher levels of conscious awareness, they begin to gain remarkable qualities and characteristics that ensure not only their own well-being but also that of the entire community. Kegan (1994) described the observable outcomes of higher levels of consciousness in four levels: individual taker (lowest level), individual doer, team player, and leadership excellence (highest level). While this pyramid is most useful for categorizing the behavior of middle- and secondary-school students and college students, younger children can also begin to demonstrate higher levels. Teachers and counselors should first assess the level of a student or client and not overwhelm them and push them to higher levels too fast. Being at a particular level is not good or bad; the categorization is just a point from which a pathway can be mapped.

### Consciousness Building Blocks

Each level builds upon the previous level.

*Level 1: Individual Taker/Struggle (Usually the
Level at Which the Child Enters Middle School)*
Here are the characteristics of the student:

- Going through the motions of responsible behavior
- An attitude of move the mind the body will follow
- Expectations set almost exclusively by the faculty and parents
- Setting the foundation for the discovery of unique potential
- Passive learner, yet finds aspects of nonacademic learning rewarding
- Not living in integrity with his self
- Does not accept certain realities about himself or his situation or the world
- Has little or no direction in life or understanding that we are driven by the principle of "move the mind, the body will follow"
- Has little or no understanding of his own emotional state of mind
- Does not love himself, respect his self, or honor his self as important

*Level 2: Individual Contributor/Effort*
Here are the characteristics of the student:

- Beginnings of a positive attitude
- Expectations shared among student/teacher/parent
- Creativity begins, beginning to taking charge of his life
- Begins to get excited about certain domains, such as sports, academics, self, or family
- Experiences himself as a doer in one or more domains
- Becomes an active learner, finds joy in learning about self, others, and some academic subjects

*Level 3: Team Player/Individual Contributor/Doer*
Here are the characteristics of the student:

- Expresses a positive attitude more often than not
- Drives his own expectations with some input by teachers and parents
- Feels creativity kick in, takes charge of own life
- Envisions a positive future
- Excited about taking charge of his life
- Experiences himself as a doer
- Learns actively about self and others, and all subjects
- Becomes creative problem solver in numerous contexts
- Honors self and others

*Level 4: Highest Level of Consciousness—Leadership Excellence*
Here are the characteristics of the student:

- Becomes the majority shareholder in student/faculty/parent partnership
- Experiences himself as a giver, assuming primary responsibility for the growth of takers
- Self-directed, with minimal help from parents and teachers
- Prepared for a great life, awarded a diploma
- Expresses his concept of his best or highest self
- Impacts the world in order to manifest his unique potential
- Creates learning opportunities for himself and others to address family, community, society, and world problems
- Accepts all his own weaknesses, challenges, and current reality
- Experiences his unique purpose in life
- Lives a life of integrity, following his own moral code
- Excited about creating a great life in spite of modern-day complexities
- Questions the assumptions of wholeness, completeness, and the priority of self in order to construct a whole, complete and an *a priori* self
- Masters the demands of modern life
- Recognizes his multiple selves and the need to create possible selves
- Able to see conflict as a signal of his overidentification with a single system
- Has a sense of relationships and connections prior to and constitutive of the individual self
- Identifies with the transformative process of his being
- Identifies with the heart more than the head as a result of the transformation of his being
- Wants to see humankind transform from the lower levels of consciousness to the higher levels
- Learns to stand on his own two feet emotionally, intellectually, economically
- Takes responsibility for his life
- Sees himself as a creator of culture rather than only being shaped by culture

Adapted from Kegan, *In Over Our Heads*, 1994.

These outcomes of higher consciousness, moving from Level 1 to 4, emerge during middle school on through college; this higher awareness is not only desirable but also entirely possible to produce through schooling.

## Process of Transforming the Self

The process of transforming the self of children, adolescents, and adults in a school or counseling setting involves change and change dynamics. An old adage from psychotherapy serves to underscore the first step in transforming a student or patient: How many psychologists does it take to change a light bulb? The correct answer? "One, but the light bulb has to want to change!"

How then do we as teachers, counselors, and medical professionals, empower the "light bulb" to want to change? We engage the first axiom of structural dynamics (Odum, 1988) that *tension seeks resolution* (Figure 4). This initiates the change process, the emotional desire to attain a future state, goal, or dream.

Many psychological problems that people are experiencing are due to their resistance to change. Change is always occurring. As seen through the information processing model, our sensory perception is constantly taking in new information and doing something with it—processing it in some way, automatically and unconsciously. More energy goes into resisting this processing of new information than into accepting a new reality and using it for our purposes. Often, we have too much information to process without the proper tools to assist us, so we go numb, unconscious, and dissociate our minds from the circumstances. The iSelf model, as taught through the SAC, helps us to first process the abundant information required to live in modern society and then transform ourselves to achieve higher levels of consciousness. Through this heightened consciousness, we can move toward the person we want to become and, more directly, are meant to be. At the bottom line, our job as service providers is to facilitate the change process.

Through classroom lessons, activities, psychological and physical health assessments, or therapeutic conversations, the service provider, whether teacher, psychologist, or physician, works with students, clients, or patients to formulate a desired future state. Importantly, you must keep in mind that change most often takes one of three forms: adaptation between the person and his circumstances, crisis, or envisioning and creating a vision or dream of a desired future state. As human beings, we have the power to choose which way we will change.

## Applications of SAC in K–16 Schooling

I have taught the principles of SAC at the university level to preservice and in-service master teachers and counselors through undergraduate and graduate coursework, as well as in numerous professional development workshops. Teachers have taken the SAC and used it as a framework to develop lesson plans and learning activities for a variety of subjects, including high school social studies, middle school science, elementary literacy, counseling practices, and college educational psychology classes.

## Teaching Educational Psychology Best Practice

When we teach college-level courses in general, educational, or developmental psychology, introduction to psychology, human development and learning, or any college level course that focuses upon children, adolescents, and adults, we should utilize the *self-referential method*, a teaching best practice to enhance learning and well-being outcomes. Numerous researchers have studied the impact of using self-references upon learning outcomes (Reeder, McCormick, & Esselman, 1987; Rogers, 1981; Rogers et al., 1977; etc.). In any academic subject, reading text and prose is required. The richness and depth of learning or encoding depends on making connections and relating to the self of the student. According to Rogers (1977), "judging a word in relation to self, however, produced the best recall of all." Reed and colleagues echoed this notion: "Self-reference represents an especially rich and deep level of encoding" (Reed, McCormick, & Esselman, 1987).

When college students in teacher education programs are introduced to educational psychology, they benefit from learning how to make meaningful connections between dry, conceptual textbook content and attributions of themselves. When future teachers learn how to do this for themselves, they are then able to teach to the selves of their students—enhancing both academic and well-being outcomes in future generations of children.

## Three Examples of Self Across the Curriculum

Here is a sample lesson plan illustrating how to use SAC at the university level to lead preservice and in-service master teachers and seasoned counselors through undergraduate and graduate coursework.

### Example 1: University Undergraduate Educational Psychology and Human Development and Learning Courses

*Title of Lesson*
"Learning Literacy Through the Self: Learning the Self Through Literacy"

*Lesson Goals*
This lesson introduces the central issues in development of the self through literacy and learning literacy through the self during the early childhood stage

of human development. (Students will be asked to use our class discussion and presentation in class and Ormond [2011] text chapters 9, 10, and 12 as references.) Students will develop and demonstrate an ability to teach literacy concepts and empower self-understanding through a developmentally appropriate lesson activity.

*Resources*
Students will be asked to draw upon chapters 9, 10, 12, and 13 in the Ormond (2011) text; a handout titled "Acquiring Literacy Skills That Have a Purpose and Deal With Real-Life Experiences" (Newman, Copple, & Bredekamp, 1998); the children's book they chose and used for their literacy connection project (another assignment during this course); and the "Learning Literacy Through Meaning" video on demand available on our course webpage link and at the Annenberg Learner website (http://www.learner.org/resources/browse.html#FL).

*Methods/Representations of Learning*
Each student or student pair will be asked to prepare one lesson activity that would take approximately 20 to 30 minutes to deliver to a class of elementary school 3rd graders:

1. Lesson activity will develop three distinctions of self discussed in class and described in text: self-concept, self-esteem, and self-efficacy.
2. Lesson activity will help the student *assess and develop* at least one attribute in each of the three developmental domains: socioemotional, physical, and cognitive development, from early childhood to late adolescence and early adulthood.
3. Lesson activity will develop these literacy skills: phonemic awareness, phonological awareness, and semantic cues.
4. Lesson activity will be of professional educator quality, suitable for inclusion into professional teaching portfolios.

*Analysis of Lesson*
This lesson produced numerous outstanding lesson plans by preservice teachers who went on to become certified as early childhood, middle school, and special education teachers. Many used their lesson plans proudly, as exemplars of excellence in their professional portfolios.

Teachers in my graduate level courses have taken the SAC processes and developed lesson plans and learning activities for their classrooms, and I use two examples to demonstrate how the SAC can be implemented in high school social studies and middle school science.

Here is an example of a 9th-grade social studies lesson developed by a new teacher with fewer than 3 years experience teaching (used with permission).

## Example 2: High School Social Studies

*Title of Lesson*
"Features of a Civilization"

*Duration*
Three class periods

*Lesson Goals*
This lesson teaches students a broader view of themselves and their potential contributions to the world by connecting book concepts to real-world problems. It also imparts social studies content standards on civics and government and empowers students to develop a self-concept, creativity or critical thinking, feelings of love and belonging to a group, self-efficacy, locus of control, and purpose in life through teaching content standards.

*Resources*
Students will participate in in-class presentations and whole-class discussion. Teacher will provide writing and discussion prompts for students to use in group discussions.

*Activity/Representations of Learning*
1. Create student teams made up of four to six students. In group discussion, students should rank the importance of different features of civilization.
2. During these discussions, students should be encouraged to express passion about their views and discuss, argue, and debate with respect and consideration for other viewpoints. These discussions should defend *why* the group ranked features in a particular order. Through this discussion, students will develop a deeper understanding of their purpose in life, their values, and possibly interests that would lead them to their future careers.
3. Lesson activity will help you *assess and develop* at least one attribute in each of the three developmental domains: socioemotional, physical, and cognitive development.

4. The following questions will prompt a follow-up discussion:
    a. What did the students find difficult or challenging about ranking the features of a civilization in order of importance?
    b. What were some issues each group faced when doing this activity?
    c. What were the reactions to seeing/hearing other groups' rankings, and how did they compare across the groups?
    d. Do the students think there is a "correct" answer to the ranking? Why or why not?

*Analysis of Lesson*

The teacher who designed this lesson reported that students did a great job of using and developing iSelf components developed through this portion of the lesson: self-efficacy, through developing their beliefs about their own views, and purpose in life, values, and self-determination, as students felt a greater sense of belonging, feeling they were in control of their views and direction of discussions and gaining competence in formulating their own beliefs and arguing for them. Other important civilization features, like those in our constitution, serve to deepen not only social studies standards content knowledge but also the relationship between personal attributions and our constitution (e.g., pursuit of happiness and equality). Happiness is a positive psychology attribute; equality indicates meaning in life, and both are explored through this activity.

At the beginning of each lesson, the teacher utilizes a writing prompt, or bell ringer exercise, to support students in connecting with prior learning and deepen personal meanings from the content.

*History Journal Prompt 1 (Day Three Lesson)*

Which feature of a civilization do you think is most important to the success/functionality of the civilization as a whole? Which feature of a civilization do you think is least important? Explain why.

Alternatively, if you are having difficulty with this, you may instead reflect on the role of a couple of the features or comment on our discussion about the role of government in our society: what it should be versus what it is.

*Analysis of Journal Prompt*

Several iSelf components were developed through this portion of the lesson; students related the features of civilization back to these iSelf distinction/attributes to find meaning in life. One student wrote an essay response that created a new civilization based on the feature of "justice," calling it "Justice-ism" and describing what that civilization would be like to live in. The teacher then also referenced how this is the basis for self-concept: having a future dream to create a world that reflects this feature, maybe through law or advocacy. The teacher imparted purpose and direction to a student's life through the lesson by referencing to iSelf distinctions in this way. The teacher also reported that students were able to relate the bigger ideas explored in the lesson to the real world by asking "why" questions.

*The Self-Referential Method Used in a Social Studies Lesson*
The SAC uses a self-referential method to help impart iSelf attributions through lessons. Applying the iSelf model to this "Features of a Civilization" lesson, or any lesson, is really as simple and as straightforward as developing any lesson using a three-stage, "backward" planning method.

Think through what self-system and positive psychology attributes you would like to impart in a particular lesson in the same way you choose academic content standards from your district's supplied list (or one that is supplied for you by the Pennsylvania Department of Education or National Council for the Social Studies Standards [http://www.socialstudies.org] or Common Core standards). Just as you review the content standards, review the iSelf attributes that you feel you could impart, either because of your commitment to imparting these or because they lend themselves to a particular lesson and meet the personalized needs of your students.

For example, in the civilizations lesson previously described, you can help students gain a self-concept and meaning in life, just to mention two. To illustrate, when you ask which features of a civilization are the most and least important, you can relate this question back to the iSelf attribute of "meaning in life." List those self-attributes that you will assess, either formatively or summatively, as assessment evidence. Be precise in what you are looking for and how you will assess it (e.g., worksheets, essays, team projects). Throughout, when delivering the lesson, describe what iSelf attributes you hope to impart; this could be a simple general reminder, or you may want to name specific self-attributes at specific points in the lesson. Be sure to pose essential questions using our prescribed and recommended method of a "self–other–all" framework. For example, students could write an essay response about creating a new civilization based on a feature they admire, such as "justice," and then describe what life would be like in that civilization for the student, her close family members, her friends, and world at large. The "self–other–all" referencing approach helps students connect more deeply with the content and can go so far as to potentially inspire them to a future career.

Also, at the beginning of the lesson, make certain that you phrase and pose essential questions using our prescribed and recommended method of "self–other–all," which would also work so very well in this civilizations lesson.

Additionally, you will want to list those self-attributes that you will assess, either formatively or summatively, as assessment evidence. Be precise in what you are looking for and how you will assess: worksheet, essays, asking the essential questions, and so on.

Throughout, when delivering the lesson, describe what iSelf attributes you will impart or make references to during various parts of the lesson. This could be a simple general reminder to do this or specific self-attributes at specific points in the lesson.

As with any method, the more you practice, the greater facility you will gain. I would strongly suggest attempting to apply the self-theory attributes in all your lessons. Incorporate iSelf attributes directly into your formal lesson plan, and see what works and what does not. As with any lesson, some things work better than others. You will also find that you have a particular motivation to impart one or a set of self-distinctions—perhaps meaning in life, or self concept, or self-esteem—whereas others are not that important to you immediately. The point being, try different ones and see what works!

In a different setting, here is an example of a 6th-grade science lesson developed by a master teacher with 10 years of experience teaching (used with permission).

### Example 3: Middle School Science Lesson

*Title of Lesson*
"Energy Conservation Is All Around Us!"

*Lesson Duration*
Five class periods

*Lesson Essential Questions*
- How can I use resources more responsibly? (self)
- How can I teach my family to save energy? (other)
- How can I make a difference in the world? (all)
- What do students need to learn to be able to answer these essential questions?
- Assessment prompt 1: Many of us waste a lot of energy and resources each day.
- Assessment prompt 2: By changing behaviors and materials, we can make a big difference.
- Assessment prompt 3: Every person has the ability and the responsibility to take action regarding saving energy and resources.

*Activating Strategy*
Students will draw a picture of a place (e.g., bedroom, kitchen, store, classroom) and label all the items that use energy. Here are the key vocabulary terms:

- Renewable resources
- Nonrenewable resources
- Wind energy
- Hydroelectric
- Geothermal
- Solar energy
- Conservation
- Energy efficiency
- Fossil fuels

*Teaching Strategies*
- Graphic organizer
- Vocabulary matrix
- Cause-and-effect fishbone
- Self-referential (self–other–all)
- Concentric circles (diagram and worksheet)

*Instruction*
- Guest speakers launch lesson
- Students apply knowledge at home with take-home kits
- Students calculate how much energy and money they have saved as individuals, within their families, and as a class
- Many summarizing strategies are applied throughout lesson
- Students use their book to learn ways that energy is being wasted and how they can conserve

*Assignments and Assessments*
- *Vocabulary acrostic.* Students create vocabulary acrostics to summarize what they've learned about a given word or concept; they share these with the class.
- *Vocabulary matrix.* Students complete a matrix to learn vocabulary words; the matrix has four columns: word, definition, example, and picture.
- *Cause-and-effect fishbone.* Students show how things they do can have a direct effect on helping themselves, their families, and the world.

- *Concentric circles.* Students use concentric circles to answer the following questions: How does saving energy help me? How can I help my family? How can I make a difference in the world?

*Extending Thinking Activity*
- The energy-saving concentric circles graphic organizer demonstrates the integration of concepts.

*Analysis of Lesson*
Note that the teacher who designed this lesson placed the "self–other–all" approach in the essential questions and discussed these with the class. This alone got their attention. In the environmental sciences lesson, the teacher observed that one student, Daniel, demonstrated self-efficacy and leadership and new levels of engagement and motivation. The teacher asked the class three essential questions demonstrating the self-referential teaching method:

1. How can I use resources more responsibly (applying what is learned to self)?
2. How can I teach my family to save energy (applying what I have learned to others)?
3. How can I make a difference in the world (applying what is learned to all)?

Daniel, in response to these questions, immediately took charge of the classroom and the learning; he organized the entire class into groups and assigned jobs. The lead classroom teacher reflected that she was literally stunned to see Daniel so energetic, dynamic, proactive, and positive when he had previously been a polite, quiet, and reserved student.

Daniel wrote a newsletter that solicited input from all his classmates on researched data about recycling in their community, the entire nation, and potential problems and solutions. Please keep in mind that Daniel was only in the 6th grade! He organized a school-wide recycling program and invited all classrooms to participate, and all did—100% involvement. He sent home copies of a letter to parents to participate in recycling in their homes with their children. He earned the highest grade in the class on all criteria in the teacher's rubric. Prior to this, he was a somewhat withdrawn student, seemingly going through the motions in every class activity. Daniel had always been a talented student academically but was not using his intelligence to his full potential. Through applying the self–other–all and self-referential methods to his own learning, he discovered through his own experience numerous self-theory and positive psychology concepts that empowered him to achieve academically and develop important personal qualities, such as leadership and self-expression.

*Middle School Homework*
This same teacher spent 10 minutes one morning talking about "intrinsic motivation" to her class. Up until this conversation, her students had difficulty getting homework done on time and at a high quality. That very same day, 90% of her students had their homework completed prior to leaving for the day, with the remaining 10% bringing it into class the next day. This had never happened in this class—or in any other class she had taught in her 10 years of experience.

## Analysis and Reflection

What is common among these examples from K–16 classrooms is that each of the teachers was able to impart iSelf attributes through everyday lessons and activities, thereby placing their students interests and sense of fun, creativity, leadership, and responsibility at the center of their teaching. They personalized the learning for each of their students using iSelf distinctions with dramatic results.

# CHAPTER 7

# Personalized Learning

As chairman of the Health, Education, Labor, and Pension Committee, Senator Tom Harkins of Iowa called for whole-child learning, and the Illinois state legislature also proclaimed that educating the whole child is important. Nevertheless, there are no specific formal programs currently under development to support educating the whole child through schooling.

One promising initiative did get under way in 2012, however. Funded by the U.S. Department of Education's Race to the Top program, support was given to school districts to implement reforms to personalize learning. While the goals remain extrinsic—closing achievement gaps and better preparing students for college and careers—the initiative accommodated for students intrinsic goals, such as the opportunity to pursue personal interests. Engaging the learner through technology and personalized learning plans creates excitement about learning and prepares students for college and career success. However, there is no underlying theoretical framework that provides for a shared understanding of personalized learning. In this chapter, I outline a researched personalized learning framework and associated best practices.

Personalized learning holds the promise to focus upon the whole child—those psychological and physical well-being needs of each child, adolescent, or young adult—with the aim of full and unique potential for a high-quality life. Because these goals are not mutually exclusive, it could also satisfy the educational aims of our society to see people graduate from high school or college, get a job, and participate in our democracy—all while addressing critical well-being needs as well.

If our educational aims explicitly reflect our well-being, societal needs, and such 21st-century needs as interpersonal and intrapersonal skills and higher-order cognitive skills (e.g., problem solving and creativity), then we should define the most effective framework and model to get there.

The framework for personalized learning includes the iSelf model distinctions discussed previously, learner-centered principles, and Quaglia's eight characteristics of student aspirations and potential, which will be discussed in this chapter.

An ideal personalized learning plan (PLP) is developed using the iSelf model in which student self-knowledge is elevated to a higher role and framework to formulate educational experiences that are aligned with student purpose and dreams. This may be done in combination with *The APA Learner-Centered Psychological Principles* (McCombs, 2003), in which personally meaningful learning and student learning modalities/styles and personally meaningful learning are honored and respected. Additionally, success in the classroom will be assessed using Ryff's psychological well-being scales, along with Rosenberg's self-esteem scales and the *Assessment of Learner-Centered Practices* (ALCP). Ideally, all these authentic assessments would be utilized in grades 9–12 and continued into the first 2 years of undergraduate education, which will hopefully help to address student retention rates.

*Personalization* is closely related to two additionally important terms: *individualization* and *differentiation*. All three terms require a shift in focus from a teacher-centered approach to an authentic, student-centered approach. What is often missing in personalized learning is the ability to take a deeper look at the inner self of the learner, to know who they are and want to become. Therefore, the focus of personalized learning should be on each student's needs across all domains: social, emotional, physical, and academic. A personalized learning program should enable students to do the following:

- Maintain high standards of mental and physical health and well-being, learning lifelong methods to further develop this well-being
- Become ready for college, career, and life, demonstrating numerous competencies in each domain
- Become self-confident members of their community, contributing to the greater societal good
- Know themselves and their strengths, weaknesses, and future hopes and dreams
- Have the flexibility to learn in both traditional and nontraditional ways, in and outside of the classroom, to support their unique strengths and needs

A true student-centered focus requires that we tailor lessons not only to a student's abilities, interests, and preferences but also to the self-components and attributes of the iSelf model—future life dreams, self-esteem, emotional intelligence, and others. Additionally, personalized learning is a way to increase students' understanding of their own hopes and dreams in life, to enable them academically, professionally, and socially to become the types of people they aspire to be with all the self-attributions they have and would like to develop.

Teachers are requesting new methods to help support their students both academically and developmentally. Personalized learning will provide educators with the support and tools to focus on whole-child needs. It raises the level of respect and admiration for teachers, in that they will be producing good people who have an understanding of who they are and feel empowered to maintain their mental and physical well-being. Personalized learning will also allow teachers themselves to more directly manifest their own true missions of producing the best possible academic and developmental outcomes. Further, personalized learning will allow our system of education to accommodate the goal of learning in and out of the classroom through extended learning opportunities such as independent study, internships, private instruction, performing groups, community service (service-learning), and online instruction. If we are able to truly personalize learning in these ways, students will take control of their own learning and responsibility for their life-course trajectories.

## Learner-Centered Psychological Principles

In 1997, the American Psychological Association (APA) funded research into a framework for individualizing learning though K–12 schooling. This key research combines numerous factors and principles that complement the iSelf model and illustrate ways of implementing psychological principles in K–16 schooling using the SAC model.

The following 14 psychological principles from the APA pertain to the learner and the learning process. All 14 learner-centered principles should be included in personalized learning plans. They focus on psychological factors that are primarily internal to and under the control of the learner, rather than conditioned habits or physiological factors. However, the principles also acknowledge external environment or contextual factors that interact with these internal factors. Intended to deal holistically with learners in the context of real-world learning situations, these principles are best understood as an organized set of principles; no principle should be viewed in isolation.

The 14 principles are categorized by factors that influence learning: cognitive and metacognitive, motivational and affective, developmental and social, and individual difference factors, influencing learners and learning. Finally, the principles are intended to apply to all learners, regardless of age or background, children, teachers, administrators, parents, and community members involved in our educational system.

Note that the following text is adapted from the American Psychological Association's Board of Educational Affairs (1997) and McCombs (2003) and is used with permission from Taylor & Francis:

### Cognitive and Metacognitive Factors

*1. Nature of the Learning Process*
*The learning of complex subject matter is most effective when it is an intentional process of constructing meaning from information and experience.*

Not all learning processes are the same. For example, habit formation arises in motor learning, whereas other learning involves the generation of knowledge, or cognitive skills and learning strategies. Learning in schools emphasizes the use of intentional processes that students can use to construct meaning from information, experiences, and their own thoughts and beliefs. Successful learners are active, goal directed, and self-regulating, and they assume personal responsibility for contributing to their own learning. The principles set forth in this chapter focus on this type of learning.

*2. Goals of the Learning Process*
*The successful learner, over time and with support and instructional guidance, can create meaningful, coherent representations of knowledge.*

The strategic nature of learning requires students to be goal directed. To construct useful representations of knowledge and to acquire the thinking and learning strategies necessary for continued learning success across the life-span, students must generate and pursue personally relevant goals. Initially, students' short-term goals and learning may be sketchy in an area, but their understanding can be refined over time by filling gaps, resolving inconsistencies, and deepening their understanding of the subject matter so that they can reach longer-term goals. Educators can assist learners in creating meaningful learning goals that are consistent with both personal and educational aspirations and interests.

*3. Construction of Knowledge*
*The successful learner can link new information with existing knowledge in meaningful ways.*

Knowledge widens and deepens as students continue to build links between new information and experiences and their existing knowledge base. The nature of these links can take a variety of forms, such as adding to, modifying, or reorganizing existing knowledge or skills. How these links are made or develop may vary in different subject areas and among students with varying talents, interests, and abilities. However, new knowledge must become integrated with the learners' prior knowledge and understanding or else this new knowledge remains isolated and cannot be used effectively or transferred readily to new situations. Educators can assist learners in acquiring and integrating knowledge by a number of strategies that have been shown to be effective with learners of varying abilities, such as concept mapping and thematic organization or categorizing.

*4. Strategic Thinking*
*The successful learner can create and use a repertoire of thinking and reasoning strategies to achieve complex learning goals.*

Successful learners use strategic thinking in their approach to learning, reasoning, problem solving, and concept learning. They understand and can use a variety of strategies to help them reach learning and performance goals, and they are able to apply their knowledge in novel situations. They also continue to expand their repertoire of strategies by reflecting on the methods they use to see which work well for them, by receiving guided instruction and feedback and by observing or interacting with appropriate models. Learning outcomes can be enhanced if educators assist learners in developing, applying, and assessing their strategic learning skills.

*5. Thinking About Thinking*
*Higher-order strategies for selecting and monitoring mental operations facilitate creative and critical thinking.*

Successful learners can reflect on how they think and learn, set reasonable learning or performance goals, select potentially appropriate learning strategies or methods, and monitor their progress toward these goals. In addition, successful learners know what to do if a problem occurs or if they are not making sufficient or timely progress toward a goal. They can generate alternative methods to reach their goal (or reassess the appropriateness and utility of the goal). Instructional methods that focus on helping learners develop these higher-order (metacognitive) strategies can enhance student learning and personal responsibility for learning.

*6. Context of Learning*
*Learning is influenced by environmental factors, including culture, technology, and instructional practices.*

Learning does not occur in a vacuum. Teachers serve a major interactive role with both the learner and the learning environment. Cultural or group influences on students can impact many educationally relevant variables, such as motivation, orientation toward learning, and ways of thinking. Technologies and instructional practices must be appropriate for the learners' level of prior knowledge, cognitive abilities, and their learning and thinking strategies. The classroom environment, particularly the degree to which it is nurturing or not, can also have significant impact on student learning.

### Motivational and Affective Factors

*7. Motivational and Emotional Influences on Learning*
*What and how much is learned is influenced by motivation? Motivation to learn, in turn, is influenced by the individual's emotional states, beliefs, interests and goals, and habits of thinking.*

The rich internal world of thoughts, beliefs, goals, and expectations for success or failure can enhance or interfere with the learner's quality of thinking and information processing. Students' beliefs about themselves as learners and the nature of learning have a marked influence on motivation. Motivational and emotional factors also influence both the quality of thinking and information processing as well as an individual's motivation to learn. Positive emotions, such as curiosity, generally enhance motivation and facilitate learning and performance. Mild anxiety can also enhance learning and performance by focusing the learners' attention on a particular task. However, intense negative emotions (e.g., anxiety, panic, rage, insecurity) and related thoughts (e.g., worrying about competence, ruminating about failure, fearing punishment, ridicule, or stigmatizing labels) generally detract from motivation, interfere with learning, and contribute to low performance.

*8. Intrinsic Motivation to Learn*
*The learners' creativity, higher-order thinking, and natural curiosity all contribute to motivation to learn.*

Intrinsic motivation is stimulated by tasks of optimal novelty and difficulty and those that are relevant to personal interests and provide for personal choice and control. Curiosity, flexible and insightful thinking, and creativity are major indicators of the learners' intrinsic motivation to learn, which is, in large part, a function of meeting basic needs to be competent and to exercise personal control. Intrinsic motivation is facilitated by not only those tasks that learners perceive as interesting and personally relevant and meaningful but also those that are appropriate in complexity and difficulty to the learners' abilities and those that they believe they can successfully perform. Tasks that are comparable to real-world situations and meet needs for choice and control also feed intrinsic motivation. Educators can encourage and support learners' natural curiosity and motivation by attending to individual differences in learners' perceptions of optimal novelty and difficulty, relevance, and personal choice and control.

*9. Effects of Motivation on Effort*
*Acquisition of complex knowledge and skills requires extended learner effort and guided practice. Without learners' motivation to learn, the willingness to exert this effort is unlikely without coercion.*

Effort is another major indicator of motivation to learn. The acquisition of complex knowledge and skills demands the investment of considerable learner energy and strategic effort, along with persistence over time. Educators should strive to facilitate motivation by using strategies that enhance learner effort and commitment to learning and while achieving high standards of comprehension and understanding. Effective strategies include purposeful learning activities, guided by practices that enhance positive emotions and intrinsic motivation to learn, and methods that increase learners' perceptions that a task is interesting and personally relevant.

## Developmental and Social Factors

*10. Developmental Influences on Learning*
*As individuals develop, there are different opportunities and constraints for learning. Learning is most effective when differential development within and across physical, intellectual, emotional, and social domains is taken into account.*

Individuals learn best when material is appropriate to their developmental level and is presented in an enjoyable and interesting way. Because individual development varies across intellectual, social, emotional, and physical domains, achievement in different instructional domains may also vary. Overemphasis on one type of developmental readiness—such as reading readiness, for example—may preclude learners from demonstrating that they are more capable in other areas of performance. The cognitive, emotional, and social development of individual learners and how they interpret life experiences is affected by prior schooling, home, culture, and community factors. Early and continuing parental involvement in schooling (or lack thereof) can influence these developmental areas, as does the quality of language interactions and two-way communications between adults and children. Awareness and understanding of developmental differences among children with and without emotional, physical, or intellectual disabilities can facilitate the creation of optimal learning contexts.

*11. Social Influences on Learning*
*Learning is influenced by social interactions, interpersonal relations, and communication with others.*

Learning can be enhanced when the learner has an opportunity to interact and collaborate with others on instructional tasks. Learning settings should allow for social interactions, respect diversity, and encourage flexible thinking and social competence. In interactive and collaborative instructional contexts, individuals have an opportunity for perspective taking and reflective thinking that may lead to higher levels of cognitive, social, and moral development, as well as higher self-esteem. Quality personal relationships that provide stability, trust, and caring can increase a learner's sense of belonging, self-respect, and self-acceptance, thus providing a positive climate for learning. Family influences, positive interpersonal support, and instruction in self-motivation strategies can offset factors that interfere with optimal learning, such as negative beliefs about competence in a particular subject, high levels of test anxiety, negative gender expectations, and undue pressure to perform well. Positive learning climates can also help to establish the context for healthier levels of thinking, feeling, and behaving. Such contexts help learners feel safe to share ideas, actively participate in the learning process, and create a learning community.

## Individual Differences Factors

*12. Individual Differences in Learning*
*Learners have different strategies, approaches, and capabilities for learning that are a function of prior experience and heredity.*

Individuals are born with and develop their own capabilities and talents. In addition, through learning and social acculturation, they acquire their own preferences for how they like to learn and the pace at which they learn. However, these preferences are not always useful in helping learners reach their learning goals. Educators need to help students examine their learning preferences and expand or modify them, if necessary. The interaction between learner differences and curricular and environmental conditions is another key factor affecting learning outcomes. Educators need to be sensitive to individual differences, in general. They also need to attend to learner perceptions of the degree to which these differences are accepted and adapted to by varying instructional methods and materials.

*13. Learning and Diversity*
*Learning is most effective when differences in learners' linguistic, cultural, and social backgrounds are taken into account.*

The same basic principles of learning, motivation, and effective instruction apply to all learners. However, language, ethnicity, race, beliefs, and socioeconomic status all can influence learning. Careful attention to these factors in the instructional setting enhances the possibilities for designing and implementing appropriate learning environments. When learners perceive that their individual differences in abilities, backgrounds, cultures, and experiences are valued, respected, and accommodated, in learning tasks and contexts, their levels of motivation and achievement are enhanced.

*14. Standards and Assessment*
*Setting appropriately high and challenging standards and assessing the learner as well as the learning progress—including diagnostic, process, and outcome assessment—are integral parts of the learning process.*

Assessment provides important information to both the learner and teacher at all stages of the learning process. Effective learning takes place when learners feel challenged to work toward appropriately high goals; therefore, teachers must appraise not only the learners current knowledge but also their cognitive strengths and weaknesses in order to select instructional materials of an optimal degree of difficulty. Ongoing assessment of the learners' understanding of the curricular material can provide valuable feedback to both learners and teachers about progress toward the learning goals. Standardized assessment of learner progress and outcomes assessment provides one type of information about achievement levels, both within and across individuals; these data can inform various types of programmatic decisions. Performance assessments can provide other sources of information about the attainment of learning outcomes. Self-assessments of learning progress can also improve students self-appraisal skills and enhance motivation and self-directed learning.

### Tying Things Together Using the iSelf Model

Conveying all these cognitive and metacognitive abilities seems like a daunting task for teachers, especially when they are primarily concerned with meeting academic standards. Using these learner-centered principles in conjunction with the iSelf model, we can personalize learning to help these abilities and attributions emerge; then, enhanced academic performance occurs as a natural outcome. To personalize learning for students means to focus upon the inner self of each student first and academics second—a considerable mind-set shift for most.

### Realization of Importance: Good Intentions Are Not Enough

Proactive education leaders are becoming aware of the critical link between student well-being, academic achievement, and positive life-course trajectories. Underscoring this important link, West Virginia state superintendent of schools Dr. Jorea Marple asserted, "It's important that we look at the child holistically." The West Virginia Board of Education and the Department of

Education have established as one of their priorities to personalize the education for each and every child (adapted from *The Legislature*, June 30, 2011, p. 1).

Our students are under high levels of stress in their daily lives, and their ability to learn is impeded due to numerous external factors. As they are nationwide, these stressors are acute in West Virginia: For example, 60% of children live in poverty and, as a result, suffer from chronic stress (*The Legislature*, 2011, p. 2). Poverty and stress not only affect student academic achievement, but student well-being attributions are also negatively impacted. Personalized learning should include assessing the stressors and pathways or interventions to resolve.

New Jersey is enacting school redesign and reform initiatives through the use of personalized learning plans that help students address their individual personal, academic and career development needs and goals: "Personalized learning plans have the potential to engage students, parents and school personnel in the planning and development of the academic career and overall future of each child in New Jersey" (American Federation of Teachers of New Jersey, April 2, 2009).

Yet many other states are still struggling with the concept of personalized learning and how to implement it statewide. Many education leaders recognize the need for changes and new initiatives and views, as captured in their statements about the whole-child, personalized learning and 21st-century learning. However, it is also clear those good intentions are not enough and that they are struggling to find an effective framework to facilitate effective implementation.

### Need for a Framework: Searching for Best Practices

Even though educational leaders are singing the praises of personalized learning initiatives, they do not have a thorough understanding of best practices, nor do they have a consistent, integrated model and framework that provides focus, direction, and sustainability to achieve the goals and visions. There is not a model that represents a best practice.

Of West Virginia's personalized learning efforts, state superintendant of schools Jorea Marple asserted, "We're working hard to be able to develop model projects all around the state" (quoted in *The Legislature*, June 30, 2011, p. 2), but without a conceptual framework to better understand personalized learning and desired outcomes, it will be difficult to formulate this project and measure its usefulness. This is a common problem throughout the United States.

In a recent speech about strategic priorities (*Teacher Leadership Institute*, July 22, 2011), Marple described personalized learning as *response to intervention* (RTI). Used appropriately, RTI offers an intervention method for those students struggling to meet school basic proficiency standards; it is not suitable as a personal empowerment intervention. The way RTI is used presently, including in the state of West Virginia, is punitive. Instead of using it as a punitive tool, it should be used as an empowering one.

Marple also stressed a need to "differentiate our instruction," suggesting that these three strategies will meet the vision of whole child—holistic, personalized learning. RTI and differentiated instruction are teaching methods and ways to impart information; they are not models for understanding the inner selves of children or methods for teaching children about the self. The iSelf model is a best practice for understanding the inner selves of children, and the SAC is the best method to impart self-distinctions.

Educators in Kentucky and New Jersey, among other states, use personalized learning to develop a contract between students and their school to set their own academic goals, but this does not address whole-child dimensions or self-knowledge attributions. This contract serves as an industrial age work contract rather than a pathway to learning how to live a life of health, well-being, happiness and flourishing to one's highest potential.

### Teachers Unions' Views Inhibit Personalized Learning

Teachers and teachers unions are also struggling to define personalized learning so as to develop a model that is applicable and effective across many schools and districts nationwide. Teachers unions have been the focus of much criticism for blocking innovation and creative new approaches to educating our youth. Personalized learning represents a unique opportunity to take a leadership role in defining this body of work as well as using it to propel the transformation of our entire system of education.

The two largest teachers unions, American Federation of Teachers (AFT) and the National Education Association (NEA), say they strongly believe in the personalized learning model and efforts by the U.S. Department of Education to promote the model throughout schools nationwide. Further, the NEA's vision communicates the obsolescence of NCLB given that the initiative has done little to graduate young people who can meet the challenges of the 21st century. However, what is clear from these statements from the AFT and NEA is that they are not aware of the need to create a new education paradigm that focuses upon the whole child: the mind, body, and soul.

For the NEA, producing a well-educated citizenry equipped to meet the challenges of the 21st century means imparting higher cognitive functioning through classroom teaching and learning best practices and to include education outcomes in technology skills are given priority to meet the competencies needed in future jobs. The "promise" is still the same: that if a student performs well academically through schooling, she will be rewarded with a good quality of life and positive life-course trajectory. But there is very little evidence that our education system can deliver on this promise, regardless of what new language or concepts we use to express a new vision for education. Within the present paradigm of thinking, it is more of the same.

In the following statement from an NEA hearing, we can find, on the positive side, a commitment to students' strengths and needs, as well as an awareness of the problems—the shortcomings of NCLB, unacceptable dropout rates, and inequities for minorities. But the actions suggested use words of measurement and control, steeped in industrial age, 19th-century thinking, and practices.

**The National Education Association (NEA) vision statement: "Meeting the Needs of the Whole Child"**
The No Child Left Behind Act (NCLB) shifted the emphasis of public education from developing well-rounded individuals, prepared to succeed in life, to testing low-level, basic skills in just two subjects: reading and math. Immediate and dramatic change is needed to undo NCLB's harmful effects—to refocus our education system on developing a well-educated citizenry equipped to meet the challenges of the 21st century. To this end, NEA proposes a new ESEA [Elementary and Secondary Education Act] purpose statement:

"The public education system is critical to democracy and its purpose, as reflected in this Act, is to maximize the achievement, skills, opportunities, and potential of all students by building upon their strengths and addressing their needs, and to ensure that all students are prepared to thrive in a democratic society and diverse, changing world."

Today's hearing, Improving America's Secondary Schools, will explore the challenges facing America's middle and high schools, and how ESEA reauthorization can help states and districts address those challenges.

Without question, among the most serious challenges is the extraordinarily high dropout rate in the United States. Each year, 1.2 million students drop out of school; that's 7,000 per school day.

School dropouts are at a severe disadvantage compared to their peers who earn a diploma. They are more likely to be unemployed, and, over the course of a lifetime, a high school dropout will earn a quarter of a million dollars less in income than a high school graduate. The dropout crisis is also hurting our economy; a decade's worth of high school dropouts will cost the country over three trillion dollars in lost income.

This crisis disproportionately affects students who are low-income, minority or have disabilities. While only 70 percent of America's students graduate from high school on time, that number drops to just over 50 percent for Hispanic, Black and Native American students. Students from low-income backgrounds are 10 times more likely to drop out of high school than their more affluent peers.

Research shows that the middle grades are a critical time to influence whether students graduate from high school. The decision to drop out is rarely the result of a single life event; in fact, many students exhibit academic warning signs years before they leave high school. We need to look at ways to identify these students through the use of early warning data systems. As early as sixth grade, such systems can use information on, for instance, absence rates or course failures to identify students who are struggling. And this information can be used to target appropriate interventions to get students back on track.

ESEA reauthorization offers an important opportunity to improve outcomes for millions of students by turning around the lowest-performing secondary schools. About 2,000, or 12 percent, of American high schools produce over 50 percent of the nation's dropouts. These so-called dropout factories serve mostly low-income and minority students. Twenty-eight percent of the nation's students of color are enrolled in one of these dropout factories, and these schools account for more than half of Black and Hispanic high school dropouts. Eighty-four percent of these lowest-performing high schools serve high-poverty student populations.

In addition to addressing the dropout crisis, we need to look at how we can meet the needs of all middle and high school students. As we heard in previous hearings, too many students currently are graduating ill-prepared for the challenges of higher education and the workforce.

In this reauthorization of ESEA, I intend for us to address the full spectrum of students' educational needs. We need to do more to ensure that every child gets a high-quality education early in life, and we need that support to start at birth, if not sooner. In addition, we must do more for our secondary school students. Currently, only about ten percent of Title I funds go to high schools, although they educate about one-quarter of low-income students. (NEA, 2011)

The NEA's use of the concept "strengths" should refer to students' iSelf model psychological attributes, such as purpose in life, dreams for their lives, creativity, self-determination, self-esteem, and others, and not necessarily their literacy or mathematical strengths. While the goal to "ensure that all students are prepared to thrive in a democratic society and diverse, changing world" is noble, such sentiments tend to focus solely on ensuring that students graduate and do not drop out and have the sensibilities to contribute to the democratic process of participation in our civic institutions.

Rather, a true whole-child goal would emphasize that we need to educate people with the mind-set and sensibilities to grow and change, and not be entrenched forever in a single belief system. Consider someone who never even questions their views on gun laws or listens to others' views on gay and lesbian rights. These sensibilities should also consist of including people of numerous cultures and backgrounds into the mainstream, fully accepted, not marginalized or disrespected. A "changing world" means that our schooling processes and pedagogy should focus upon the psychological and physical well-being of people. This holds the promise of a better life, rather than just educating for new technologies and jobs.

The NEA lacks understanding of the *whole child* and effective ways to implement personalized learning to educate people who are equipped to handle future 21st-century challenges. The iSelf model offers a much needed framework that will add substance to their organization's mission and impact. The iSelf model, along with personalized learning, whole-child focus, the use of SAC, and learner-centered principles, will produce people who are well prepared to meet the challenges of the modern era and flourish. What I am proposing is that the framework for personalized learning should be the iSelf model, and I challenge the NEA, AFT, and others to take a leadership role in shaping the next education paradigm.

Why is there such a lack of awareness of the importance of seeing our children as holistic beings with numerous and varying needs, not just as products to inculcate with math and language arts skills? Our children have genuine and critical needs to prepare them for the 21st century, which means more, much more than STEM knowledge and skills. Educational psychologists know about the importance of personalized learning and psychological components, yet, for the most part, teachers and policy makers do not. If they do, they do not know how to incorporate them into actionable teaching and learning.

## Teachers and Personalized Learning

According to the National Board for Professional Teaching Standards (NBTS; 2007), "research shows that the single most important school-related factor in raising student achievement is the quality of the teacher in the classroom. Today, in the era of high standards and increased accountability, boosting teacher quality is more crucial than ever before" (p. 4).

Teacher quality may be a factor, but in personalized learning, it really isn't the most important factor—at least not the way the NBPTS means it. The responsibility for learning needs to shift to the student. Two personalized learning teaching best practices would be to formulate personalized learning plans using a psychological framework and to learn coaching skills versus direct instruction platform skills.

## Shift to Coaching

A basic principle of personalized learning is that there will be a shift in the teaching model, from "sage on the stage" to "guide on the side." Teachers will become learning coaches in settings that will also incorporate flipped learning, revised seat-time requirements, and new models of extended learning opportunities (ELO), along with 21st-century learning needs that include the whole child, including socioemotional health and well-being needs. Teachers would be likely to welcome this shift, not only because they know that the NCLB 2014 proficiency goals are impossible to meet, but also, and perhaps more important, because they became teachers to empower people, not teach to the test.

In 2009, I conducted a study in a central Pennsylvania middle school regarding teacher beliefs about students' self-attributes. Many of the teachers interviewed reported that students' academic levels were lower than those of past years, as demonstrated in student artifacts:

> I know I am not perfect and I have said things because I can get so frustrated.... I said I have been doing this for like 10 years, and I don't want to say that the kids are not as smart as they were 10 years ago, but there has been a definite decrease in ability.... Like our low group, I have never had a low group like this one. (Brzycki, 2009)

Another teacher, who took some time off between teaching jobs, commented on the significant difference she observed in both student academic abilities and well-being:

> I do want them to achieve in math and do well in my classroom but the way society is right now, something has to change. It is like I said, having had those 11 years off really was an eye opener to me coming back into teaching. (Brzycki, 2009)

One teacher offered keen insights, commenting that declining student performance may be due to the concentration on standardized tests and less time dedicated toward children's integrated, experiential understanding:

> We have our kids separated by ability and [in] what we consider the high groups they score usually advanced on the PSSAs [and] that is how they are

grouped. Every year when I get [these supposed higher groups] in language arts I feel their ability, their skill, their knowledge is getting lower and lower, you can see it. . . . it is because we're having to focus on the standards and not so much the child and that interaction, and you know, being able to build on that. (Brzycki, 2009)

Later on in this same interview, she indicated the following:

As far as the writing . . . we are noticing a major decline. However, their test scores in 5th grade on the writing are showing that they are improving, yet when they get to me and I am trying to review different things, they cannot write a sentence, a complete sentence. They can do capitals sometimes, they use punctuation sometimes, but they are lacking the complete thought by the time they get to sixth grade. Why is that? That, two years ago, three years ago, that was not an issue, not an issue at all, and now we are seeing it a lot more. Yet their scores are going up. I am not understanding that. (Brzycki, 2009)

These sentiments express that we have become good at teaching students to perform well on required tests, but their understanding, knowledge, and abilities have deteriorated. The high-order transfer of knowledge and transfer of knowledge are not occurring in schooling, to the detriment of children's futures.

Teachers want personalized learning in their classrooms but feel constrained by current NCLB policies and the excessive focus on testing, including time spent preparing students for testing, at the expense of children's well-being. Many teacher comments shed light on the out of balance emphasis:

You know you don't get in here [get the opportunity to teach at such a wonderful middle school] because you have to teach to the stupid test. The kids aren't getting what they need to get. I mean there is a reason why a lot of kids are not getting proficient on the PSSAs [Pennsylvania System of School Assessment]. It is because their minds are elsewhere or you know we are not teaching them. I don't feel personally that we are teaching them what they need. I don't even know what they need. (Brzycki, 2009)

This teacher is offering insights into the heart of the issue: the mind—the level of cognition that is needed to perform intellectually, the working memory space, the use of creativity, and metacognitive critical thinking—is not available. There is so much going on in the minds of adolescents, pediatrician Mel Levine likened it to "a stuffed closet, and this is a common neurodevelopmental affliction within this [middle school] age group" (Levine, 2002, p. 309). The iSelf model in schooling would help clear out the "closet" or at least organize it.

Further, this teacher is expressing another common frustration that teachers do not know which strategies will reach their students, intellectually or personally. In addition, she did not really know what her students need in either domain, the intellectual/cognitive or the emotional/developmental.

Two additional comments add another perspective on increasing pressures felt by teachers, who on the one hand believe deeply in empowering the development of their students, while on the other hand are being asked to adhere to increased lesson planning requirements:

> You can see that too through the years. They don't care and I don't have the time to make them care anymore because of you know, you got to get it done, got to get it done! I don't know what to do about it other than you know just keep trying and try and figure out ways around it. How can I...do the littlest thing, but it is [frustrating], I can't even put into words how frustrating it is. . . . For teachers, the time and the caring that you can put into helping their development along is getting smaller and smaller. (Brzycki, 2009)

Lest we give up, remember what is at stake. Findings in this study about teacher beliefs and student attitudes are consistent with the views of Barbara McCombs (2003) that bear repeating:

> When the educational paradigm or reform agenda puts something other than the learner or learning at the center of instructional decision making, all learners suffer. Students know that the system is not about them and is not responsive to their needs. In such a system, learners recognize they are not important, because who they are and what they need are not at the heart of the learning process. At worst, they feel left out, ignored or alienated; at best, they feel the system is impersonal and irrelevant. (McCombs, 2003, p. 96)

That students "feel left out, ignored, or alienated" explains why approximately 20% of teachers interviewed for this study stated that students' well-being and academic performance are lower now than in past years. Emotions play a key role in developmental change during adolescence and in learning academic information but, unfortunately, the balance in schooling is toward cold cognition or the absence of emotions in a learning situation (McCombs, 2003; Peterson, Stahlber, & Dauenheimer, 2000; Pintrich, Marx, & Boyle, 1993; Pintrich & Schunk, 2002).

Teacher education programs and professional development coursework need to help teachers personalize learning for all students and are predicated on the changes occurring in our society for a new model of education that will address the new 21st-century needs of our students.

## Personalized Learning and Potential

An effective personalized learning framework requires educators to consider the potential of all students—psychological and physical well-being and academic—the whole child. While the NEA speaks of unleashing the potential of all students "by building upon their strengths and addressing their needs, and [ensuring] that all students are prepared to thrive in a democratic society and diverse, changing world," its current paradigm cannot support these goals.

Throughout this book, we have defined potential as the "capacity, propensity, and capability" to grow and learn about one's self, the whole person—mind, body, and soul. Achieving one's full potential and flourishing in life is not about getting higher grades. Rather, potential means the fully unique human potential, in all dimensions: physical, intellectual, emotional, psychological, and spiritual. The NEA and the entire educational system comes from a mind-set of seeing potential primarily as capability—a person's effectiveness in manifesting an intended outcome, such as getting good grades, acquiring skills, or becoming a better student.

We need to shift our focus and also explore students' capacity, the existence of what is possible to learn and become. We should also help students uncover their propensity: the set of personal beliefs, values, and intrinsic motivations to develop and apply skills toward an intended outcome.

## Eight Conditions to Empower Student Potential

Personalized learning that incorporates potential truly places students at the center of their learning—academically, personally, and professionally. The Quaglia Institute has created eight conditions (Table 1) that make a difference in increasing student aspirations and their ability to reach their fullest potential. These eight conditions correlate quite closely with the iSelf model attributes.

The Quaglia conditions and the iSelf attributes can be learned and expressed through a number of work products, artifacts, or ways of representing knowledge—student-produced videos or other multimedia productions, written essays and poems, and music and dance, among others.

**Table 1.** Eight Conditions to Empower Potential

| Eight conditions to empower full potential | Correlating iSelf model attribute |
|---|---|
| Belonging | Self-determination, self-efficacy |
| Heroes | Inspiration, self-efficacy |
| Sense of accomplishment | Self-efficacy, self-esteem |
| Fun and excitement | Happiness, affect, emotions |
| Curiosity and creativity | Creativity, dreams, identity |
| Spirit of adventure | Dreams, possible selves |
| Leadership and responsibility | Character, commitment |
| Confidence to take action | Self-esteem, self-efficacy |

Adapted from New Hampshire Department of Education, *Personalized Learning Presentation*, 2009.

## The Role of Technology

The growing use of technology in the teaching and learning process has opened the opportunity to focus upon each person's needs. Best practices are still emerging on how to integrate online learning into classroom instruction and how to personalize learning through the use of personalized learning plans.

The nature of the 21st-century classroom is rapidly changing. Online technology integration in K–12 classrooms is growing dramatically, with virtually all teachers in all subjects or content areas utilizing some form of online learning, usually in a blended format. The National Education Association (NEA) recognized the implications in its policy statement on distance education:

> Licensure in a subject matter being taught is a necessary condition for any teacher, but it is not a sufficient condition for a teacher involved in distance education. Teachers who provide distance education should in addition be skilled in learning theories, technologies, and teaching pedagogies appropriate for the online environment. (NEA Policy 13, sec. Student Learning, 7a)

The work being done by Khan Academy to implement flipped classroom methods represents this shift of responsibility. Khan's work integrates online technology into daily lessons seamlessly and holds much promise to meet the whole-child learning needs required from a 21st century, transformed model of education, with new learning environments.

## Transforming Learning Environments With Technology

Today's educators must provide a learning environment that takes students beyond the walls of their classrooms into a world of endless opportunities. Technology promotes classroom transformation by ensuring that digital-age students are empowered to learn, live, and work successfully today and tomorrow. The key findings in a meta-analysis and review of online learning studies conducted by the U.S. Department of Education (2009), included the following:

- Students in online conditions performed modestly better, on average, than those learning the same material through traditional face-to-face instruction.
- Instruction combining online and face-to-face elements had a larger advantage relative to purely face-to-face instruction than did purely online.
- Effect sizes were larger for studies in which the online instruction was collaborative or instructor directed than in those studies where online learners worked independently.
- The effectiveness of online learning approaches appears quite broad across different content and learner types.
- Online learning can be enhanced by giving learners control of their interactions with media and prompting learner reflection.

Adapted from U.S. Department of Education, 2009.

A U.S. Department of Education study, *Learning Powered by Technology*, called for a more individualized approach to teaching:

Personalization refers to instruction that is paced to learning needs (i.e., individualized), tailored to learning preferences [i.e., differentiated], and tailored to the specific interests of different learners. In an environment that is fully personalized, the learning objectives and content as well as the method and pace may all vary. (U.S. Department of Education, 2010, p. 12)

Digital-age children are experiencing enhanced learning achievement outcomes when taught using technology. Additionally, the type of learning experience and the teachers' pedagogical approach influences student learning outcomes. When courses are designed around active learning in which the learner builds knowledge through inquiry-based manipulations of digital artifacts (e.g., online drills, simulations, games, or microworlds), students are able to control their learning. The multimedia approach enables the student to go deeper into understanding material or concepts, with numerous opportunities to engage cognitive processes applied self-referentially.

When learning becomes personalized, students use lesson materials for self-inquiry and self-understanding; they become intrinsically motivated and self-directed and more able to engage their whole self in the experience of learning. Today's students already self-direct their learning by conducting Internet searches that interest them, that help them learn and grow based on their own motivations. Our system of education and teaching and learning processes now need to play catch-up to meet the growing expectations of our youth for new pathways for learning. No longer can we control the learning; we need to facilitate what our children want to learn.

Another example of effective technology integration into classroom lesson plans is the use of online discussion boards in learning management systems (LMS) such as Moodle, Blackboard, Sakai, among others. For example, a teaching and learning best practice that utilizes "personal purpose" (a positive psychology attribution) asks students to reflect upon and then post to an online classroom discussion their purpose in life and how taking this course and how its concepts and exercises will help either further define or manifest their purpose in life. This practice can be done in any course in any program, and it places the responsibility for learning on the learners to personalize the material to help manifest their own purpose. From here, students and teachers can discover those learning experiences, either those already a part of the course design and included in the syllabus or those located outside the course materials that will further provide experiential learning to manifest that purpose. Additionally, many learning activities (experiences) should enable students to make differences in their community through not only demonstrating competencies but also expressing their purpose and dreams. As dean of a school of education, I was able to implement this best practice very successfully, resulting in increased student retention and exceptional demonstration of competencies learned through our programs of study; we were empowering superior counselors, teachers, and educational leaders.

Student-personalized learning plans are easily managed by using technology as an administrative tool, to request input into the plan electronically and then search for appropriate learning activities either inside or outside of the classroom and course syllabus. Such systems can also keep track of learning outcomes that relate to competencies, knowledge, and well-being outcomes, to name a few.

## Personalized Learning Plans

In Table 2, I present an example of a personalized learning plan (PLP) from New Hampshire, where such plans were implemented in 147 schools and reached almost 50,000 students (as of 2009). New Hampshire uses an "electronic portfolio" to administer the components of the learning plan for each student across the state, coordinated by the student's school and school district.

The New Hampshire PLP is an example of a best practice that incorporates numerous self-attributes found in the iSelf model. New Hampshire's Department of Education appears to understand the needs of the 21st-century learner and the importance of placing the student at the center of the new educational paradigm.

In the New Hampshire PLP, the students' individualized education plans (IEP, or 504 plans) are only considered a *subset* of their PLP. This is significant in that the IEP/504 is often used to define limitations in both the student and the school system. The PLP allows for a broader set of skills, talents, and interests to define the student, which is a more empowering view of the person in schooling. In the "student voice" section of the PLP, we find something that apparently no other state is doing currently: The student's own perspective is prominent. In writing this page, a student can define who she is and learn about herself through the process. Specifically, she can both learn about and express her identity, self-concept, self-understanding, life purpose and meaning, and happiness; she can discover what inspires her, what gives her hope, and what she dreams of becoming. She can also reflect upon her interests and where she excels and what life experiences are most meaningful and important to her and why.

Teachers use the PLP "Plan" section to conduct research about what learning opportunities or learning experiences are available to help a student manifest her personal, academic, or career attributions. These learning activities could be drawn from other teachers' lessons or from a growing database of extended learning opportunities. The "Providers and Individuals Involved" section points to the opportunities for supported partnerships beyond one teacher and one school. The use of extended learning opportunities is growing nationwide, particularly in those states where seat-time requirements in the form of Carnegie units have been eliminated; these opportunities can also be modified to allow for a shift to personalize learning. I have also seen teachers work with students who are very capable of developing their own plan for how to achieve learning goals. This, once again, places the student in charge over her own learning and destiny in life and thereby enables an important iSelf model attribution, self-determination (Deci & Ryan, 1985; Ryan & Deci, 2000). The more we can give students autonomy when choosing what they

**Table 2.** Example of a Personalized Learning Plan from the New Hampshire Department of Education

| | |
|---|---|
| **Senate Bill 18** <br> **Alternative Learning Plan** <br><br> **Template for New Hampshire** <br> (Our intention is that the information suggested here will be integrated into an electronic portfolio template. **This is guidance only for districts to adapt as needed.**) ||
| | |
| | |
| **Student:** | |
| **SASID:** | |
| DOB: | |
| Current Grade Level: | |
| **Originating High School:** | |
| Address: | |
| Phone: | |
| Student Residential Address: | |
| Phone: | |
| E-mail: | |
| **Assigned Mentor:** | |
| **Date Plan Originated:** | |
| **Other Existing Plans (IEP [Individual Education Plan], 504, IPE [Individual Plan for Employment], ISS [Individual Service Strategy]):** | |
| **Key Contact People Connected With Other Plans:** | |
| | |
| | |
| | |
| | |
| | |
| | |
| **Transcript Attached?** | Yes/No |
| **Attendance Report Attached?** | Yes/No |

**Table 2.** Example of a Personalized Learning Plan from the New Hampshire Department of Education (*continued*)

| Student Voice Page | |
|---|---|
| "This Is Me" | Written Essay |
| "My Life and Welcome to It" | Student Intro Video |
| "Where I'll be in 5 years" | |
| **My Goals**—List 3 goals of your personal top priorities in the following areas: | |
| Personal | |
| Academic | |
| Career | |
| **My Interests**—Tell us something about yourself—the kinds of things you like to do in your spare time | |
| **My Dreams**—If you could do anything you want with no roadblocks, what would that be? | |
| **Previous Life Experience**—Include paid and unpaid work, volunteer experiences, and adventures where you learned something new | |
| | |
| | |
| | |
| | |
| | |
| | |

**Table 2.** Example of a Personalized Learning Plan from the New Hampshire Department of Education (*continued*)

| Plan | |
|---|---|
| Start Date: | End Date: |
| **Description of Plan Goals** | |
| Short Term | Long Term |
| Personal— | Personal— |
| Academic— | Academic— |
| Career— | Career— |
| | **Degree Attained:** |

| Description of Goal Steps | Start Date | Goal Type |
|---|---|---|
| Goal #1 | | |
| Goal #2 | | |
| Goal #3 | | |
| Goal #4 | | |

**Progress Benchmarks**

Goal #1 reviewed by _____ on (date)_____

Progress achieved/needed:_____Initials:___

Goal #2 reviewed by _____ on (date)_____

Progress achieved/needed:_____Initials:___

Goal #3 reviewed by _____ on (date)_____

Progress achieved/needed:_____Initials:___

Goal #4 reviewed by _____ on (date)_____

Progress achieved/needed:_____Initials:___

**Providers and Individuals Involved**

| Service Name | Start Date | End Date | Provider Name & Payment Source | Description |
|---|---|---|---|---|
| | | | | |
| | | | | |
| | | | | |
| | | | | |

**Table 2.** Example of a Personalized Learning Plan from the New Hampshire Department of Education (*continued*)

| Other | |
|---|---|
| Experiential Learning Credit Pending? Descriptions and Dates: | |
| | |
| | |
| Other Services Needed to Accomplish Goals: | |
| | |
| | |
| | |
| Services/Supports/Referrals Needed to Achieve Goals After Graduation: | |
| **Signature Page** | |
| **Person's Completing Plan** | Should include student, parent/guardian, mentor, guidance counselor, teacher(s), and superintendent |
| Name (Please Print) and Role | Signature and Date |
| | |
| | |
| | |
| | |
| | |
| | |

want to do and control in how they do it (while also providing an empowering student–teacher relationship), the more students will be intrinsically motivated to achieve and take responsibility for their own future success.

Personalized learning plan best practices require placing student self-psychology at the center of all learning goals and planned learning activities. Teaching methods such as project-based learning and differentiated learning and the use of technology when either delivering instruction or measuring student progress are secondary considerations. When student dreams and interests guide the teaching and learning, learning is accelerated and deepened.

## CHAPTER 8

# WELL-BEING AND PROTECTIVE AND RISK FACTORS

> The individual has within himself vast resources for self-understanding, for altering his self-concept, his attitudes, and his self-directed behavior—and that these resources can be tapped if only a definable climate of facilitative psychological attitudes can be provided.
>
> —Rogers, 1986, p. 135

Is it possible to improve both well-being *and* academic outcomes from schooling? What best practice or practices are available to assist us when producing these outcomes? Do we need to attend to both well-being outcomes and academic outcomes equally, or should we elevate one over the other and why? What broad-spectrum approaches (BSAs) and protective factors have been identified through research?

What I will attempt to do in this chapter is paint a picture of the harsh realities regarding the well-being of our society—children, adolescents, adults—by looking at objective measures using key indicators. I will also explore how self-knowledge and the iSelf model could assist policy makers and practitioners in improving physical and psychological outcomes.

Throughout this book, I have discussed numerous research studies that support the use of self-esteem and other self-knowledge attributes when promoting health and well-being as a preventative approach. Leading researchers from Europe, where they are ahead of the United States in their thinking about well-being, find that self-esteem is an important protective factor:

> Self-esteem is an important risk and protective factor linked to a diversity of health and social outcomes. Therefore, self-esteem enhancement can serve as a key component in a broad spectrum approach (BSA) approach in prevention and health promotion. The design and implementation of mental health

programs with self-esteem as one of the core variables is an important and promising development in health promotion. (Mann, Hosman, Schaalma, & de Vries, 2004, p. 368)

With compelling evidence making the direct connection between self-esteem and mental and physical well-being, it is my hope that this book inspires action by policy makers and practitioners alike.

How do we know when we have achieved a state of well-being? The research literature on well-being states and antecedents is sorely missing in both psychology and education. Even psychological well-being college courses often fail to consider the component parts of the self. Physical and psychological well-being is typically defined by the *absence* of some condition or ailment in the body or mental state.

Well-being is a combination of social, emotional, spiritual, psychological, and physical health, where we have the understanding of the influence each has upon the other. It is a combination of thoughts and experiences where one is clear when a state of well-being is manifest or present. Well-being is also an experience of flourishing on the positive end of a scale. Positive psychologists often point to traditional psychology and psychotherapeutic methods that attempt to bring patients from a negative state of well-being to zero, on a scale of −5 to 0 to +5. Positive psychologists and strength-based methods of counseling attempt to bring a client from zero to a +5. Well-being is present when you feel happy, exemplified when you do the following:

- Learn and grow personally and professionally
- Feel positive about yourself and have positive self-esteem
- Have relationships that nurture yourself and others
- Know that you are manifesting your unique purpose in life and have evidence of that in your life
- Use circumstances in which you are unsuccessful to learn more about yourself
- Have vitality and energy to strive for a better quality of life
- Experience the goodness of yourself and others
- Are not concerned about what others think
- Know that you are on your chosen pathway toward manifesting your full potential in life
- Have activities in your life where you experience a state of being at one with the world (sometimes referred to as a "state of flow")
- Experience yourself as separate from and bigger than the circumstances in your life

- Are able to express unconditional love to others
- Can feel happy

Yale University psychologist and professor James Hillman (1996; 1999) contributed significantly to our understanding of well-being, how to recognize when it is present, and how to achieve this state. As an archetypal psychologist, Hillman asserted that we all have a "daimon," or inner consciousness that, when listened to, tells us when we are living consistently with our guiding purpose in life. Additionally, I have found that we all have a natural drive (part of a DNA, if you will) to achieve balance among our personality, morality, physicality, character, and soul. When I provide clients and students with the concepts in the iSelf model, I have found that the DNA of the person—the soul—is engaged and finds its way through time, trial and error, and considerable self-reflection and contemplation to its natural state. This is highly rewarding, as you can imagine; through my teaching and counseling, my primary responsibility is to trust the soul of the people in my care.

As you read the rest of Chapter 8, please refer to this definition of well-being (and consider your own) when making the determination of whether our society and our children are experiencing well-being.

## Well-Being: Obesity

Learning how to transform one's self is important if we want to create a positive life-course trajectory. We tend to go through our everyday lives as we have for years and generations with the same assumptions about life, that this is "just the way it is." Take, for example, the fact that numerous stories are broadcast on the television nightly news highlighting stories on the obesity epidemic while scientists research causes and new solutions to the problem. Nevertheless, we do not even consider that we may have the power within us to change our situations or our "personal protective factors." I do not mean through prescription drugs, although they may be appropriate for short-term management of certain diagnoses until you can get your mind and body in balance once again.

When I give presentations on the total picture of the health and well-being of children and adults in our society, my audience often sits in stunned disbelief, unsure of how to react or where to start with questions or brainstorm about possible solutions. The truth is so difficult and the problems are so large that we do not know how to address them. Do we take each problem and attempt to develop strategies to involve the correct medical professionals, community resources, and programs to teach or inform how to correct and heal things? If so, how? For example, the problem of obesity in our society is generally due to a lack of self-awareness and directly correlates to our emotions and depressive states of mind that lead us to unhealthy eating and living habits. It is a chain reaction: Poor self-esteem leads to emotional depression or upset, which leads to eating poorly.

One highly touted childhood obesity program, endorsed by the U.S. Department of Health and Human Services (HHS) and by researchers at the University of Texas Health Science Center, in conjunction with University of California–San Diego, Tulane University, and the University of Minnesota, under the auspices of the National Institutes of Health (NIH), is the Coordinated Approach to Child Health (CATCH) program, which is in place in 1,500 elementary schools in Texas and several hundred others across the United States. CATCH emphasizes changing environmental factors to support children's health, minimize the risk factors, and increase the protective factors. And what are these protective factors? Assistant Secretary of Health Howard Koh, a leading voice in child well-being in this country, identified the following: vegetable intake, ample amounts of physical activity, access to affordable and healthy food, and accessible places to play. While a worthy list, these are all *external* factors; no mention is given to *internal*, personal factors, such as motivation, happiness, and feeling good about one's self. The CATCH program is delivered through the lens of environmental risk and protective *external* factors. Is this sufficient? While a good start and important in the entire scope of possible interventions and supports, it does not address the most impactful view, the inner self. With approximately 28% of adolescents in high school reporting that they are sad and hopeless (Child Trends Data Bank, July 2012), it should be a significant part of the students' thinking and paradigm of reality to understand their emotions and to have a guide or mentor to discuss states of mind. In Texas, where the CATCH program is mandated in all public elementary schools, obesity statistics have fluctuated. Between 2000 and 2002, 25.6% of Texas children were obese; this percentage declined to 23.5% from 2003 to 2004 but increased again to 23.8% between 2009 and 2011, after millions of dollars had been invested into the program by numerous state agencies, community groups, and committed health partners.

One CATCH success story is that of 4th-grade children in El Paso, Texas, who experienced a 7% reduction in obesity over an 8-year period (Hoelscher et al., 2004; Ogden et al., 2012). However, given the large effort, the amount of community groups, and large expenditures, these results seem modest. As often happens, we are caught up in the hype and hustle of getting things moving and involving people around a cause, but our outcomes fall short. Shifting the paradigmatic view to one where the inner self and self-knowledge are the center of education and intervention programs would produce extraordinary results, or at least better than the externally focused programs. Given the overwhelming scope of the problem, with evidence that more information imparted through education programs about nutrition, diet, and exercise produces minimal results, we need new initiatives based on a model of an integrated, whole self.

## Why We Remain Blind to the Problem

There are two reasons why we remain blind to the depth and scope of the problem of obesity in the face of our professional commitment to health and well-being: (1) we have not realized that we need a new paradigm with which to view the issue through a self-esteem or self-model lens, and (2) those with a stake in keeping our existing approaches (i.e., physicians, therapists, and educators) do not have the incentive to change their views. Yes, with all the mounting research and billions of dollars spent on the problem of obesity and obesity-related illnesses, we have built quite an industry and thus have avoided reaching a tipping point where we are compelled to take action.

Regarding programs to intervene and prevent obesity, medical professions have dropped the ball in using robust research highlighting self-esteem as a critical protective factor. Education policy makers and educators apparently prefer to ignore a 21st-century model that includes physical well-being outcomes, opting to keep the level of mediocrity and sameness in the way we look at and work with children, focusing solely on academic achievement. It is morally wrong and a great injustice to young people in our society today and tomorrow, especially when you consider the abundance of research that is available that demonstrates the correlation and causality of self-attributions to health and well-being. Additionally, we now have a psychological model (iSelf) and curriculum (SAC) that educators can utilize now to address health and well-being problems.

Consider these future health forecasts: 42% of Americans are projected to be obese by 2030, driving associated health care costs upwards to an estimated $550 billion. These numbers alone offer reason enough to try some new preventative programs.

In recent studies of the direct impact that foods have on our mental states of mind, 88% of people said improving their diet benefited their mental health (The Food and Mood Project, 2011). Therefore, it makes sense to develop new programs that focus upon the self and all attributions, and at a minimum, to teach the connection between foods and states of mind, along with teaching which foods work for different blood types and DNA.

## How Are We Doing?

When evaluating the effectiveness of a particular system or paradigm, you must take a look at the results, what is actually present in terms of evidence, and ask, "How are we doing? Is it working?" By numerous measures, including those presented in this section, we can assert that something is not working.

A highly publicized HBO documentary on obesity, *Weight of the Nation*, reported a dramatic increase in obesity rates since 1980. When looking for causal relationships between our systems, our mind-set, and the problem of obesity, I suggest that the education paradigm and they way we treat and educate our children contributes significantly.

Consider recent research that points to the critical issue of obesity and obesity-related illness among children, adolescents, and adults, including the following troubling statistics:

- Obesity in the United States has increased from 13% to 34% in the past 50 years.
- Since 1980, the percentage of children who are overweight has more than doubled, with the rate in adolescents more than tripling. If the rate continues to increase at this pace, 80% of adults could be overweight or obese by 2030, potentially costing the U.S. health care system over $950 billion and accounting for 16% to 18% of all health care expenditures (Wang et al., 2008).
- According to the CDC, approximately 60% of children are currently overweight, of whom 20% are obese. Broken down by age, 18% of adolescents (12 to 19 years of age), 20% of children (6 to 11 years of age), and 10% of preschool children (2 to 5 years of age) are obese. Children and adolescents who are overweight are more likely to become overweight adults.
- Obesity and being overweight leads to increased risk for other illnesses, such as type 2 diabetes, stroke, heart disease, and cancer.
- 18% of adolescents aged 12–19 are obese.
- 20% of children aged 6–11 are obese.
- 10% of children aged 2–5 are obese.
- Being overweight and obese are becoming a risk factor for both health and psychological and emotional well-being, where studies clearly demonstrate that overweight children are more likely to suffer from psychological and emotional diagnoses, including depression.
- One in five children has abnormal cholesterol levels, indicating a higher risk of future heart disease.
- Approximately two-thirds of U.S. adults are overweight, over half of whom are clinically obese.
- Since 1980, the prevalence of global obesity has doubled, indicating that the issue is not confined within the borders of the United States.

- By state, obesity prevalence ranged from 21% in Colorado to 34% in Mississippi in 2010. No state had a prevalence of obesity less than 20%, and 36 states had a prevalence of 25% or more; 12 of these states (Alabama, Arkansas, Kentucky, Louisiana, Michigan, Mississippi, Missouri, Oklahoma, South Carolina, Tennessee, Texas, and West Virginia) had a prevalence of 30% or more.
- The South has the highest prevalence of obesity (29.4%), followed by the Midwest (28.7%), Northeast (24.9%), and the West (24.1%).
- In Louisiana, only 56% of students had a healthy BMI, with 44% having an unhealthy BMI. About 22% are obese, and only 37% of students meet the minimum standard for cardiovascular fitness.

Source: U.S. Department of Health and Human Services, 1999; Kataoka, Zhang, & Wells, 2002; National Institute of Mental Health, 2010; http://www.bullyingstatistics.org; The Center for Evaluation and Education Policy, Indiana University School of Education; http://whatworks.wholechildeducation.org; CDC, 2012a, http://www.cdc.gov/obesity/data/adult.html.

When taken together as a whole picture of the health and well-being of people in our society, a strong and compelling case can be made to change what we are doing, through both the medical profession and the system of education and schooling practices. The physical and financial costs of not creating new interventions are too high, and we have to question whether or not our abilities to solve the problems of behavior-based illnesses are beyond our present paradigm of reality. Is this the reality we want to create? Do these alarming statistics represent our best?

Recall that *A Nation at Risk* caused a dramatic shift in our view of education at the time it was published in 1983. We called for the educational system to be managed and assessed more like a business, using the total quality management (TQM) methods first made popular by Deming and Juran in Japan. We went to a detached view of children, treating them more like products produced from efficient education factories, which led to the correlated increases in obesity. When we are working with children and we adopt total quality management methods and associated teaching and learning practices, we objectify children, assessing them primarily based on what is measurable, quantifiable, and narrow, in multiple-choice math and language arts tests. Psychologically, children learn that they are not important because their whole person is not being considered, only certain kinds of intellectual skills. They also learn to be externally motivated, through the fear of failing tests or the reward of meeting others expectations, without understanding the intrinsic rewards of learning for the sake of learning.

What I am asserting is that our education policies, methods, and practices are largely responsible for the obesity, health, and well-being tragedy among our youth. Recall this one statistic alone: Since 1980, the percentage of children who are overweight has more than doubled, with the rate in adolescents more than tripling (Wang et al., 2008). Our education paradigm does not care about children's psychological or physical well-being, and we have the results to prove it.

Through black-and-white thinking and disregard for the whole child, we have done a grave disservice to our youth and to our society that will be felt for many years to come. Much like the shocking events of 9/11 drove our nation further toward a black-and-white way of thinking and elevated our primal fears, our educational practices have caused young people to erect walls of defense to keep them safe. These are characteristics of a deficiency in the psychological attribute known as *resilience*, which allows us to keep our selves open to change, growth, and improvements. Resiliency is "a class of phenomena characterized by patterns of positive adaptation in the context of significant adversity or risk" (Masten & Reed, 2005). Since 1983, and certainly since 9/11, we have reacted with fear of worldwide competition and perceived enemies of our values, instead of being proactive and initiating a new wave of theories and approaches to bring all humans closer together.

Our educational policies and methods and cultural influences further perpetuate the cycle of fear with a constant focus on external factors. Children have learned that their emotions, their paradigms of reality or understanding of the world, and their selves are not important. Given the considerable health and well-being statistics in our society today, our children have learned these lessons well, unfortunately.

There are real and serious consequences for living out of fear, especially if we do not have the emotional intelligence to effectively manage this and other emotions. Most acutely, these consequences are manifesting as deteriorating physical health. For example, nearly 50% of all children in Philadelphia, Pennsylvania, are overweight or obese according to Mayor Michael Nutter; in some of the poorer neighborhoods, 90% of adults are overweight (*Weight of the Nation*, 2012). Of the 10 states with the highest obesity rates, 9 rank among our nation's poorest.

What to do? Initiate policies to achieve economic parity? Or invest in a program of teaching self-understanding? The former, while well intentioned, assumes that poverty is a cause of obesity when the real cause is fear of economic survival. If we shift the paradigm in our society to helping people see the importance of the whole person, rich inner life, and psychological and physical well-being, and away from the constant focus upon survival and external means to achieve well-being, then people will live with dignity and flourish.

In another example of what happens when we focus upon external supports when addressing obesity, Elsie Taveras, a pediatrician and obesity researcher at Children's Hospital Boston clinic, said that the advice she gives her patients can be very difficult for them to follow after they head back home (*Weight of the Nation*, 2012). The advice doled out to Taveras's young patients is more of the same and is consistent with medical best practices: Change your eating and exercise habits. This advice is important, but only a small piece of a very large and complex problem, and only useful if the individual self-schema has a structure to incorporate the habits in support of self-directed goals.

Since certain communities have such acute obesity problems, the correlation of socioeconomic status and race must come into consideration. If so, then the iSelf model implemented in these schools could be the equalizer— not more standards or higher standards or teaching math through rap music. We would provide all children—regardless of their race, ethnicity, or social status—with hope, access to their dreams, a glimpse into their unique purposes in life, and the type of mind that will allow them to develop a life-course trajectory beyond that which is presently being taught through schooling.

A new mind is most definitely needed to help us understand the modern stressors and complex emotions that are attacking our health and well-being at a systemic level. In the case of obesity, our physical biology has not evolved quickly enough to accommodate our eating habits. Consider that stores of fat used to ensure our survival and that of our young. But we have moved along the evolutionary time line and outside evolutionary needs in that past 50 years; in the 1970s, 5% of children were obese and now over 30% are. The human body is not designed to carry weight that is two times our body size. Therefore, phylogenetically, if our physical biology cannot change quickly enough to accommodate our new eating habits, then we need a new mind, one that helps us to understand all the stressors and complex emotions inherent in modern society in order to combat at a systemic level our health and well-being.

The health consequences of being overweight include increased prevalence of asthma, cancer, cardiovascular disease, diabetes, dementia, kidney failure, arthritis, impaired cognitive functioning, and others. We need to confront the obesity epidemic head on, not simply through traditional dietary recommendations, but with a new set of recommendations and preventative methods, such as teaching how to be well, both mentally and physically. If we continue to do more of the same, we will propagate a mind-set of abdicating personal responsibility for health to the medical professionals. There is a pervasive mind-set involving the relationship between the self, significant others, and socioconstructed realities, as characterized by what one study participant said: "I am the 5th generation that has had heart disease due to obesity, my mother had it, and her mother had it, therefore I will too." Do we want a 6th generation?

## Intersection of Obesity and Mental Health

Childhood and adolescent obesity is strongly correlated with social and psychological problems, such as discrimination, use and abuse of relationship power dynamics, poor self-knowledge, low self-esteem, and ineffectual coping mechanisms to meet the economic and other survival challenges of modern society. As psychologist Janet Greeson states, "it is not what you are eating, it is what's eating you" (Greeson, 1993).

Numerous studies underscore the impact of poor self-esteem upon a host of preventable illnesses. One study of 6,500 participants in England found that 10-year-olds with emotional problems who felt less in control of their lives were most likely to gain weight over the next 20 years, with girls affected more than boys. Professor and lead researcher Dr. Andrew Ternouth recommended that "early intervention for children suffering low self-esteem, anxiety, or other emotional challenges could help improve their changes of long-term physical health" and "strategies to promote social and emotional aspects of learning, including the promotion of self-esteem, are central to a number of recent policy initiatives" (Ternouth et al., 2009, p. 8). With the growing and compelling researched-based evidence pointing to the correlations between self-esteem and health, it is ethically and morally the right thing to teach self-knowledge through our system of education.

To further underscore the critical nature of the obesity, let's look at the financial consequences of this problem. Consider these economic facts:

- $190 billion in annual medical costs are due to obesity.
- $1,850 more per year accrue in medical costs for an overweight person than for someone of healthy weight.
- $4 billion annually is needed for additional gasoline as cars carry heavier people.
- The annual average cost of absenteeism per worker is $1,140.
- 75% of the nation's $2 trillion medical care costs are for behavior-based illnesses (eating habits, sedentary lifestyle, alcohol use, and smoking).
- In the 10 cities in the United States with the highest obesity rates, direct costs are about $50 million per 100,000 residents.
- If the rate of increase in childhood obesity continues as it did in the period from 1970 to 2004, then 80% of today's children could be obese by 2030, costing $861–957 billion, or 16%–18% of all health care expenditures (Wang et al., 2008).

- In 2006, 9.1% of all annual medical spending was for childhood-obesity-related procedures. This number rivals costs associated with smoking, which range from 6.5% to 14.4% of annual medical spending.

### Risk and Protective Factors for Health and Well-Being

In a study on the role of schools in preventing childhood obesity sponsored by the National Association of State Boards of Education, Wechsler and colleagues report "childhood overweight also is associated with social and psychological problems, such as discrimination and poor self-esteem" (Wechsler, et al., 2004, p. 5). Yet, when presenting their list of recommendations, the researchers do not include personal protective factors at all, let alone those that include self-knowledge, self-understanding, self-esteem, or the enlightened view that we create ourselves and our realities in life. All the study's recommendations, which include policies and strategies, pertain to those factors outside or external to the individual, thereby reinforcing that the issue of obesity and being overweight is outside the control and personal responsibility of each individual. If nothing is done, then the U.S. economy will be "weighed down" through neglect of the health and well-being of our children and the increases in health care expenditures.

The CDC has recommended strategies to combat the epidemic of overweight and obese children and adolescents, but most are grounded in environmental protective factors that are external to the self of the individual. This is troublesome because the CDC has researched the critical link between self-esteem and psychological well-being to illness, and yet none of the agency's efforts have incorporated these psychological self-attributes into their general recommendations or recommendations for schooling. Examples of some of the initiatives they have supported include locating schools within easy walking distance of residential areas; improving the availability of affordable, healthier food and beverage choices; and restricting availability of less healthy foods and beverages in public service venues, among others. These *external* factors will stick only if individuals have the tools to understand them in the context of their own identity, life purpose, self-awareness, and emotional intelligence, among other *internal* attributions and personal factors.

### Personal Factors

*Personal factors*, unique to each individual, include an individual's knowledge, skills, experience, history, and genetic makeup. Personal factors contribute to either risk or protection:

1. *Self-Knowledge and Skill*
    - *Knowledge*, including knowledge about what can and should be done and its consequences, as well as knowledge of available resources; deeper awareness of self-attributions throughout the life-span; personality type
    - *Beliefs*, such as ideas about the causes of problems or the consequences of choices, including those self-beliefs that either limit or free up new possibilities for health, well-being, and success; hopes and dreams
    - *Skills*, including being able to influence one's environment, set and accomplish goals, and utilize or apply self-distinctions in one's life directly
    - *Education and training*, such as years of formal education or specialized training in the self-distinctions through K–16 schooling or counseling

2. *Experience and History*
    - *Experience*, such as history of abuse and neglect, or care and caring; ability to learn about self and others and make changes; family dynamics and beliefs that allow for unique identity formulation and self-expression separate from these
    - *Cultural norms and practices*, including understanding what behaviors are appropriate and acceptable in family, social groups, and various social settings, such as school and peer and community gatherings
    - *Social status*, such as history of discrimination or privilege in work, social, or service situations; socioeconomic levels and improvements from one level to another (social mobility)

3. *Biology/Genetics*
    - *Type and degree of existing health*, including current health status, blood type, blood pressure, BMI
    - *Cognitive, mental or physical ability*, such as the ability to process information; mobility or physical impairment; mental well-being or illness; strengths and weaknesses, talents and abilities, hopes and dreams
    - *Chronic illness*, including requirements for care or specialized needs
    - *Gender and age*, as they might increase risk or protection throughout life-span development
    - *Genetic predisposition*, such as having a family history of diabetes, alcoholism, and depression

    Adapted from The Community Tool Box, a service of the Work Group for Community Health and Development at the University of Kansas, http://ctb.ku.edu/en/tablecontents/sub_section_main_1156.aspx.

Some of the personal factors that influence the development of obesity and being overweight include physical activity, diet, and regular health screenings. Just as important, some of the modifiable risk factors include self-esteem, purpose and direction in life, self-understanding, and ability to take proactive/ positive actions.

Protective factors are often the opposite side of risk factors. Therefore, some of the protective factors for obesity would include diet and getting regular aerobic exercise, high self-esteem, knowing unique purpose and dreams in life, clear self-understanding, personalized education plan in school, and efficacy in the world. All these risk and protective factors occur on an individual level.

### Environmental Factors

*Environmental factors* are factors that bring risk or protection to a specific group of people in a community; they can be specific to an individual or more general in nature. The *environment* refers to the conditions in which individuals live—their households, neighborhoods, or towns, and the larger community. These may include aspects of the *social environment*, including the norms and behaviors of families, friends, and others in the community. Aspects of the *physical environment* include access to resources, exposure to hazards, and overall living conditions. Environmental factors fall into the following categories:

1. Support and Services
   - *Availability and continuity of social support and ties*, such as connecting with family, friends, neighbors, and those with different experiences; schooling; availability of self-knowledge or iSelf through education or counseling
   - *Availability of appropriate services*, such as for basic and specialized needs
   - *Availability of resources*, including human and material resources

2. Access, Barriers, and Opportunities
   - *Physical access and barriers*, including distance and physical access to services
   - *Communication access and barriers*, including languages spoken and access to interpreters (if appropriate)
   - *Competing requirements for participation*, including those circumstances that make involvement difficult, such as having to work or care for children, or equality of involvement—all having equal access

3. *Consequences of Efforts*
   - *Social approval and disapproval,* such as whether family and peers encourage or discourage particular behaviors
   - *Incentives and disincentives,* including monetary and material gain or loss and likely prospects for getting desired benefits, including self-interest and such motivations as growth and development
   - *Time costs and delays,* including the time and effort for taking action, meeting needs, and getting access to services; also including health and well-being consequences of not getting access to self-knowledge on a timely basis

4. *Policies and Living Conditions*
   - *Policies,* such as those that affect who has access to self-knowledge education or counseling or benefits; rules and laws affecting workplaces and communities; national, state, and local educational policies that focus upon internal or external preventative factors and eligibility requirements for services
   - *Financial barriers and resources,* including not having enough money for needed goods and services; how resources are allocated
   - *Exposure to hazards,* including to toxic chemicals, air pollutants, or risky situations
   - *Living conditions,* such as decent housing, food, clothing, heating and cooling, and clean drinking water
   - *Poverty and disparities in status,* such as not having enough money for basic needs and disparities or differences in income and social status

Adapted from The Community Tool Box, a service of the Work Group for Community Health and Development at the University of Kansas, http://ctb.ku.edu/en/tablecontents/sub_section_main_1156.aspx.

Some of the environmental risk factors that influence the chances of becoming overweight or obese include community norms that favor large portions of unhealthy food (such as "Super Sizing" at fast-food restaurants); poor access to adequate and culturally appropriate self-knowledge education, counseling, health care; and family and community norms that favor a sedentary life style.

On the flip side, some of the protective factors that influence being overweight include being from a community that traditionally eats a healthy diet (think of the Mediterranean diet, which includes a lot of seafood, olive oil, and fresh vegetables), community norms that include exercise and activity, and open access to state-of-the-art, caring, and culturally appropriate self-knowledge education, counseling, and health care.

Most obesity prevention programs focus on environmental factors with limited results. Further, the personal factors, "experience and history" and "biology genetics," are difficult to change. Of all the personal and environmental factors, the most effective ones for true protection against obesity and obesity-related illnesses are those within self-knowledge and skill and, more to the point, the integrated self-attributes of each person. With a healthy self, we can rise above the personal and environmental factors over our life-span.

Any external environmental changes must be accompanied by tools for self-understanding, encouraging intrinsic thinking and decisions. We need to trust each individual. To do so, we need to combine health and well-being services with schooling and self-knowledge education and counseling, to underscore the necessity to see health and well-being as a primary responsibility of public schooling in our society within the new and emerging paradigm. Schooling is a primary protective factor if self-knowledge is taught and teachers are rewarded for placing mental and physical well-being at the center of their work.

## Well-Being: Psychological

"Depression is a major public health issue," asserts Kelly Posner, an assistant professor at Columbia University College of Physicians and Surgeons in New York. "The fact that people are getting the treatments they need is encouraging. She added that 25% of adults will have a major depressive episode sometime in their life, as will 8% of adolescents—remarkably high numbers" (Cohen, 2007). If this constitutes a "major public health issue," then why are our government agencies not working on more interventions? Here are some additional psychological well-being statistics:

- More than 14 million children and adolescents have mental health issues.
- Approximately 20% of all youth are impacted by a mental disorder to the extent that they have difficulty functioning.
- About 80% of these children with mental disorders do not get the help they need.
- Depressive disorder is the leading cause of disability among Americans age 15–44.
- Suicide is one of the leading causes of death among children under the age of 14 in the United States.
- From 2003 to 2004, there was a 76% increase in teen suicides among 10- to 14-year-old girls.

The U.S. Department of Health and Human Services (HHS), along with other government agencies, often attempts to address one mental health problem at a time, separated from the whole self, as it does with depression and suicide. For the past 40 years, HHS has had the "Healthy People" initiative in place, which is described as "a comprehensive set of national 10-year health objectives" and "a roadmap for prevention" (HHS, Healthy People 2020 webinar, May 1, 2012). The agency developed a Signs of Suicide (SOS) program to employ environmental protective support and service to address the mental health issue of suicide. The SOS program is a community intervention strategy in support of government policy and targets for reducing childhood and adolescent suicide in our society. Like so many other programs of similar designs, its performance was less than satisfactory. Robert H. Aseltine, director of the Institute of Public Health and principal investigator of the SOS program, reported the effects of the SOS program on knowledge and attitudes about depression and suicide were not significant. He also reiterated that SOS is a *suicide* prevention program, not a *depression* prevention program, underscoring how we examine isolated variables instead of taking a holistic view of the causal relationship between depression and suicide, in this case.

I suspect the limited impact stems from isolating depression from suicide and from failing to educate youth about the causal relationship, along with not teaching self-knowledge, a primary protective factor.

A more effective program would be one that does address that relationship, promoting such protective factors as knowing one's purpose in life, having the emotional intelligence to empathize with a group of people and take action to help, and building self-esteem, among others. A program that teaches children and adolescents that self-esteem impacts depression, emphasizing the relationship among inner self psychological well-being attributions, would lower incidences of depression and suicide.

In this same HHS webinar, it was reported that this program was implemented in 100% of St. Louis Missouri schools, proudly reported as an indicator of effectiveness; note the emphasis upon the environmental factor of schools and community supports in lieu of mental health indicators. With the Healthy People 2020 initiative, HHS takes the external view for assisting human well-being. Nowhere does the initiative mention the importance of the internal view or inner self of children and adolescents as the most effective prevention strategy to consider. The advertised goal of Healthy People 2020 is to create a roadmap for *all* leading health indicators, which are "critical health issues that, if addressed appropriately, will dramatically reduce the leading causes of preventable health disease and illnesses" (Webinar slide). With the abundance of research conducted and reported by the CDC and NIH on the causal relationship between inner self-dimensions and disease, why has HHS not implemented mental and physical health programs that teach self-knowledge as a primary protective factor?

According to Howard Koh, assistant secretary of health, the two determinants of mental health are *social factors*, such as interpersonal relationships, family, and community dynamics, and *economic factors*, such as housing quality and employment opportunities. Koh understands that "mental health and physical health are inextricably linked" and "from a federal level, that mental health and behavioral health in its totality is a major priority of this administration and department." Nevertheless, the Healthy People initiative aims to provide a roadmap for both mental and physical health in our society but clearly overlooks the importance of the number one protective factor for both mental and physical health: that of self-knowledge, self-understanding, and self-esteem.

Our current paradigm for viewing and solving mental health issues is from the circumstantial, related to factors external to the self, instead of taking the iSelf's view of the inner person, the self-components and their dynamic. This may account for why suicide rates increased from 1999 to 2008 by over 12% (National Vital Statistics System Mortality, CDC, 2012b). In men, rates increased four times higher than those of women, while women have a much higher rate of attempted suicides versus completed suicides. Additional statistics support the need for a new, transformed view: Approximately 20% of children will experience mental health disorders in their lifetimes, and in 2010, 11% of adolescents between 16 and 17 years of age reported major depressive episodes (MDE).

As Table 3 indicates, 29% of adolescents in high school grades 9 through 12 reported feeling sad or hopeless almost every day for an extended period (2 or more weeks in a row) in the last year (Child Trends Data Bank, July 2012).

With approximately a third of adolescents in high school feeling so sad or hopeless that they withdrew from their daily responsibilities and activities, or worse, without mental health counseling, many adolescents became so resigned that they started to go through the motions of making it look like they were "OK" to parents and teachers, engaging in passive aggressive behavior. Adolescents are skilled at making it look like they are "OK" to prevent their parents from worrying too much or to avoid the stigma associated with having difficulties in life. Passive-aggressive behavior has its emotional roots in anger and sadness, but since adolescents do not have ready access to ways to process these complex emotions, it shows up as having an "attitude," laziness, or apathy.

As an addition to Table 3, you should note that the data do not include the 27% of high school students who dropped out of school. If we consider dropping out as an emotional breakdown or reaction, then well over 50% of all adolescents in our society are experiencing emotional and mental health

**Table 3.** Percentage of High School Students Who Felt Sad or Hopeless, 1999-2011*

|  | 1999 | 2001 | 2003 | 2005 | 2007 | 2009 | 2011 |
|---|---|---|---|---|---|---|---|
| **All Students** | 28.3 | 28.3 | 28.6 | 28.5 | 28.5 | 26.1 | 28.5 |
| *Race/ethnicity* | | | | | | | |
| White, non-Hispanic | 24.9 | 26.5 | 26.2 | 25.8 | 26.2 | 23.7 | 27.2 |
| Black, non-Hispanic | 28.9 | 28.8 | 26.3 | 28.4 | 29.2 | 27.7 | 24.7 |
| *Grade* | | | | | | | |
| 9 | 27.4 | 29.4 | 28.0 | 29.0 | 28.2 | 26.6 | 27.6 |
| 10 | 29.3 | 27.2 | 29.7 | 28.9 | 28.9 | 26.1 | 28.7 |
| 11 | 27.1 | 28.7 | 28.9 | 28.8 | 27.1 | 27.3 | 28.8 |
| 12 | 29.4 | 27.0 | 27.4 | 26.4 | 29.4 | 24.3 | 28.9 |

*Felt so sad almost every day for two or more weeks in a row that they stopped doing some usual activities.

problems that are not being addressed by educators, counselors, or medical professionals. Isn't this justification for teaching self-knowledge and emotional intelligence through K–16 schooling? We are losing more than 50% of our youth and their future potentials to contribute their unique talents to a better world, simply because our paradigm does not allow for placing the well-being of people at its center.

Depressive episodes are common at numerous transition periods in life, across the life-span. These can be due simply to changes in diet and food reactions, or these can be due to changing identities and uncertainty about how a new one will be accepted by friends and family. Or worse, depression may be due to incidences of abuse or negative changes in family dynamics.

### Psychological Well-Being From Adolescence to Adulthood

If we do not learn how to be well in childhood or adolescence, our mental health will continue to deteriorate into adulthood. If children have not been taught to access the number one protective factor—self-knowledge and self-esteem—how can we expect young adults and adults to know how to take responsibility for their own health and well-being?

The issue of depression among children, adolescents, and adults requires our attention. Depression affects more than 11 million people per year in the United States, costing about $45 billion per year in treatment and lost productivity—a toll slightly larger than the costs of heart disease (Greenberg,

Stiglin, Finkelstein, & Berndt, 1993). A CDC study found those states with high depression rates also have higher than average rates of obesity, heart disease, diabetes, and other illnesses. Approximately 10% of the study's participants had depressive episodes in the 2 weeks prior to taking the survey (CDC, 2006; 2008). Lela McKnight-Eily, a clinical psychologist and epidemiologist at the CDC, states the following:

> Depression can both precipitate and exacerbate the symptoms of a chronic disease. For example, if someone is depressed and they have diabetes, they may be less likely to stick to their treatment regimen in terms of their insulin and eating appropriately. Those things are definitely linked. (CDC, 2011)

The pervasiveness of poor adolescent mental health is acute and getting worse, requiring our attention and best efforts to develop a prevention and intervention approach that has both short-term and longer term systemic results at the ontological level (the "being" of human beings), instead of the usual pathological approaches that simply medicate symptoms.

To further underscore the problems, from 2003 to 2004, there was a 76% increase in suicide among 10- to 14-year-old girls, a 32% increase among 15- to 19-year-old girls, and a 9% increase among 15- to 19-year-old boys (CDC, 2007). As a past teacher of 4th graders at a school for a wide range of learning and emotional disabilities, I would have noticed if one of my 10-year-old students was experiencing emotional or psychological difficulties; hopefully other caring teachers would notice as well. I am appalled that teachers today are not being taught how to observe and preliminarily diagnose the inner, mental, and psychological conditions of their students. Educators at all levels have forgotten what business they are in, why they are teachers, and what they should be imparting to their students beyond content knowledge.

According to the respected organization Suicide.org, a U.S. teen takes his or her life every 100 minutes. Suicide is the third-leading cause of death for young people ages 15 to 24. Approximately 20% of teens experience depression before they reach adulthood, and between 10% and 15% suffer from symptoms at any one time. Only 30% of depressed teens are being treated for the disease.

Risk factors for depression and suicide among teens vary; for example, teen girls develop depression twice as often as boys, yet almost all teens experience at least one or more of these factors in their adolescent years (between 11 and 24 years of age):

- Abuse and neglect
- Chronic illness or other physical conditions

- Family history of depression or mental illness (with between 20% and 50% of teens suffering from depression having a family member with depression or some other mental disorder)
- Untreated mental or substance-abuse problems (with approximately two-thirds of teens with major depression also battling another mood disorder such as dysthymia, anxiety, antisocial behaviors, or substance abuse)
- Trauma or disruptions at home, including divorce or deaths of parents
- Low self-esteem or confidence
- External locus of control orientation (versus internal)
- Lack of meaning and direction in life through unformed life purpose and/or dreams

A study led by Jean Twenge (2009; 2010), a San Diego State University psychology professor, found that five times as many high school and college students are dealing with anxiety and other mental health issues as youth of the same age who were studied in the Great Depression era. To derive these data, Twenge analyzed the responses of more than 77,000 college students who took the Minnesota Multiphasic Personality Inventory from 1938 through 2007 (Twenge et al., 2010). These findings add further evidence to support the theory that modern life is too stressful, too complex, and changing too fast for the minds that are being trained through our education system to meet the myriad of 21st-century challenges.

### The iSelf Paradigm, Psychological Well-Being, and Physical Health Dynamics

Today's youth find themselves focused on external goals such as wealth, fame, success; emotional dependency upon technology; attainment of school-based measures; and college selection and loans, to name a few. Without being able to focus on internal goals, such as feelings, self-understanding, relationship intimacy, and purpose and dreams in life, among others, it is no wonder that young people are experiencing that it all feels beyond their control to live a high quality of life, a flourishing life to the level of their unique potentials and what they can envision.

The increase in mental health issues such as anxiety and depression underscores the need for a cultural and paradigmatic shift from external motivations and measures of success to internal motivations and measures, such as self-knowledge, among others called for in the iSelf model.

## The iSelf Model and Borderline Personality Disorders

While studying the association and correlation between mental health and disorders and physical health, I have analyzed which of the mental health diagnoses described in the American Psychiatric Association's *Diagnostic and Statistics Manual, 4th edition* (DSM-IV), could be readily addressed through the implementation of the iSelf model in either an educative classroom setting or a counseling therapeutic setting.

In one of my cases handled through my clinical counseling practice, "Mary" had been diagnosed with borderline personality disorder (BPD), which is defined and described by the National Institute of Mental Health (NIMH) as follows:

> Borderline personality disorder (BPD) is characterized by pervasive instability in moods, interpersonal relationships, self-image, and behavior. While a person with depression or bipolar disorder typically endures the same mood for weeks, a person with BPD may experience intense bouts of anger, depression, and anxiety that may last for only a few hours to a day. (NIMH, 2011)

Through an eight-session learning and treatment plan using the iSelf model and positive psychology attributes in particular, we focused on her self-image, self-esteem, and emotional understanding of her family dynamics and purpose and dreams for her life. Mary made a dramatic transformation in her life. She went from being withdrawn and angry when with her family to participating in family outings and preparing meals. Additionally, she went on a college visitation tour with her mother, toward whom she had the most anxiety and anger. Mary's BPD symptoms were minimized and addressed at the ontological, being level, and she has not had repeating symptoms in the 10 years since the intervention.

There are many more people of all ages, adolescents, young adults, and adults who are walking around with undiagnosed, untreated borderline personalities. They suffer in silence because BPD is difficult to diagnose and then apply the appropriate intervention. More to the point, it is difficult for mental health care providers to receive reimbursement from health care companies for this diagnosis. This explains why other diagnoses are more prevalent for closely related, yet more acute symptoms, such as bipolar and depression, thereby qualifying for insurance reimbursements. Every day that goes by is another day that children, adolescents, and young adults have not been helped, have not been provided a model of understanding themselves so that they can put into context the complexities of modern life and heal themselves.

Approximately 9.1% of the adult U.S. population has been diagnosed with personality disorders. Personality disorders represent "an enduring pattern of inner experience and behavior that deviates markedly from the expectations of the culture of the individual who exhibits it," according to the DSM-IV. These patterns tend to be consistent across varied situations and are typically perceived to be appropriate by the individual, even though they may markedly affect their day-to-day life in negative ways. What makes these personality disorders so difficult to diagnose, provided with this description, is that all teenagers, when very honest, will indicate that they have either the "inner experience" or "behavior" that "deviates markedly" from their families or "culture," if not for the external behavioral controls established by family, schools, or culture. So, at the inner self, ontological level, to address those inner experiences of difference helps young people feel better about whom they are, which leads to improved self-esteem.

These disorders encompass antisocial personality disorder, avoidant personality disorder, borderline personality disorder, and emotionally unstable disorder, and are characterized by the lack of one's identity. Erikson (1968; 1980) and Marcia (1966; 1991) would say that this is a normal process—seeking one's identity—at the adolescent stage of development. I would draw your attention to the use of the phrase "inner experience that deviates markedly from the expectations of the culture" as a very gray area in which to clearly diagnose and prescribe a course of action.

### Emotionally Unstable Borderline Personality Disorder

One additional diagnosis where a prevention program would assist is emotionally unstable borderline personality disorder. Most, if not all, people experience some sort of emotional crisis, such as divorce in the family, witnessing or experiencing violence, and emotional, physical, and sexual childhood abuse. Typical symptoms include swinging from one emotional crisis to another, dependency, separation anxiety, unstable self-image, chronic feelings of emptiness, and threats of self-harm, such as self-mutilation, of which cutting is an example. While some children receive the emotional unstable diagnosis, in many cases, we accept these symptoms as normal for our children, in this modern time, in human history. *Yet they are not normal*—they are acute symptoms of children in crisis and a characteristic outcome of a culture and a society and a school system that is in need of a paradigm shift so as to be able to heal our people.

Approximately 8% to 10% of individuals diagnosed with emotionally unstable disorder end their lives in suicide. In adulthood, job losses, interrupted education, and broken marriages are common.

The primary risk factors for emotionally unstable disorder are having a very stressful or chaotic childhood (e.g., physical and sexual abuse, neglect, hostile conflict, and early parental loss or separation). Mood disorders, substance-related disorders, eating disorders (usually bulimia), post-traumatic stress disorder, attention-deficit/hyperactivity disorder, and other personality disorders frequently co-occur with emotional unstable disorder.

I would assert that these risk factors and co-occurrences are common and affect most in our society. The incidences are underreported because we are accepting this state as the new normal: We accept these symptoms, allow them to persist, or treat them with medications without regard to developing prevention programs.

Because we have so many people in the world who will never be diagnosed with personality disorder and teachers themselves are not trained to address these pervasive needs, we need to give teachers and students a better model for prevention. The iSelf model offers a teacher or counselor access to the inner experience and life of their students or clients. With the iSelf model, teachers and counselors and direct service professionals can shift their focus to a student's inner life and experiences when designing their interventions and prevention programs. This creates a healthier balance for how we work with young people—before they qualify for DSM-IV diagnoses.

## Better Assessments

There are two common assessment tools used to diagnose emotional and behavioral issues in children between the ages of 4 and 17: the Schedule for Affective Disorders and Schizophrenia for School-Age Children (K-SADS) and the Strengths and Difficulties Questionnaire (SDQ). In a study sponsored by the CDC, 7% of children between 4 and 17 years of age had high scores using the SDQ: "Emotional and behavioral problems are among the most prevalent chronic health conditions of childhood and often have serious negative consequences for a child's academic achievement and social development" (CDC, 2012, p. 1).

These children are those who have utilized mental health services and been diagnosed properly. I would argue that the number of children who actually fall into this category is triple or more; thus, the voiceless child would have difficulty expressing his or her need for help.

I would propose educators be trained in and given the opportunity to use these two assessments periodically for all school children, thereby making it a part of personalized learning plan as well as the well-being portfolio of each child. Additionally, each student's portfolio would include the Ryff Well-Being Scales assessment, along with the Quaglia Institute's student aspirations survey on his or her dreams in life, administered annually. (Note the latter is now used in New Hampshire as a part of its Personalized Learning initiative). We do have the means to know our teens at deeper levels than their report card or standardized test scores show in either a school or clinical setting through the utilization of well-being assessments, such as attributional style questionnaires (ASQs), Beck depression inventories (BDIs), dysfunctional attitudes scales (DASs), hopelessness scales (HSs), psychological well-being scales, Rutter B scales for diagnosing emotional problems, LAWSEQ self-esteem scales, Brzycki's context paradigm for assessing purpose and dreams in life, CAROLOC for assessing locus of control, Rotter's locus of control scales for measuring locus of control orientation or attribution, and others.

## Antidepressant Medication

Adults and children have mental health issues that they do not have the mindset to process and understand. Yet medical professionals and their patients often take the easy route to gaining a sense of emotional balance within the self, to gaining a sense of well-being absent of anxiety or stress—they prescribe and take prescription drugs.

As with obesity and depression, drug use statistics are overwhelming but serve to enhance and round out our view of the alarming state of well-being in our society. Therapeutic drug use to address mental health issues is increasing and leading to prescription drug abuse, with 47.9% of the U.S. population using at least one prescription drug in the past month, 21.4% using three drugs, and 10.5% using five or more. The most frequently prescribed therapeutic classes are antidepressants (CDC, 2011). To underscore the reliance upon drugs for minor mental health issues in 2008, drug therapy was prescribed in 76% of hospital outpatient departments visits and 74% of physician office visits.

We can deduce that a narrow scientific medical model has influenced both diagnosis and therapy. Numerous studies support the use of cognitive behavioral therapy (CBT) or other short-term intervention models for depressive and anxiety disorders, including generalized anxiety disorder, moderate depressive episodes, and severe depressive episodes. One study found that cognitive therapy prevents relapse after the termination of therapy and may have a greater preventative effect than antidepressant drugs (Blackburn, Eunson, & Bishop, 1986). Another study indicates the following:

> Unlike pharmacotherapy, cognitive therapy teaches a set of skills that can be applied long after the end of therapy. Because the majority of depressed individuals suffer multiple episodes, the capacity of an intervention to prevent future episodes is at least as important as its ability to treat the current episode. (Seligman, Schulman, & DeRubeis, 1999, p. 2)

This is significant when we consider that the iSelf, implemented through schooling, is a method of preventing depression, among other possible mental health disorders. Skills learned in a classroom setting provide lifelong protection and place the responsibility and advocacy for psychological, attitudinal, explanatory, hopelessness, and other functional changes in the being and cognition of students on the students themselves.

The fact that a narrow medical model pervades intervention strategies for depressive and personality disorders explains why there is such a high rate of multiple episodes. The iSelf model is a preventative model that teaches how to create a paradigm of thinking, being, and reality that brings into balance the psychodynamics that create depressive episodes. Depression is an antecedent to numerous health behaviors; therefore, it is important to put into place those protective factors that will help prevent the long list of these related behavior-based illnesses and chronic health issues.

A real-life story highlights the mind-set and inherent beliefs of many Americans. Maryland anesthesiologist and senior fellow at Washington's Hudson Institute, Ronald Dworkin, tells the story of a woman who didn't like the way her husband was handling the family finances. She wanted to start keeping the books herself but didn't want to insult her husband.

Her doctor suggested she try an antidepressant to make herself feel better. She got the antidepressant, and she did feel better, according to Dworkin, who told the story in his book *Artificial Unhappiness: The Dark Side of the New Happy Class*. But in the meantime, Dworkin says, the woman's husband led the family into financial ruin.

"Doctors are now medicating unhappiness," said Dworkin. "Too many people take drugs when they really need to be making changes in their lives" (Cohen, 2007). This story and sentiment underscores the value of implementing the iSelf model in schools as a preventative tool for learning how to handle states of anxiety, where students learn about and develop positive emotional intelligence through a paradigm of self to process complex emotions around stressors in life. The story of family financial ruin may well have ended more positively if the woman had learned self-efficacy and self-understanding and if the husband had learned self-responsibility, purpose in life, and character.

According to a government study, antidepressants have become the most commonly prescribed drugs in the United States. They are prescribed more than drugs to treat high blood pressure, high cholesterol, asthma, or headaches. In a 2011 study, the CDC looked at the 2.4 billion drugs prescribed in visits to doctors and hospitals in 2005. Of those, 118 million were for antidepressants. High blood pressure drugs were the next most common, with 113 million prescriptions.

The use of antidepressants and other psychotropic drugs—those that affect brain chemistry—has skyrocketed over the last decade. Between 1995 and 2002, the most recent year for which statistics are available, the use of these drugs tripled, the CDC reported. These findings offer further evidence that we do not have the modern minds required to handle increased complexities and stressors and of a medical model that does not value a person's ability to heal oneself, naturally, by gaining equilibrium among all component parts of the mind, including brain chemistry.

### Prescription Drug Abuse: Cultural Acceptance of Prescribing Happiness

Prescription drugs are the second most abused category of drugs in the United States, following marijuana, with a fourfold increase in those admitted to drug rehabilitation centers over the past decade (SAMHSA, 2010). Among 12th graders, 6 of the 10 most abused substances are pharmaceutical drugs (University of Michigan, 2010). This epidemic among adolescents and adults demonstrates that we do not have the ability to know how to meet the challenges inherent in our lives. We are too focused upon the external world, taking external advice that offers quick solutions to common emotional and psychological issues and concerns. Instead of teaching people that they have it within themselves to change, to take control over their own destinies in life by tapping into their inner lives, we teach them to believe that prescription drugs, especially antidepressants, must be acceptable if prescribed so readily by the medical professionals. Consider these startling statistics that underscore our health and well-being epidemic:

- In 1998, 2.2% of people in the United States reported abusing prescription pain relievers, but that number has climbed steadily over the years. By 2008, nearly 10% reported abusing common prescription drugs, such as Vicodin, Oxycontin, or morphine.
- Approximately 11% of people in the United States are taking antidepressants, according to the CDC.
- Antidepressant use has surged almost 300% when you compare the figures from the 3-year period ending in 2008 to the 6 years ending in 1994, the year the eye-opening memoir *Prozac Nation* was published.
- More than 1 in 5 women between the ages of 40 and 59 are taking an antidepressant, the highest rate for any group. Overall, women and adolescent girls are 2.5 times more likely than men and adolescent boys to be taking one of the pills.
- Nearly 4% of adolescents (ages 12 through 17) are on an antidepressant.

- Antidepressants are the second most prescribed type of drug in the United States, right behind pills for high cholesterol, according to data from IMS Health. In 2011, 255 million prescriptions for antidepressants were dispensed in the United States, a 2% increase from 2009.
- Most of the people taking antidepressants—60%—have done so for at least 2 years; fewer than one-third of people taking a single antidepressant have seen a mental health professional in the past year.
- In a survey of more than a thousand Californians, the majority of whom had a history of depression, nearly half said they would not tell their family doctor about symptoms of depression. The primary reason? 23% said they feared that they would be prescribed antidepressants.
- In 2010, the United States has spent $11.6 billion on antidepressants and $7.2 billion on treatment for ADHD, according to IMS Health, which tracks prescription drug sales.

Source: Hensley, 2011.

A prevention program in public schools is worth the investment, given the critical nature of the psychological and physical well-being of our children and adolescents (as well as the associated billions spent on antidepressants). The problem is not going away and is in fact growing. Sad or hopeless children and adolescents have a higher probability of becoming sad or hopeless adults who require prescription drugs to ameliorate. Doctors are more likely to prescribe antidepressants instead of counseling or talk therapy because it is quicker and easier and because they are encouraged by the health care system that rewards the psychopharmaceutical intervention over counseling. Rather than accepting the entrenched position, we can give children integrated self-protective factors to help propel them on a pathway to flourishing, to manifesting their full potentials, and psychological and physical well-being.

## Bullying

Bullying is a mental health issue affecting young children, adolescents, and young adults, and we do not know how to address this growing epidemic. This past year, I received an e-mail from one of my former students, who was now a lead teacher in a K–3 elementary school and in need of assistance in addressing the epidemic bullying problem in her school. Her tone was panicked, yet the school had three psychologists on staff who were hired experts in antibullying. What is going on that a group of very competent teachers and three psychologists in a small rural community could not address the issue of bullying among 5- to 8-year-old children?

I propose taking a much broader view of the bullying problem, looking at stressors and those risk factors in children's lives that would create such a departure from their childlike natures. Schools and schooling processes are risk factors for K–16 students.

Children are under stress to perform, to meet specific learning standards through their schooling. We disregard children's socioemotional needs and excessively highlight their intellectual growth and demonstration of skills or competencies, creating a chilling environment that contributes to bullying behaviors and victimization.

A student of mine finishing up her M.Ed. degree, "Cassie," was assigned to a 3rd-grade public school classroom to observe children who were learning how to read and to assist when needed. One of Cassie's students, "Michael," had scored low on the Dynamic Indicators of Basic Early Literacy (DIBELS) assessment used extensively in elementary schools to measure reading fluency—this test measures the rate and accuracy of reading. Rate of reading is a count of the number of words read within a given time span, and accuracy is the ability to read a word aloud that matches the print on the page. The tests measure reading fluency as though it can be converted to a simple "hit" or "miss" measure. Words read correctly are "hits" and an error is a "miss;" the more times a child can hit the right word in one or two minutes, the better the child's fluency scores are (AIMS web training, 2004).

A skilled educator is trained to use these assessments and data derived from these for use in data-driven instruction. This means that if Michael scored low, where the number of misses in a minute is high, then a reading intervention and associated strategy is used to boost the DIBELS scores. The lead classroom teacher was upset with Michael and declared that he could not read and needed special remediation.

Upon observing Michael's emotional upset and sense that he had been defeated, Cassie took it upon herself to take Michael into a quiet corner of the classroom and read the book *Frog and Toad Together* (Lobel, 1983) with him. Cassie observed that Michael could read and, more important, understand and comprehend what he was reading—just not quite as fast as is required for DIBELS and for early childhood educators feeling the stress to improve reading scores.

Did Michael's teacher really know him? The reading material required for assessment was detached from the reader's experience of the story, words, and meanings—and from the whole child who is reading. When Cassie read with Michael, the material became more pertinent and personal, with a more meaningful and direct transfer of content to Michael's personal experience. Therefore, this produced better literacy results as well as less stress, anxiety, and potential harm to Michael's sense of self-belief system that he was a good person and could read.

How does this case relate to increased incidences of bullying in our education system? In all a child's primary cultural learning sources (schooling among them), learning is detached and decontextualized from the learner, from the whole child's mind, body, and soul. When learning becomes solely about acquiring content and is not related to the child's own experiences or emotional responses and relevant development potential, then the child feels that he is objectified—that he is somehow less important than the number of hits and misses in a minute.

In the context of Michael's classroom dynamics, as the class was moved ahead with other higher-level reading material, Michael felt bad about himself when he realized that he had not measured up to his teacher's expectations for DIBELS performance. He felt shamed in front of his classmates, his peer group. Cassie reported that Michael felt marginalized, separate from the group and therefore not belonging. He was questioning himself as a competent learner and, more directly, as a good person; the seeds of fear and self-doubt were planted.

The classroom is where children of all ages and abilities learn to construct or create a self, a mind, and brain. Michael will automatically respond emotionally to these circumstances, either positively or negatively. This visceral effect will impact his learning pathways and his ability to develop a mind that is comfortable and motivated to learn both interpsychosocially and intrapsychologically. Without his teacher or parents helping him interpret these learning and socioemotional experiences in a way that enables a positive self-construct, he will become frustrated and react emotionally. Michael may become angry, wanting to demonstrate to himself and his classmates that he has some abilities. To cover up his shame in not being as able as his peers, he could find another way to demonstrate efficacy and regain his footing with his classmates, as a pathway to feel good about himself.

This scenario is replayed over and over again in classrooms throughout the United States, whenever children have difficulty meeting the expectations of their teachers, parents, or classmates. Our children do not have the mental mind-set or psychological paradigm with which to process and understand these omnipresent stressors. They have not been taught how to construct a self, a healthy self, which consists of self-concept, identity, purpose and dreams in life, and emotional intelligence, among other iSelf attributions. Because the vast majority of children are fundamentally good people and aspire to be good to their highest potentials, they become upset when they do not measure up to external expectations; they often want to act out with aggressive behaviors. The more they feel the effectiveness of treating others badly because they themselves feel bad, the more this becomes a cycle of learned reactions and behavior that defines who they are. We are not allowing our children to be children, to develop without forcing them to learn information that is so separate from their own experiences and such a far transfer from their realities.

Michael could, on the other hand, retreat into silence, withdraw, and isolate himself from the stressors and external forces as a natural defense mechanism. If the circumstances are too much for his psyche to be able to handle, he will learn how to cope through *dissociation*, a clinical term meaning that the mind separates or detaches feelings and emotions from the circumstances in his life experience, especially specific experiences that threaten his sense of self. I call this "adaptive dissociation." This leads to one of numerous dissociative disorders, including dissociative identity disorder and depersonalization disorder, among others. According to a recent updated study with recommendations for the updated DSM-IV manual,

> dissociation is a disruption of and/or discontinuity in the normal, subjective integration of one or more aspects of psychological functioning, including— but not limited to—memory, identity, consciousness, perception, and motor control. In essence, aspects of psychobiological functioning that should be associated, coordinated, and/or linked are not. (Spiegel et al., 2011, p. 826)

We can see, then, how Michael's psychobiological functioning between identity and consciousness most likely could result in a dissociative state, which could produce an unawareness of either bullying or withdrawal behaviors. Dissociative disorders rob children of happy, healthy development. So many children are in a constant state of anxiety or trauma because they do not have the mind-set or psychological tools to process and understand modern life.

We know that motivation and enjoyment are critical to learning to read and to all learning, and the child who enjoys reading (and learning) is likely to read on his own and will gain the practice necessary to become a lifelong, skilled reader (Fox, 2008). Michael's case provides an example. If we teach literacy, then we can also simultaneously teach positive emotions and identity through learning to read. If teachers focus on personalized learning and the cultivation of love for learning, they are in fact critical protective factors in the lives of children, adolescents, and young adults.

*How Extensive Is Bullying?*
We cannot know the full extent of the impact that bullying has on the psychological well-being of a young person, but we do know it destroys the psyche. Even minor incidents of bullying change the paradigm of reality of young people because they do not have the defense mechanisms in place to understand acts of inhumane treatment. Children, while they can test limits, naturally treat each other with all possible kindness and love, unconditionally. Something happens in our homes or schools to change this mind-set. That something occurs when we impede the natural expression of one's natural goodness, the instincts for growing in the direction of one's life's purpose and dreams, and the drive to be well—psychologically and physically. The impact of man's inhumanity to man is felt as evidenced by these realities:

- In 2010, approximately 160,000 children missed school every day out of fear of being bullied.
- Approximately 2.7 million students are bullied each year, with about 2.1 million students taking on the role of the bully.
- 15% of all students who don't show up for school report cite their fear of being bullied as the reason.
- Approximately 71% of students report bullying as an ongoing problem.
- Suicide continues to be one of the leading causes of death among children under the age of 14 in the United States and is tied to bullying.
- Only half of high school students feel they are an important part of their school community.
- More than 20% of students say there is no adult at their school who cares about them and knows them well.

Source: U.S. Department of Health and Human Services, 1999; Kataoka, Zhang, & Wells, 2002; National Institute of Mental Health, 2010; http://www.bullyingstatistics.org; The Center for Evaluation and Education Policy, Indiana University School of Education; http://whatworks.wholechildeducation.org; CDC, 2012a, http://www.cdc.gov/obesity/data/adult.html.

*Two Cases*
Phoebe Prince was new to this country, having just moved to western Massachusetts from Ireland. Soon thereafter, she found herself being tormented by a group of six students, both at school and through social networking. Phoebe was different; she had a different set of values and view of the world and about relationships. She was kind, and in our very aggressive and growing increasingly more aggressive culture, she did not know how to handle what

was coming at her, the force of the meanness, the ridicule, and the demeaning and emotionally damaging comments. She did not have the mental mind-set to know how to handle the aggressive, violent American culture.

Many children and adolescents have been conditioned, hardened by our culture, and have unconsciously developed a series of defense mechanisms: bullying or demeaning others to gain personal power and influence in a group. Many young people act like the others in their peer group to avoid being viewed as different; they are afraid to take moral stands, and they dissociate emotions from personal experiences or circumstances. Dissociation is perhaps the most common defense mechanism today because so many children, adolescents, and adults do not understand their emotions or how to process them when confronted with complex relationships and situations.

I recall Don McLean's ballad, *Starry, Starry Night*, "But I could have told you, Vincent [Phoebe], this world was never meant for one as beautiful as you." The way people treat each other, man's inhumanity to man, was not within Phoebe's paradigm of reality to comprehend. After months of harassment from the other students at her Massachusetts high school, Phoebe hung herself.

We have become such a violent society that we do not know another way, another paradigm—one built upon kindness and peace and man's humanity to man. Maybe this is why Phoebe died at this time?

In 2012 in Greece, New York, a group of middle school students verbally and physically abused Mrs. Klein, a 68-year-old school bus monitor, caught the incident on film, and posted it to YouTube. Our public response was to use social media to raise $400,000 for her vacation to recover from her pain and suffering. I couldn't help recalling when President George Bush asked Americans to "go shop" after 9/11. We typically respond emotionally through an economic lens. Economics drive our lives versus person-centered approaches to address the pain, emotional damage, and sense of moral outrage.

To demonstrate just how ingrained this beliefs system is, Mrs. Klein was also showered with material goods from the corporate sector. In a seemingly generous act that also functions as a public relations strategy, Southwest Airlines extended an offer to fly Mrs. Klein and her family members for a 3-day vacation at Disney World. I am guessing that this was about a $20,000 gesture, which could have been better spent on sponsoring an antibullying program in New York schools or establishing a scholarship in Mrs. Klein's name to students who help stop bullying in middle schools. This would have been the longer-lasting gesture and one that reinforces good behavior and good human beings through culturally recognized rewards.

Further, strong cultural influences from television shows that glorify and honor the bully or domination behavior serve to communicate that this is what is good in our society. This is not merely a moral argument; these influences are literally shaping our minds to become this way, to learn domination as a self-construct—that this is how I should construct myself to win in our society. Learning occurs everywhere, not just in school, so therefore our minds, our brains, and our selves are literally being shaped by cultural influences. We have become a desensitized nation of adolescents and young adults who have become dissociated through the onslaught of cultural media and schooling influences. This new normal explains why young people are desperately attempting to heal their internal state and condition and attempting to feel their full feelings through the use of social media. But because we have not taught children how to know themselves or how to heal, their bullying behaviors cross over into social media and extend the dysfunctional behaviors.

*Why Do People Bully?*
According to the American Academy of Child and Adolescent Psychiatry (March 2011, no. 80, Facts for Families), close to half of all children will experience school bullying at some point while they are at primary or secondary school. At least 10% of children are bullied regularly. Even if this type of behavior is learned, it is a symptom of a person's internal state of mind where something is out of balance among the set of complex self-components.

I have observed that those of my students and clients who treat other people in an abusive manner do so because they do not feel good about who they are; their self-concept and self-esteem have not been formulated or perhaps it has been damaged through living life. When intervening in the lives of children or adults who are in abusive relationships, I have found they have numerous regrets or resentments in their life. These regrets may be centered on themselves or their circumstances. They do not have their own personal dreams or purpose in life and therefore feel as though their life has no meaning. Life has beaten the spirit out of them, and they do not have the resilience necessary to come back or the tools to manifest their own sense of why they are here, their *daimon*.

*What Is Childhood Bullying?*
Bullying is a mind-set where efficacy is demonstrated through mistreatment of others, usually targeting someone perceived to be weaker in some manner. The perceived weaknesses are most readily related to the self of the victim. The aggressor senses that the victim already feels bad about himself, or holds different views and beliefs, or is highly emotional and reacts quickly to outside or external upsets. The aggressor most often has the same or similar weaknesses within himself, and in order to not address his own internal hurt,

he lashes out externally toward another. Bullying is a mental disorder, not just bad behavior.

Bullies get what they want through some sort of coercion or force; often all that is wanted is for the bully to establish a perceived superiority over another person to compensate for their own weaknesses. While some may think that bullying consists only of physical domination, there are verbal and emotional forms of bullying as well. With the rise social media, children are now being bullied online through e-mail, in online chat rooms, and on Facebook. It is even possible to be bullied through text messaging on a cell phone.

For the most part, boys prefer to use physical intimidation tactics in their bullying. They will use physical aggression to force others to do what they want or to feel in charge of a situation. Girls, on the other hand, are more likely to use verbal abuse and other subtle methods to harass and belittle others. Girls are also more likely to be adept at emotional bullying by ostracizing their victims because they know the importance of relationships to the female psyche.

*Signs of Child Bullying*
Many parents are concerned that their child might be a victim of a child bullying. Some of the signs that a child is being bullied are as follows:

- Becoming withdrawn
- Showing fear when it is time to go to school
- Increasing signs of depression
- Decline in school performance
- Speaking of another child with fear
- Noticeable decline in how the child sees him or herself
- Signs of physical altercations, such as bruises, scrapes, and other marks

Source: http://www.bullyingstatistics.org/content/child-bullying.html.

It is more difficult to spot signs of verbal or emotional bullying, but parents and teachers should be on the lookout for indications that a child's self-esteem and self-image are faltering, as well as a reluctance to go to school.

*Research on Bullying*
In a study about bullying conducted by Clemson University's Institute on Family and Neighborhood Life, psychology professor Susan Limber (2004) found that too many children do not believe there is a system in place to protect them, especially as they get older. For example, 30% of boys in grades three through five said their teacher had done little or nothing to reduce bullying,

as compared with almost 60% of boys in grades 9 through 12. Where is our outrage over the mistreatment of children in a schooling setting?

The U.S. Department of Education and the HHS have established special outreach initiatives to prevent bullying. Secretary of Education Arne Duncan has stated "enough is enough" and has proudly announced an updated website dedicated to preventing bullying in schools. The Clemson University website for the initiative says the following:

> The Olweus Program (pronounced Ol-VEY-us; the E sounds like a long A) is a comprehensive, school-wide program designed and evaluated for use in elementary, middle, or junior high schools. The program's goals are to reduce and prevent bullying problems among school children and to improve peer relations at school. The program has been found to reduce bullying among children, improve the social climate of classrooms, and reduce related anti-social behaviors, such as vandalism and truancy. Schools are also gathering data about implementing the program at the senior high school level. The Olweus Program has been implemented in more than a dozen countries around the world, and in thousands of schools in the United States. (http://www.clemson.edu/olweus)

Through its four core components, the Olweus program focuses upon external or environmental factors and is a behavior-based program in which children are encouraged to monitor their own and their classmates' behaviors and report incidents of aggression. It does not address the inner psychological dynamics and well-being of children, at the being level, or provide for an ontological shift in the mind-sets of children. A more systemic, long-term approach would not only reduce bullying behaviors but also mold the mind-set that helps prevent numerous psychological disorders, dissociation, depression, and anxiety, among others. This demonstrates that educators and psychologists do not have a paradigm of understanding that would allow us to focus upon the inner life of children. Sadly, there will be many more Phoebe Princes and Mrs. Kleins.

What happens in classrooms and playgrounds between children is carried forward into adulthood in the workplace, in Congress, and in all our social and cultural institutions. The behavior and the mind-set that this behavior is acceptable originate from poor self-esteem and lack of self-knowledge; the bully unconsciously overcompensates with boisterous, entrenched attitudes.

The primary protective factor that could eliminate bullying in schools is to teach and empower self-esteem and establish a system of education where children know that their mental and physical well-being is the priority.

### Responsive Classroom *Bullying Prevention*

*Responsive Classroom* strategies, however, do indeed address the inner life of children and come from a very different place or paradigmatic view than the Olweus program: Socioemotional with iSelf model distinctions form the foundation of *Responsive Classroom*'s body of work; behaviorism with external controls and rewards are the guiding principles of the Olweus program.

I am surprised that more teachers have not used the body of work known as the *Responsive Classroom*, which was created by the Northeast Foundation for Children (NEFC) in 1981. I can immediately determine upon walking into a classroom if the teacher uses *Responsive Classroom* methods. There is a different culture, a mood, an atmosphere of dignity and respect, of happiness, of genuine friendships.

The theoretical foundations of this work appear to be well grounded in Maslow's Hierarchy (1954), along with numerous positive psychology distinctions. Maslow posited that children need safety and security, and limits and stability, along with a strong sense of belonging and cooperation, so they can build loyal, affectionate relationships. They must be reassured as they build self-affirmation and self-esteem, achievement and status, while leading toward personal growth and self-actualization (Figure 6).

Positive psychology and the self-attributions, akin to those in the iSelf model, underlie the *Responsive Classroom* procedures and activities, forming the psychological, theoretical frame for this body of work. *Responsive Classroom* strategies include asking children to reflect upon their dreams for their lives and for the school year. These are posted for all to see, which serves to assist young people when formulating an identity during these early years and to inspire an extraordinary future. These further act as tools to trigger group discussion for relationship building and to open up new possibilities for new, broader, and bolder dreams that inspire all. During morning meeting activities, children check in with their emotional states of mind, which teaches emotional intelligence and positive behaviors and views. With such a strong focus on relationship-building and positive language and behavior, teachers have numerous opportunities to discuss deeper, more meaningful, very personally empowering topics with individual students or through whole-class discussions. Instead of these deeper discussions being distrusted by children or considered weird, they are welcomed. In fact, they are perceived as personally important and natural and as a natural part of the growth and development of the whole child.

In classrooms where *Responsive Classroom* strategies are not used, issues arise in discipline, behavior management, and power dynamics; instead of

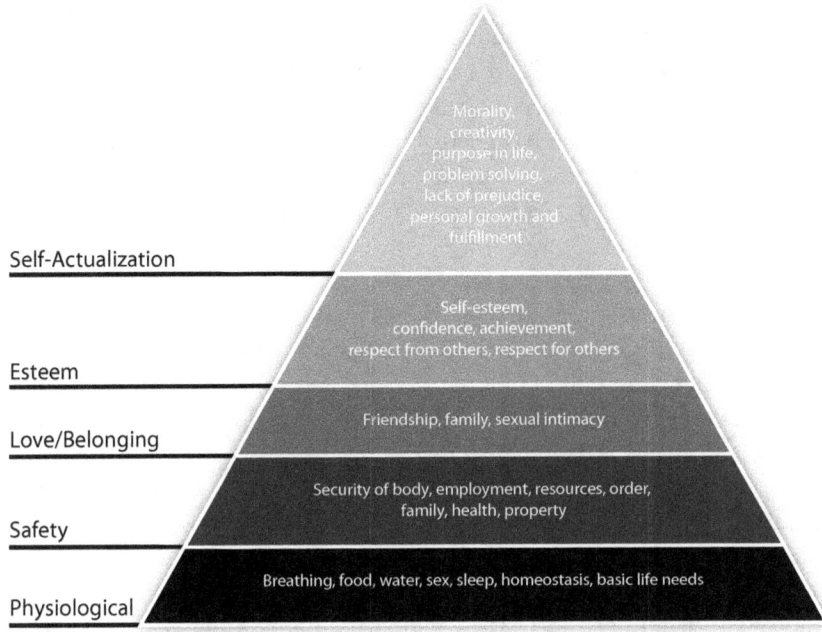

**Figure 6.** Maslow's Hierarchy of Needs (Adapted from Maslow, 1943)

distinctly human qualities being highlighted, narrow curricula standards guide the classroom discussions and influence the culture negatively.

Any teacher or counselor knows that if a real, genuine, caring relationship is established, then students and clients sense that they can grow and develop because of the warm, facilitative environment or context that has been cultivated. The space created triggers students' own natural instincts to see mind and soul grow. The students know that they are in control of their own destinies in life, and they are intrinsically motivated; they do not feel as if they are being manipulated into believing something that teachers themselves do not believe: that teaching to the test will help people thrive and flourish.

It is precisely because of the culture that is created through a real interest in each and every child's well-being that *Responsive Classroom* strategies and methods work to reduce incidences of bullying behavior. Instead of being unconsciously influenced by the power dynamics and falsehoods of their classroom environment, children are both unconsciously and consciously aware that they come first; they matter to the teacher, to each other, and to themselves. There is no need to gain an advantage over another student in the classroom if all needs of every child are observed and met. With their well-being considered, they are happier, more productive young people.

In my view, *Responsive Classroom* is grounded in many of the iSelf model attributions in that it produces happier, engaged, loving children. And while I am not affiliated with the Northeast Foundation, I find it effective. For the remainder of this chapter, I present additional information from the *Responsive Classroom* website for the readers review and use (http://www.responsiveclassroom.org):

What's the Connection Between Northeast Foundation
for Children (NEFC) and the *Responsive Classroom* Approach?
Northeast Foundation for Children (NEFC) is a nonprofit organization whose mission is to create safe, challenging, and joyful elementary schools. NEFC does this by developing the *Responsive Classroom* approach, a way of teaching that emphasizes social, emotional, and academic growth in a strong and safe school community. NEFC offers workshops, on-site consulting, books, videos, and other resources for educators who want to learn to use the *Responsive Classroom* approach.

NEFC was founded in 1981 by a group of public school educators who wanted to share the practical strategies they'd developed for teaching social and academic skills together. They opened a laboratory school in Greenfield, Massachusetts, called Greenfield Center School. Soon after, NEFC began publishing books and offering workshops about the practices that were being used at the school. In the early 1990s, NEFC secured its first major contract to work with public school teachers in Washington, DC. The term *Responsive Classroom* was coined in conjunction with that work.

What's Distinctive About the *Responsive Classroom* Approach?
The *Responsive Classroom* is a general approach to teaching, rather than a program designed to address a specific school issue. It is based on the premise that children learn best when they have both academic and social-emotional skills. The *Responsive Classroom* approach consists of a set of practices that build academic and social-emotional competencies and that can be used along with many other programs. These classroom practices are the heart of the *Responsive Classroom* approach:

- *Morning meeting.* Gathering as a whole class each morning to greet one another, share news, and warm up for the day ahead
- *Rule creation.* Helping students create classroom rules to ensure an environment that allows all class members to meet their learning goals

- *Interactive modeling.* Teaching children to notice and internalize expected behaviors through a unique modeling technique
- *Positive teacher language.* Using words and tone as a tool to promote children's active learning, sense of community, and self-discipline
- *Logical consequences.* Responding to misbehavior in a way that allows children to fix and learn from their mistakes while preserving their dignity
- *Guided discovery.* Introducing classroom materials using a format that encourages independence, creativity, and responsibility
- *Academic choice.* Increasing student learning by allowing students teacher-structured choices in their work
- *Classroom organization.* Setting up the physical room in ways that encourage students' independence, cooperation, and productivity
- *Working with families.* Creating avenues for hearing parents' insights and helping them understand the school's teaching approaches
- *Collaborative problem solving.* Using conferencing, role playing, and other strategies to resolve problems with students

What Theory Is *Responsive Classroom* Based On?
The *Responsive Classroom* approach is not based on the work of one particular theorist. It draws on the work of many great teachers and educators, articulating a collection of sound and tested classroom practices in a way that is accessible and practical for today's teachers. It also incorporates research and thinking from child development and constructivist educators (such as Piaget, Gesell, Montessori, Dewey, Erikson, and Vygotsky).

How Widely Is the *Responsive Classroom* Approach Used?
Since 1981, thousands of classroom teachers and hundreds of schools and school districts have begun using the *Responsive Classroom* approach. These schools are in urban, suburban, and rural settings nationwide.

How Many People Work for Northeast Foundation for Children?
About 30 people make up our in-house staff, plus over 100 consulting teachers who give workshops and provide coaching at schools.

Is There Research on the Effectiveness
of the *Responsive Classroom* Approach?
Several research studies have been conducted on the effectiveness of the *Responsive Classroom* approach. Most recently, researchers at the University of Virginia's Curry School of Education released results from a quasi-experimental

longitudinal study funded by the DuBarry Foundation. The study compared children at three schools using the *Responsive Classroom* approach with those at three control schools. This research yielded six key findings about children and teachers at schools using the *Responsive Classroom* approach:

1. Children showed greater increases in reading and math test scores. Children taught using the *Responsive Classroom* approach for 2 or 3 years scored higher in reading and math on the Connecticut Mastery Test. The gains were greater over 3-year periods than over 2-year periods and greater in math than in reading.
2. Teachers felt more effective and more positive about teaching. Teachers who used the *Responsive Classroom* approach felt more effective in teaching discipline, more able to create a positive school climate, and more able to influence decision making at their schools.
3. Children had better social skills. After just one year of the *Responsive Classroom* approach, children showed greater growth in prosocial skills and assertiveness. They were more comfortable trying new things in school, and their teachers reported feeling closer to them.
4. Teachers offered more high-quality instruction. Teachers using the *Responsive Classroom* approach appeared to offer more emotional and instructional support for learning. Examples include creating a positive classroom climate and offering better feedback and more instruction involving concept development.
5. Children felt more positive about school. Children whose teachers used more *Responsive Classroom* practices had improved attitudes about school. They liked school more and enjoyed their peers and their teachers more.
6. Teachers collaborated with each other more. Teachers using the *Responsive Classroom* approach reported more frequent formal collaboration with each other. They placed greater value on collaboration and felt more involved in decision making at their schools.

On the strength of these findings, in 2007, the U.S. Department of Education's Institute of Education Sciences and the National Science Foundation awarded $2.9 million to Dr. Rimm-Kaufman and her team for an expanded 3-year follow-up study.

## CHAPTER 9

# NEW MODELS: FUTURE POSSIBILITIES

New initiatives and practices hold promise and do indeed represent the 21st-century learning model called for in the new educational paradigm to shift responsibility for learning to the student. The Self Across the Curriculum (SAC), personalized learning, *Responsive Classroom*, flipped classrooms, and real-world learning are well suited to reducing high school dropout rates, increasing retention in colleges, and engaging students in their own learning, careers, and well-being.

### Educational and Health Policies Return on Investment

When analyzing the K–16 educational policies and best practices that have been used over the past 30 years, we need to look at the return on that investment for NCLB in terms of academic achievement outcome statistics. The limited return should not make any sense at all to concerned parents, policy makers, teachers, or business executives. Let's take a percentage of these expenditures and conduct professional development training on the integrated self (iSelf) and Self Across the Curriculum (SAC) models, thus transferring the responsibility for learning to the student. Rather than curricula standards and the Common Core, we should focus our spending on building competencies that represent 21st-century well-being skills and personalized learning attributes, among others.

The financial costs of administering standardized tests required in NCLB or in the next form of the ESEA are too high, given the return. For example, Florida spent $59 million on NCLB in 2011, but only 39% of 10th graders passed the Florida Reads test (one of up to 62 tests administered in the state of Florida). Texas spent $93 million in 2012 administering standardized tests, which is 10-fold greater than what it cost only 9 years ago. What if we took a percentage of these expenditures and implemented the Self Across the Curriculum? What might be possible, and what would be the return on this investment in terms of student well-being and better, happier people?

Consider these NCLB expenditures, given the results: The share of U.S. 4th graders reading below proficiency in 2011 was 68%, and in math, the share of 8th graders below proficiency was 66% (Kids Count 2012, Annie E. Casey Foundation), further evidence that the system is not working within the paradigm we are now using. Take West Virginia's case as an example, after 10 years of policies focused primarily on academic achievement:

> The West Virginia Legislature finds that: West Virginia students continue to face an achievement gap between themselves and students in other states and internationally, beginning, in many cases, in middle school. For example, according to the National Assessment of Educational Progress (NAEP) report, The Nation's Report Card: Science 2009, West Virginia students' scores are consistent with the national average in fourth grade, but have dropped into the lower fifteen states by eighth grade (Senate Bill Number 516, February 18, 2011)

As of June 2012, 24 states have been approved for waivers from NCLB requirements, with an additional 13 pending approval. The model is breaking down under the weight of the costs and in light of such mediocre results in achievement on standardized tests nationwide. Not surprisingly, this model of education has not been able to deliver on its false promise of a better life to those who do well on the tests. In many ways, we have done almost everything "right" in terms of applying the business world's total quality management practices to education. We are hopefully discovering that education is not a business; it is about the condition of human beings. Education is a *human potential service* with the new purpose of achieving health, well-being, and happiness, so that all souls in our care may flourish.

### Déjà Vu

Although the Common Core (Council of Chief State School Officers, 2006) movement attempted to do something different than previous NCLB reforms, with different goals for college and career readiness, in reality, it offers more of the same within the current standards-based education paradigm. One of the loudest criticisms of NCLB and the standards-based system of education has been that it attempts to make all children learn the same thing and usually in the same way. Similar cries are being heard about the Common Core, which, in essence, makes all people common—not exceptional or unique. Certainly the Common Core emphasizes the four critical Cs in teaching—critical thinking, collaboration, creativity, and communication—but these have actually been taught to teachers for decades, where these methods and competencies are the basis for good teaching. Understanding by design, differentiated instruction, and project-based learning methods already include these qualities.

In any standards movement, education narrowly focuses on the curricula, the standards, and the assessment of these, and forgets to foster the unique gifts and contributions of each child and their future possibilities.

Policy makers who support the Common Core initiative want to create a society of people who think in a similar manner to meet total quality management efficiency standards. To empower people to think for themselves in their own unique ways would require a transformed mind-set that challenges long-held beliefs about people and how to educate them.

The Common Core movement is actually about money and control over the production of knowledge. Each state cannot afford to develop its own standardized tests and then purchase associated resources and materials, such as tests, textbooks, and exam graders. Costs can be contained if the 48 states (those states who have adopted the Common Core) agree on the standards, assessment, and one text because of the efficiencies of production. We still operate from the industrial efficiency paradigm of the 19th century when making very important decisions that will impact quality of life—people's lives in the 21st century—resulting in deteriorating mental and physical health and well-being.

## Real-World Learning Model

We need to envision a transformed system of education that can support learners in gaining self-knowledge for personal and professional potential so they can demonstrate real competencies rather than memorized curricula standards. One possible model is known as *real-world learning*.

*Real-world learning* follows the concept of extending the process of education beyond traditional school environments and formally adopts rules for measuring and rewarding student achievement in "real-world" learning environments. The goal is to weave into the fabric of education a greater variety of learning experiences that will help prepare students for the real world—during and after formal, traditional classroom education. Real-world learning should provide the following:

1. Multiple pathways to learning for career and college success, including online courses, work-based learning, service-learning, project-based

learning, apprenticeships and internships, and numerous extended learning opportunities
2. Numerous and varied experiential learning opportunities that are out in the real world in combination with in-classroom instruction
3. Personalized learning plans using the American Psychological Association's *Learner-Centered Psychological Principles* in combination with the iSelf model
4. Student development partnerships that involve the local community in a student's middle school, high school, and college learning experiences. For example, businesses like Air Products and Chemicals, Inc. have expressed strong interest in creating such partnerships in their local communities to train youth. Foundations, such as the Annenberg Foundation, and state and local government may also subsidize programs in conjunction with businesses that may not otherwise be able to fund student training.
5. Better, more useful assessments of student growth, development, and performance, including portfolios, well-being scales, self-esteem instruments, dreams surveys, employer evaluations, standardized test scores. These types of instruments are known as "authentic assessment," versus those that focus upon test scores and grades and "value-added" assessments.

Real-world learning allows students to learn experientially out in the world to give meaningful context to what they learn in the classroom. At its core is the personalization and individuation of teaching and learning processes in which teachers are facilitators of learning in the coaching model of teaching. This is an important point, as McCombs asserted: "Empirically tested and research-validated teacher and student surveys have verified that students' perceptions of their teachers' learner-centered classroom practices are the most significant predictors of student motivation and achievement" (McCombs, 2003, p. 97).

Every student has a personalized learning plan that is customized to every student in every subject. By offering an expanded curriculum with enhancements that include learning outside of the typical classroom setting, real-world learning "provides many more curriculum offerings to meet the desires of each student" (New Hampshire Department of Education, 2011). This model can actually work with Common Core and ESEA legislative requirements because every child has a personalized learning plan. Real-world learning ensures that the states curriculum frameworks for each subject, as well as for math and language arts Common Core standards, are met through a wide variety of learning experiences both inside and outside the classroom and school setting.

Real-world learning has implications for federal and state policy makers to consider in achieving school reform goals, and hopefully building a new model and new purpose for 21st-century education. It produces systemic change that personalizes learning for each student and rewards student achievement in authentic learning environments. This model is well suited to address numerous goals, but particularly those related to increasing student engagement and improving high school infrastructure to increase student achievement; by having access to multiple enrichment pathways, students are more likely to stay engaged and achieve postsecondary success (Council of Chief State School Officers, 2006, p. 5).

Real-world learning engages not only students but the entire community, with families, businesses, and other organizations sharing best practices with schools. Many partnerships can be formed through the proposed student development partnerships to offer experiential or extended learning opportunities that hold the interest of all learners and are personally meaningful to each.

Past chairman of the New Hampshire Board of Education Fred Bramante asked, "Why shouldn't the [local] auto dealership be the laboratory for teaching kids automotive-related studies, with the school acting as the coach, the facilitator, the overseer" (Gorenstein interview with Bramante on New Hampshire public radio, May 18, 2004)? Former governor of New Hampshire Craig Benson was in agreement, stating that he liked the idea of "transforming the entire state into a big classroom" (Gorenstein, NHPR, May 18, 2004). This is the possibility of this model: that individual student interests and talents are empowered through experiential learning. Inside the classroom, a student can learn about computers in an information technology class and about combustion engines from his physics books, but he could then apply this conceptual learning in the auto repair shop at the auto dealership. And then, because the hands-on experience helped raise his overall academic performance, he can go on to college and graduate school to learn how to design plane engines.

The need to engage students more thoroughly and to make bold changes in our system of education are supported by past National Education Association president Karen McDonough (Gorenstein, NHPR, May 18, 2004). According to noted education reformer Fred Bramante, "education reform will include new legislation and school rules covering everything from nontraditional credit opportunities to special education to the length of the school year, now mandated at 180 days" (Kittredge, *The Boston Globe*, Bramante interview, May 16, 2004).

A number of states, including New Hampshire and Iowa, have already taken bold steps and made the necessary changes to eliminate *seat time*, which has formed the basis of secondary-school graduation requirements. The

Carnegie unit, which has long been the standard measure of course credit, represents one credit for completion of a 1-year course that meets daily. Chairman Bramante, educator Milton Goldberg, former Assistant U.S. Secretary of Education Christopher Cross, and many other education reformers agree that the issue of seat time is a formidable constraint to the type of systemic reform needed to replace our outdated, 19th-century model and may inhibit the diffusion of real-world learning nationwide.

According to Fred Bramante, "[real-world learning] represents the biggest education reform effort since 1919" (New Hampshire public radio, May 18, 2004). In addition to offering new opportunities to students, real-world learning also represents a new "partnership" model of financing public school education that enables local businesses and other interested organizations to commit themselves to ensuring meaningful and profitable learning experiences for all our students. Teachers, principals, and superintendents will also see the advantages in real-world learning as the responsibility for learning is shifted from educator to student. The model can help to deliver on the promise made to the next generation's youth that their lives will be better than their parents'.

## Flipped Classrooms

As discussed earlier, much has been made about the idea of a "flipped classroom" model of teaching and learning pioneered by Khan Academy. In this innovative approach, students view online lectures as homework and then solve problems in class under the coaching guidance provided by the classroom teacher. The flipped classroom integrates technology with pedagogy, creating a solution that satisfies the need for more personalized learning. It shifts the responsibility for learning to the student, with teachers becoming facilitators and technology integrating seamlessly with pedagogy. The flipped classroom offers a fertile platform to teach self-knowledge and impart all iSelf model distinctions. To do so, however, we will need to produce videos, demonstrations, and other multimedia learning objects that apply the iSelf dynamic processes, possible future visions of psychological and physical well-being, happiness and flourishing, and online assessments of each.

## New Approach to College Success

College-aged young adults are struggling to develop their own pathways for a positive life-course trajectory, not only financially, but, more to the point, purposefully with meaningful direction. Dropout rates from colleges point to students' lack of purposeful direction. Nationwide, approximately 45% of college students earned a bachelor's degree within 6 years (Beginning Postsecondary Survey, 2009, National Center for Education Statistics at the U.S. Department of Education). At Clarion University, a Pennsylvania State System of Higher Education (PASSHE) institution where I taught, only 53% (just a bit better than the national average) of students finished within 6 years, and only 24% of students in Clarion's College of Education and Human Services completed their programs of study. At Cheyney University, another PASSHE school in suburban Philadelphia that serves a large population of inner-city minority students, only 24% of students go on to graduate (Integrated Postsecondary Education Data System, 2010).

Once again, we are not aware of the implications of these alarming statistics. Consider that by 2020, over 69% of jobs will require a college education. How do we inspire students to pursue a college education and then complete it once enrolled? A high impact practice that I have used at the college level is to teach my students how to refer what they are learning to themselves. Discussed in greater detail in Chapter 5, the Self Across the Curriculum framework with the *self-referential method* of teaching and learning can be used effectively in all college courses. Additionally, in my classes, I presented the many distinctions in the iSelf model that students used to inspire them to do whatever it takes to finish their degree. The most salient examples are the distinctions life purpose and dreams, and self-concept and identity. Once students are able to personally formulate their own purpose and dreams for their lives, they are committed, inspired, and motivated to obtain the monetary resources required to finance their education—the most often cited source of frustration causing students to drop out. Students experience a shift in their perspectives about who they are and the future difference they are called to make and can dream about making.

This is why the iSelf model represents an effective, *high-impact practice* for use by college advising departments, first-year experience programs, campus alcohol and drug awareness programs, and career advising. It draws upon an integrated model of self with positive psychology distinctions that connect with college-aged adolescents and young adults, and it utilizes strengths-based counseling and academic and career advising to empower students to create their own paths toward academic, career, and life success.

## Future Possibilities

Education in the 21st century should (1) recognize that in the world, we have all the wealth we need to take care of each person's survival needs, thereby eliminating economic survival as the purpose of education, and (2) free up our fullest human expressions possible for love, caring, kindness, healing, and understanding, to empower full, and unique and highest potentials for a better life and world—our highest visions for a flourishing life.

We seem to be on the brink of the integrated age, where information and technology and all natural resources are used for the purpose of giving more personal power to each individual. In this emerging paradigm, the individual is free to create a life of his dreams, filled with personal meaning. We need to shift this paradigm now!

In the current information age, actionable knowledge is the central resource to create the wealth that is traditionally seen as the pathway to a better society and better life. Forces are shaping the emerging paradigm or, as I suggest, the integrated age, in which to redefine the good life. In this new age, a better society will be based on the creation of personal meaning for each individual through the use of knowledge and information. Knowledge is used to make a difference in society. Each individual will take the knowledge available and create new knowledge and new services to make things better in terms of quality of life, happiness, and well-being. The iSelf model makes it possible to take that knowledge and channel it toward personal purpose and meaning making, to make a unique contribution to the world.

I would argue that implementing the iSelf model through schooling will serve to make self-knowledge actionable, toward a greater good, not toward acquiring wealth. Using the iSelf model as one's lens, the individual self uses and creates knowledge with the intent of building a better life—not always for economic value but for community value and for psychological and physical well-being.

Our economy, whether driven by material goods or knowledge, should not be the standard reference for choosing an educational paradigm or evaluating the effectiveness of that paradigm. Rather, the economy is *handled*, meaning all societies would have equal access to the means of production. A fruitful economy could and should be channeled toward the well-being and happiness of citizens. If citizens and government leaders make the well-being of people the priority in their countries, then the iSelf model will serve to change the economic priorities as well as the foundation for the guiding principle of a school system. Further, if we focus upon personal happiness and psychological and physical well-being, the economy will be driven by motivated people who want to make our society better—which is more consistent with what is possible for us to envision as we strive for self-actualization.

Two examples come immediately to mind. First, think about how difficult it has been for the U.S. economy to make a shift from fossil fuels to green fuels to supply growing worldwide energy needs. In contrast, Germany has changed its mental mind-set and made a paradigmatic shift, as evidenced by the percentage of its energy derived from renewable sources. In 2011, approximately 20% of Germany's energy was renewable; its 2030 target of 45% is especially impressive when compared with the United States, where only 8% of our energy comes from renewable sources.

Europe is also more enlightened in its view of happiness. Adrian White, an analytic social psychologist at the University of Leicester in Great Britain, discovered when he developed the first "World Map of Happiness" that Denmark is the happiest nation in the world. In comparison, the United States comes in 23rd. Despite our efforts in this country to pursue wealth as a means to happiness, financial security does not equate to personal fulfillment. No longer does the United States educational paradigm serve us in attaining a competitive advantage in international comparisons in literacy, math and science, *and* happiness. We are at a crossroad in our human history, where we can choose financial wealth or happiness and well-being.

## Which Reality to Create?

David McCullough, a teacher at Wellesley High School in Wellesley, Massachusetts, told the 2012 graduating class, "you are not special, you are not exceptional" (Wellesley Channel TV, June 7, 2012). He asserted, "astrophysicists say that the universe has no center, so you can't be it," reflecting his position as an educator whose mind-set attempts to make everyone the same by teaching everyone the same content. He speaks in service to the production model with which he is so familiar, being a product of schooling himself.

However, his students know another reality. We are indeed part of a larger existence, and the Internet and social media inventors are harnessing power in numbers, using crowd sourcing to collect information to solve problems—real-world problems. Granted, young people must pass through developmental stages to be able to understand others' views; but remember Buckminster Fuller's geodesic dome, where the entire whole relies on the strength of each and every individual part. In fact, if each person in our society is not seeing and reaching her own full potential in life, using all personal, strengths, talents, and attributions, then the society falls down.

With each student as his own center, he first generates a healthy self. Then, in envisioning purpose and dreams, he begins to care about making a difference. The depth of that awareness is a lifelong endeavor, where young people, with a variety of talents and gifts, take a giant developmental leap forward toward a future filled with new solutions to those problems handed down to them. Instead of berating his students for wanting to be special and make a difference in the universe, he should, as we all should, apologize for leaving this generation with the huge problems that we were not able to solve. More directly, we should apologize for not teaching them a model of self that would serve as a more solid foundation to create a better world with a new reality.

No matter how dreadful the schooling, some breakout individuals will always find a way to manifest genius and develop the next theories of the universe—perhaps altering, as Einstein and Copernicus did, everything that is now considered our reality. But if we want to empower this year's graduates to create tomorrow's reality, to collectively make our tomorrow better than our today, then we need to stop attempting to make everyone common and find ways to manifest all that is exceptional about each person. Then we must do all that we can to empower each person's dreams.

How can all 7 billion people on our planet realize their dreams? Well, when you are aware of yourself as deeply and thoroughly as taught through the iSelf model, your dreams shift away from the external, from material things, to internal experiences of well-being. Self-fulfillment becomes less about acquisitions, dominance, and resource exploitation, and more about integrating one's self in service to others. Maybe an idea whose time has come?

# References

American Academy of Child and Adolescent Psychiatry. 2011. "Bullying." *Facts for Families*, March 2011. Accessed October 1, 2012. http://www.aacap.org/galleries/FactsForFamilies/80_bullying.pdf.

American Federation of Teachers of New Jersey. 2012. "AFT Resolutions: Digital Learning in Pre-K–12 Instruction." Accessed October 1, 2012. http://www.aft.org/about/resolution_detail.cfm?articleid=1619.

American Psychiatric Association. 2000. *Diagnostic and Statistical Manual of Mental Disorders* (4th ed.). Arlington, VA: American Psychiatric Association.

American Psychological Association Board of Educational Affairs. 1997. *Learner-Centered Psychological Principles: Framework for School Reform and Redesign.* Washington, DC: Center for Psychology in Schools and Education.

Anderson, J., Greeno, J., Reder, L., & Simon, H. A. 2000. "Perspectives on Learning, Thinking, and Activity." *Educational Researcher* 229(4): 11–13.

Anderson, J. R. 1995. *Learning and Memory.* New York: John Wiley & Sons.

Anderson, J. R., & Lebiere, C. 1998. *The Atomic Components of Thought.* Mahwah, NJ: Lawrence Erlbaum.

Annie E. Casey Foundation. 2012. "Kids Count Data Bank." Accessed October 1, 2012. http://www.aecf.org/MajorInitiatives/KIDSCOUNT.aspx.

Atkinson, R. C., & Shiffrin, R. M. 1968. "Human Memory: A Proposed System and Its Control Processes." In *The Psychology of Learning and Motivation* (Vol. 2), edited by K. Spence & J. Spence, pp. 89–195. New York: Academic Press.

Baker. D. P. 2009. *The Quiet Revolution: The Educational Transform of Modern Society* (Draft book manuscript, Pennsylvania State University). Draft copy available from dpb4@psu.edu.

Baker, D. P., & LeTendre, J. 2005. *National Differences, Global Similarities: World Culture and the Future of Schooling.* Stanford, CA: Stanford University Press.

Baker Miller, J. 1976. *Toward a New Psychology of Women.* Boston: Beacon Press.

Bandura, A. 1986. *Social Foundations of Thought and Action: A Social Cognitive Theory.* Englewood Cliffs, NJ: Prentice-Hall.

Bandura, A. 1997. *Self-Efficacy: The Exercise of Control.* New York: Freeman.

Bandura, A., Barbaranelli, C., Caprara, G. V., & Pastorelli, C. 2001. "Self-Efficacy Beliefs as Shapers of Children's Aspirations and Career Trajectories." *Child Development* 72(1): 187–206.

Berger, K. S., & Thompson, R. A. 1995. *The Developing Person Through Childhood and Adolescence*. New York: Worth.

Berger, P. L., and Luckmann, T. 1966. *The Social Construction of Reality*. New York: Random House.

Bernanke, B. S. 2012. "Economic Measurement." Paper presented at the 32nd General Conference of the International Association for Research in Income and Wealth, Cambridge, MA, August 6. Accessed October 1, 2012. http://www.federalreserve.gov/newsevents/speech/bernanke20120806a.htm.

Blackburn, I. M., Eunson, K. M., & Bishop, S. 1986. "A Two-Year Naturalistic Follow-Up of Depressed Patients Treated With Cognitive Therapy, Pharmacotherapy and a Combination of Both." *Journal of Affective Disorders* 10: 67–75.

Blume, G. W., & Heckman, D. S. 1997. "What Do Students Know About Algebra and Functions?" In *Results From the Sixth Mathematics Assessment*, edited by P. A. Kenney & E. A. Silver, pp. 225–77. Reston, VA: National Council of Teachers of Mathematics.

Borysenko, J. 1987. *Minding the Body, Mending the Mind*. Reading, MA: Addison-Wesley.

Borysenko, J. 1994. *A Women's Journey to God: Finding the Feminine Path*. New York: Riverhead Books.

Bostock, D. 1986. *Plato's Phaedo*. Oxford: Clarendon Press.

Bourdieu, P. 1977. "Cultural Reproduction and Social Reproduction." In *Power and Ideology in Education*, edited by J. Karabel & A. H. Halsey, pp. 487–511. New York: Oxford University Press.

Bourdieu, P. 1986. "The Forms of Capital." In *Handbook of Theory and Research for the Sociology of Education*, edited by J. G. Richardson, pp. 241–58. New York: Greenwood Press.

Bradie, M., & Harms, W. 2012. "Evolutionary Epistemology." In *The Stanford Encyclopedia of Philosophy* (Spring 2012 ed.), edited by E. N. Zalta. Stanford, CA: Stanford University Press.

Branden, N. 1994. *The Six Pillars of Self-Esteem*. New York: Bantam Books.

Broadie, S. 2001. "Soul and Body in Plato and Descartes." *Proceedings of the Aristotelian Society* 101: 295–308.

Bruner, J. 1960. *The Process of Education*. Cambridge, MA: Harvard University Press.

Bruner, J. 1990. *Acts of Meaning*. Cambridge, MA: Harvard University Press.

Bruner, J. 1996. *The Culture of Education*. Cambridge, MA: Harvard University Press.

Brzycki, H. G. 2009. "Teacher Beliefs and Classroom Practices That Impart Self-System and Positive Psychology Attributes." PhD diss., Penn State University. https://etda.libraries.psu.edu/paper/9451/5058.

Brzycki, H. G. 2010. "The Self in Teaching and Learning." In *Educational Psychology Reader: The Art and Science of How People Learn*, edited by G. S. Goodman. New York: Peter Lang.

# References

Bullying Statistics. 2009. "Bullying Statistics—Stop Bullying, Harassment, and Violence." Accessed October 1, 2012. http://www.bullyingstatistics.org.

Caplan, M. 2009. *Eyes Wide Open: Cultivating Discernment on the Spiritual Path*. Boulder, CO: Sounds True.

Card, S., Moran, T., & Newell, A. 1983. *The Psychology of Human-Computer Interaction*. Hillsdale, NJ: Lawrence Erlbaum.

Centers for Disease Control and Prevention. 1999. "Improving Child and Adolescent Health Through Physical Activity and Nutrition." Accessed October 1, 2012. http://www.cdc.gov/nccdphp/dnpa/panprog.htm.

Centers for Disease Control and Prevention. 2005. "CDC Efforts to Reduce or Prevent Obesity." Accessed October 1, 2012. http://www.cdc.gov/OD/OC/MEDIA/pressrel/fs050419.htm.

Centers for Disease Control and Prevention. 2007. "Teen Suicide Rate: Highest Increase in 15 Years." Accessed October 1, 2012. http://www.sciencedaily.com/releases/2007/09/070907221530.htm.

Centers for Disease Control and Prevention. 2010. "Current Depression Among Adults—United States, 2006 and 2008." *MMWR* 59(38): 1229–1235.

Centers for Disease Control and Prevention. 2011. "Antidepressant Use in Persons Aged 12 and Over: United States, 2005–2008." National Center for Health Statistics Brief, no. 76. Accessed October 1, 2012. http://www.cdc.gov/nchs/data/databriefs/db76.htm.

Centers for Disease Control and Prevention. 2012a. "Adult Obesity Facts." Accessed October 1, 2012. http://www.cdc.gov/obesity/data/adult.html.

Centers for Disease Control and Prevention. 2012b. "National Vital Statistics System—Mortality." Accessed October 1, 2012. http://www.cdc.gov/nchs/deaths.htm.

Centers for Disease Control and Prevention, Office of Analysis and Epidemiology. 2012. "Identifying Emotional and Behavioral Problems in Children Aged 4–17 Years: United States, 2001–2007," by P. N. Pastor, C. A. Reuben, & C. R. Duran. National Health Statistics Report, no. 48. February 24. http://www.cdc.gov/nchs/data/nhsr/nhsr048.pdf.

Centers for Medicare and Medicaid Services. 2010. "National Health Expenditures 2010 Highlights." http://www.cms.gov/Research-Statistics-Data-and-Systems/Statistics-Trends-and-Reports/NationalHealthExpendData/downloads/highlights.

Child Trends Data Bank. 2012. "Adolescents Who Felt Sad or Hopeless: Indicators on Children and Youth." http://www.childtrendsdatabank.org/sites/default/files/30_Felt_Sad_or_Hopeless.pdf.

Chingos, M., & Whitehurst, G. 2012. *Choosing Blindly: Instructional Materials, Teacher Effectiveness, and the Common Core*. Washington, DC: The Brookings Institution.

Christianson, S. A, ed. 1992. *The Handbook of Emotion and Memory*. Hillsdale, NJ: Lawrence Erlbaum.

Clemson University. 2012. "Olweus Bullying Prevention Program." Accessed October 1, 2012. http://www.clemson.edu/olweus.

Cohen, E. 2007. "CDC: Antidepressants Most Prescribed Drug in U.S." Accessed October 1, 2012. http://articles.cnn.com/2007-07-09/health/antidepressants_1_anti depressants-high-blood-pressure-drugs-psychotropic-drugs?_s=PM:HEALTH.

Cohen, J. 2006. "Social, Emotional, Ethical, and Academic Education: Creating a Climate for Learning, Participation in Democracy, and Well-Being." *Harvard Educational Review* 76: 2.

Cohen, S., Doyle, W. J., Treanor, J. J., & Turner, R. B. 2006. "Positive Emotional Style Predicts Resistance to Illness After Experimental Exposure to Rhinovirus or Influenza A Virus." *Journal of Bio-Behavioral Medicine* 68(6): 809–815.

Cohen, S., Doyle, W. J., Turner, R. B., Alper, C. M., & Skoner, D. P. 2006. "Research Highlight: Emotional Style and Susceptibility to the Common Cold." In *Healthier Lives Through Behavioral and Social Science Research*. Available from the Office of Behavioral and Social Sciences Research website: http://obssr.od.nih.gov/publications/books_and_projects/books_and_reports.aspx.

Cole, M. 1996. *Cultural Psychology*. Cambridge, MA: Harvard University Press.

Coleman, J. 1988. "Social Capital in the Creation of Human Capital." *American Journal of Sociology* 94(Suppl.): S95–S120.

Coles, R. 1997a. "Basic Humanity." (Transcript of interview with David Gergen.) *Mac-Neil/Lehrer News Hour*. Accessed October 1, 2012. http://www.pbs.org/newshour/gergen/february97/coles_2-21.html.

Coles, R. 1997b. *The Moral Intelligence of Children*. New York: Random House.

Copernicus, N., & Duncan, A. M., trans. 1976. *On the Revolutions of the Heavenly Spheres*. New York: Barnes and Noble.

Corno, L., & Mandinach, E. B. 1983. "The Role of Cognitive Engagement in Classroom Learning and Motivation." *Educational Psychologist* 18: 88–108.

Council of Chief State School Officers. 2006. E-Newsletter, Spring, p. 5. Washington, DC: CCSSO.

Cremin, L. A. 1964. *The Transformation of the School: Progressivism in American Education 1876–1957*. New York: Vintage/Random House.

Cresta, B. 2004. "The National Context." Paper presented at Managed Behavioral Health Care in Massachusetts: Challenges of Maintaining Access and Quality. Schneider Institute for Health Policy. Accessed October 1, 2012. http://www.sihp.brandeis.edu/shedard/downloads.html.

Crook, T. R., Todd, S. Y., Combs, J. G., Woehr, D. J., & Ketchen, D. J. 2011. "Does Human Capital Matter? A Meta-Analysis of the Relationship Between Human Capital and Firm Performance." *Journal of Applied Psychology* 96(3): 443–456.

Csikszentmihalyi, M. 1993. *The Evolving Self*. New York: HarperCollins.

Csikszentmihalyi, M. 1997. *Creativity: Flow and the Psychology of Discovery and Invention*. New York: HarperCollins.

Damasio, A. 1994. *Descartes' Error: Emotion, Reason, and the Human Brain*. New York: Penguin.

Davis, J. V. 2003. "Transpersonal Psychology." In *The Encyclopedia of Religion and Nature*, edited by B. Taylor & J. Kaplan. Bristol, England: Thoemmes Continuum.

Deci, E. L., Nezlek, J., & Sheinman, L. 1981. "Characteristics of the Rewarder and Intrinsic Motivation of the Rewardee." *Journal of Personality and Social Psychology* 40: 1–10.

Deci, E. L., & Ryan, R. M. 1985. *Intrinsic Motivation and Self-Determination in Human Behavior*. New York: Cambridge University Press.

Deci, E. L., & Ryan, R. M. 1995. "Human Autonomy: The Basis for True Self-Esteem." In *Efficacy, Agency, and Self-Esteem*, edited by M. Kernis, pp. 31–49. New York: Plenum.

Deci, E. L., & Ryan, R. M. 2008. "Facilitating Optimal Motivation and Psychological Well-Being Across Life's Domains." *Canadian Psychology* 49: 14–23.

Deming, W. E. 1986. *Out of the Crisis*. Boston: MIT Press.

Dewey, J. 1900. *The School and Society*. Chicago: University of Chicago Press.

Dewey, J. 1902. *The Child and the Curriculum*. Chicago: University of Chicago Press.

Dewey, J. 1916. *Democracy and Education*. New York: Macmillan.

Diener, E., Lucas, R. E., & Oishi, S. 2002. "Subjective Well-Being: The Science of Happiness and Life Satisfaction." In *The Handbook of Positive Psychology*, edited by C. R. Snyder & S. J. Lopez, pp. 463–473. New York: Oxford University Press.

DiMaggio, P. 1997. "Culture and Cognition." *Annual Review of Sociology* 23: 263–287.

Dokoupil, T. 2012. "Is the Onslaught Making Us Crazy?" *Newsweek*, July 16.

Dolcos, F., LaBar, K., & Cabeza, R. 2004. "Interaction Between the Amygdala and the Medial Temporal Lobe Memory System Predicts Better Memory for Emotional Events." *Neuron* 42: 855–863.

Dolcos, F., & McCarthy, G. 2006. "Brain Systems Mediating Cognitive Interference by Emotional Distraction." *Journal of Neuroscience* 26(7): 2072–2079.

Duckworth, A. L., Steen, T. A., & Seligman, M. E. P. 2005. "Positive Psychology in Clinical Practice." *Annual Review of Clinical Psychology* 1: 629–651.

Edformation. 2004. *AIMSweb Training DVD: Illustrations and Practice Exercises for Use With AIMSweb Administration and Scoring Guides* (Video). Eden Prairie, MN: Edformation.

Edwards, V. J., Anda, R. F., Dube, S. R., Dong, M., Chapman, D. F., & Felitti, V. J. 2005. "The Wide-Ranging Health Consequences of Adverse Childhood Experiences." In *Victimization of Children and Youth: Patterns of Abuse, Response Strategies*, edited by K. Kendall-Tackett & S. Giacomoni. Kingston, NJ: Civic Research Institute.

Effrat, A. 1972. "Power to the Paradigms." *Sociological Inquiry* 42(3–4): 3–33.

Elliot, A. J., & McGregor, H. A. 2001. "A 2 by 2 Achievement Goal Framework." *Journal of Personality and Social Psychology* 80(3): 501–519.

EPE Research Center. 2008. "Graduation Rates in America's Top 50 Cities." Accessed October 1, 2012. http://www.edweek.org/info/about/research.html.

Erikson, E. 1963. *Childhood and Society*. New York: Norton.

Erikson, E. 1968. *Identity, Youth, and Crisis*. New York: Norton.

Erikson, E. 1980. *Identity and the Life Cycle*. New York: Norton.

Felitti, V. J., Anda, R. F., Nordenberg, D., Williamson, D. F., Spitz, A. M., Edwards, V., Koss, M. P., & Marks, J. S. 1998. "Relationship of Childhood Abuse and Household Dysfunction to Many of the Leading Causes of Death in Adults: The Adverse Childhood Experiences (ACE) Study." *American Journal of Preventive Medicine* 14: 245–258.

Feuer, M., & Towne, L. 2002. "The Logic and the Basic Principles of Scientific-Based Research." Accessed October 1, 2012. http://www.ed.gov/nclb/methods/whatworks/research/page_pg11.html.

Finkelstein, E. A., Fiebelkorn, I. C., & Wang, G. 2003. "National Medical Spending Attributable to Overweight and Obesity: How Much, and Who's Paying?" *Health Affairs* W3: 219–226.

Fox, M. 2008. *Reading Magic: Why Reading Aloud to Our Children Will Change Their Lives Forever.* Orlando, FL: Harvest Original-Harcourt.

Frankl, V. 1984. *Man's Search for Meaning.* New York: Simon & Schuster.

Freire, P. 2000. *Pedagogy of the Oppressed.* New York: Continuum.

Gardner, H. 1983. *Frames of Mind: The Theory of Multiple Intelligences.* New York: Basic Books.

Gardner, H. 2000. *The Disciplined Mind.* New York: Penguin.

Gersten, R., Baker, S., & Lloyd, J. W. 2000. "Designing High-Quality Research in Special Education: Group Experimental Design." *Journal of Special Education* 34(1): 2–18.

Giffin, W. M. 1906. *School Days in the Fifties.* Chicago: A. Flanagan Company.

Glas, G. 2006. "Person, Personality, Self, and Identity: A Philosophically Informed Conceptual Analysis." *Journal of Personality Disorders* 20: 126–138.

Glasersfeld, E. von. 1995. *Radical Constructivism: A Way of Knowing and Learning.* London: Falmer Press.

Goetz, T., Zirngibl, A., Pekrun, R., & Hall, N. 2003. "Emotions, Learning and Achievement From an Educational-Psychological Perspective." In *Learning Emotions: The Influence of Affective Factors on Classroom Learning*, edited by P. Mayring & C. von Rhoeneck, pp. 9–28. Frankfurt, Germany: Peter Lang.

Goldberg, M., & Cross, C. 2005. "Time Out: Rethinking the Hours America Spends Educating." Accessed October 1, 2012. http://www.edutopia.org/time-out-rethinking-hours-america-educates.

Goleman, D. 1995. *Emotional Intelligence: Why It Can Matter More Than IQ.* New York: Bantam Books.

Goodman, E., & Whitaker, R. C. 2002. "A Prospective Study on the Role of Depression in the Development and Persistence of Obesity." *Pediatrics* 110(3): 497–504.

Goodman, G., ed. 2010. *Educational Psychology Reader: The Art and Science of How People Learn.* New York: Peter Lang.

Greenberg, P. E., Stiglin, L. E., Finkelstein, S. N., & Berndt, E. R. 1993. "The Economic Burden of Depression in 1990." *Journal of Clinical Psychiatry* 54: 405–426.

Greene, M. 1995. *Releasing the Imagination.* San Francisco: Jossey-Bass.

Greer, R. D. 2002. "Designing Teaching Strategies: An Applied Behavior Analysis Systems Approach." In *Educational Psychology Series: Critical Reviews of Research Knowledge, Theories, Principles, and Practices*, edited by G. Phye. New York: Academic Press.

Greeson, J. 1993. *It's Not What You Are Eating; It's What Eating You: The 28-Day Plan to Heal Hidden Food Addiction*. New York: Simon & Schuster.

Hanushek, E. A., Peterson, P. E., & Woessmann, L. 2012. *Achievement Growth: International and U.S. States Trends in Student Performance*. PEPG report no. 12–13. http://hks.harvard.edu/pepg.

Harter, S. 1999. *The Construction of the Self: A Developmental Perspective*. New York: Guilford Press.

Harter, S., & Marold, D. 1992. "Psychosocial Risk Factors Contributing to Adolescent Suicidal Ideation." In *Child and Adolescent Suicide: Clinical Developmental Perspectives*, edited by G. Noam & S. Borst. Rochester, NY: University of Rochester Press.

Harvey, O. J. 1986. "Belief Systems and Attitudes Toward the Death Penalty and Other Punishments." *Journal of Personality* 54: 659–675.

Hawkins, D. J., Kosterman, R., Catalano, R. F., Hill, K. G., & Abbott, R. D. 2008. "Effects of Social Development Intervention in Childhood 15 Years Later." *Archives of Pediatric and Adolescent Medicine* 162(12): 1133–1141.

Heckhausen, H. 1977. "Achievement Motivation and Its Constructs: A Cognitive Model." *Motivation and Emotion* 1(4): 283–329.

Heckhausen, H., ed. 2000. *Motivational Psychology of Human Development*. Oxford: Elsevier.

Henderson, J., & Hawthorne, R. 2000. *Transformative Curriculum Leadership*. Upper Saddle River, NJ: Pearson Education.

Hensley, S. 2011. "Look Around: 1 in 10 Adults Takes Antidepressants." SHOTS: NPR HealthBlog, October 10. http://www.npr.org/blogs/health/2011/10/20/141544135/look-around-1-in-10-americans-take-antidepressants.

Herman, K. C., Lambert, S. F., Reinke, W. M., & Ialongo, N. S. 2008. "Low Academic Competence in First Grade as a Risk Factor for Depressive Cognitions and Symptoms in Middle School." *Journal of Counseling Psychology* 55(3): 400–410.

Hermes, J. J. 2008. "Report Shows Stunning Failures in High-School Graduation Rates." *Chronicle of Higher Education*. Accessed October 1, 2012. http://chronicle.com/article/Report-Shows-Stunning-Failures/40728.

Hiebert, J., & Carpenter, T. 1992. "Learning and Teaching With Understanding." In *Handbook of Research on Mathematics Teaching and Learning*, edited by D. Grouws, pp. 65–97. New York: Simon & Schuster Macmillan.

Hillman, J. 1996. *The Soul's Code: In Search of Character and Calling*. New York: Random House.

Hillman, J. 1999. *The Force of Character and the Lasting Life*. New York: Random House.

Hoelscher, D. M., Day, R. S., Lee, E. S., Frankowski, R. F., Kelder, S. H., Ward, J. L., & Scheurer, M. E. 2004. "Measuring the Prevalence of Overweight in Texas School Children." *American Journal of Public Health* 94: 1002–1008.

Home Box Office. 2012. *Weight of the Nation*. Accessed October 1, 2012. http://the weightofthenation.hbo.com/films/main-films.
Immordino-Yang, M. H. 2008. *The Relevance of Social and Affective Neuroscience to Education* (Video). Presented at USC Rossier School of Education Brown Bag Series. Accessed October 1, 2012. http://m.youtube.com/#/watch?v=KyjatC2MCYY.
Immordino-Yang, M. H., & Damasio, A. 2007. "We Feel, Therefore We Learn: The Relevance of Affective and Social Neuroscience to Education." *Mind, Brain, and Education* 1(1): 3–10.
Immordino-Yang, M. H., & Faeth, M. 2010. "The Role of Emotion and Skilled Intuition in Learning." In *Mind, Brain, and Education: Neuroscience Implications for the Classroom*, edited by D. Sousa. Bloomington, IN: Solution Tree/Leading Edge.
Immordino-Yang, M. H., & Fischer, K. W. 2009a. "Brain Development." In *Corsini Encyclopedia of Psychology* (4th ed.), edited by I. Weiner & E. Craighead. New York: John Wiley & Sons.
Immordino-Yang, M. H., & Fischer, K. W. 2009b. "Neuroscience Bases of Learning." In *International Encyclopedia of Education* (3rd ed.), edited by V. G. Aukrust. Oxford, England: Elsevier.
Izard, C. E. 1984. "Emotion-Cognition Relationships and Human Development." In *Emotions, Cognition, and Behavior*, edited by C. E. Izard, J. Kagan, & R. B. Zajonc. New York: Cambridge University Press.
Jahoda, M. 1958. *Current Concepts of Positive Mental Health*. New York: Basic Books.
Jalali, A. A., & Mahmoodi, H. 2009. "Virtual Age: Next Wave of Change in Society." Paper presented at the 2009 International Joint Conferences on e-CASE and e-Technology, Singapore, January 8–10.
James, W. 1890. *Principles of Psychology* (Vol. 1). New York: Henry Holt and Company.
James, W. 1892. *Psychology (Briefer Course)*. New York: The Library of America.
Johnson, M. H. 2001. "Functional Brain Development in Humans." *Nature Reviews: Neuroscience* 2(7): 475–483.
Kegan, J. 1994. *In Over Our Heads: The Mental Demands of Modern Life*. Cambridge, MA: Harvard University Press.
Kensinger, E. A., & Corkin, S. 2004. "Two Routes to Emotional Memory: Distinct Neural Processes for Valence and Arousal." *Proceedings of the National Academy of Sciences USA* 101: 3310–3115.
Kittredge, C. 2004. "N. H. Explores Worldly Ways to Learn." *Boston Globe*, May 16.
Kroger, J. 1996. "Identity, Regression and Development." *Journal of Adolescence* 19: 203–222.
Kuhn, T. S. 1962. *The Structure of Scientific Revolutions*. Chicago: University of Chicago Press.
Kunda, Z. 1990. "The Case for Motivated Reasoning." *Psychological Bulletin* 108(3): 480–498.
LeDoux, J. E. 1994. "Emotion, Memory and the Brain." *Scientific American*, June, 50–57.

LeDoux, J. E. 1996. *The Emotional Brain: The Mysterious Underpinnings of Emotional Life*. New York: Simon & Schuster.
LeDoux, J. E. 2002. *Synaptic Self: How Our Brains Become Who We Are*. New York: Penguin.
Lent, R. W., Singley, D. Sheu, H., & Gainor, K. 2005. "Social Cognitive Predictors of Domain and Life Satisfaction: Exploring the Theoretical Precursors of Subjective Well-Being." *Journal of Counseling Psychology* 52(3): 429–442.
Levi, J., Segal, L., Laurant, R., Lang, A., & Rayburn, J. 2012. "F as in Fat: How Obesity Threatens America's Future." http://www.healthyamericans.org.
Levine, M. 2002. *A Mind at a Time*. New York: Simon & Schuster.
Levy, M. 2012. *Big Test for Corbett Loom in Election, Tax Credit*. New York: Associated Press.
Lickona, T. 1991. *Educating for Character: How Our Schools Can Teach Respect and Responsibility*. New York: Bantam Books.
Lickona, T., Schaps, E., & Lewis, C. 2003. "Eleven Principles of Effective Character Education." Accessed October 1, 2012. http://www.character.org/more-resources/publications/11-principles.
Limber, S. P. 2004. "Implementation of the Olweus Bullying Prevention Program: Lessons Learned From the Field." In *Bullying in American Schools: A Social-Ecological Perspective on Prevention and Intervention*, edited by D. Espelage & S. Swearer, pp. 351–363. Mahwah, NJ: Lawrence Erlbaum.
Lobel, A. 1983. *Frog and Toad Together*. New York: HarperCollins.
Locker, J., & Cropley, M. 2004. "Anxiety, Depression and Self-Esteem in Secondary School Children: An Investigation Into the Impact of Standard Assessment Tests (SATs) and Other Important School Examinations." *School Psychology International* 25(3): 333–345.
Mamun, A. 2003. *Life History of Cardiovascular Disease and Its Risk Factors—Multistate Life Table Approach and Application to the Framingham Heart Study*. Amsterdam: Rozenberg.
Mann, M., Hosman, C. M. H., Schaalma, H. P., & de Vries, N. K. 2004. "Self-Esteem in a Broad Spectrum Approach for Mental Health Promotion." *Health Education Research: Theory and Practice* 19(4): 357–372.
Marcia, J. E. 1966. "Development and Validation of the Ego Identity Status." *Journal of Personality and Social Psychology* 3: 551–558.
Marcia, J. E. 1991. "Identity and Self Development." In *Encyclopedia of Adolescence* (Vol. 1), edited by R. Lerner, A. Peterson, & J. Brooks-Gunn. New York: Garland.
Marcia, J. E. 2002. "Identity and Psychosocial Development in Adulthood." *Identity: An International Journal of Theory and Research* 2: 7–28.142.
Marcia, J. E., Waterman, A. S., Matteson, D. R., Archer, S. L., & Orlofsky, J. L. 1993. *Ego Identity*. New York: Springer.
Markus, H. 1977. "Self-Schemata and Processing Information About the Self." *Journal of Personality and Social Psychology* 35: 63–78.
Markus, H., & Nurius, P. 1986. "Possible Selves." *American Psychologist* 41(9): 954–969.

Maslow, A. H. 1943. "A Theory of Human Motivation." *Psychological Review* 50: 370–396.
Maslow, A. H. 1954. *Motivation and Personality*. New York: Harper and Row.
Maslow, A. H. 1968. *Toward a Psychology of Being*. New York: John Wiley & Sons.
Masten, A. S., & Reed, M. J. 2005. "Resilience in Development." In *Handbook of Positive Psychology*, edited by C. R. Snyder & S. J. Lopez. New York: Oxford University Press.
Masters, J. C., Barden, R. C., & Ford, M. E. 1979. "Affective States, Expressive Behavior, and Learning in Children." *Journal of Personality and Social Psychology* 37: 380–390.
Mayo Clinic Staff. 2012. "Cognitive Behavioral Therapy." Accessed October 1, 2012. http://www.mayoclinic.com/health/cognitive-behavioral-therapy/MY00194.
McCarty, T. L., Wallace, S., Hadley Lynch, R., & Benally, A. 1991. "Classroom Inquiry and Navajo Learning Styles: A Call for Reassessment." *Anthropology and Education Quarterly* 22(1): 42–59.
McCombs, B. L. 2003. "A Framework for the Redesign of K–12 Education in the Context of Current Educational Reform." *Theory Into Practice* 42(2): 93–101.
McCullough, D. 2012. *You Are Not Special* (Video). Presented to graduating class, Wellesley High School, June 7. Accessed October 2, 2012. http://www.youtube.com/watch?v=_lfxYhtf8o4.
McMeil, J. D. 2005. *Contemporary Curriculum: In Though and Action* (6th ed.). New York: John Wiley & Sons.
Miller, G. A. 2003. "The Cognitive Revolution: A Historical Perspective." *Trends in Cognitive Sciences* 7(3): 141–144.
Mink, O., Owen, K., & Mink, B. 1993. *Developing High-Performance People: The Art of Coaching*. Reading, MA: Addison-Wesley.
Moore, T. 1992. *Care of the Soul: A Guide For Cultivating Depth and Sacredness in Everyday Life*. New York: HarperCollins.
Moscovitch, M., & Craik, F. I. M. 1976. "Depth of Processing, Retrieval Cues, and Uniqueness of Encoding as a Factor in Recall." *Journal of Verbal Learning and Verbal Behavior* 15: 447–458.
Murphy, P. K., & Mason, L. 2006. "Changing Knowledge and Changing Beliefs." In *Handbook of Educational Psychology* (2nd ed.), edited by P. A. Alexander & P. Winne. New York: Lawrence Erlbaum.
National Alliance on Mental Illness. 2011. "Cognitive Behavioral Therapy Fact Sheet." Accessed October 1, 2012. http://www.nami.org/factsheets/CBT_factsheet.pdf.
National Center for Education Statistics. 2005a. "Dropout Rates in the United States: 2005." Accessed October 1, 2012. http://nces.ed.gov/pubs2007/dropout05/tables/table_A3.asp.
National Center for Education Statistics. 2005b. "National Assessment of Educational Progress—The Nation's Report Card." Accessed October 1, 2012. http://www.nces.ed.gov/nation'sreportcard.

National Center for Education Statistics. 2009. "Beginning Post-Secondary Students, Drop-Out Rates." Accessed October 1, 2012. http://nces.ed.gov/surveys/bps.

National Center for Education Statistics. 2011. "The Condition of Education 2011." Accessed October 1, 2012. http://nces.ed.gov/programs/coe/indicator_scr.asp.

National Commission on Excellence in Education (with D. Gardner). 1983. *A Nation at Risk: The Imperative for Educational Reform.* Washington, DC: U.S. Department of Education.

National Education Association. 2011. "Meeting the Needs of the Whole Child." Press release, April 29. Accessed October 2, 2012. http://help.senate.gov/newsroom/press/release/?id=aec51833-aa09-4f09-a354-2d5d493bae44&groups=Chair.

National Institute of Mental Health. 2010. "National Survey Confirms That Youth Are Disproportionately Affected by Mental Disorders." Accessed October 1, 2012. http://www.nimh.nih.gov/science-news/2010/national-survey-confirms-that-youth-are-disproportionately-affected-by-mental-disorders.shtml.

National Institute of Mental Health. 2011. "Borderline Personality Disorder Definition and Statistics." Accessed December 21, 2012. http://www.nimh.nih.gov/statistics/1Borderline.shtml.

Neuman, S. B., Copple, C., & Bredekamp, S. 1998. "Learning to Read and Write: Developmentally Appropriate Practices for Young Children. A Joint Position Statement of the International Reading Association (IRA) and the National Association for the Education of Young Children (NAEYC), National Association for the Education of Young Children." Accessed October 2, 2012. http://oldweb.naeyc.org/about/positions/pdf/PSREAD98.PDF.

New Hampshire Department of Education. 2006. "New Hampshire Comprehensive Education Reform." Accessed October 2, 2012. http://www.ed.state.nh.us.education/EdReform/RWL.htm.

New Hampshire Department of Education. 2009. "Follow the Child Initiative." Accessed October 2, 2012. http://www.education.nh.gov/innovations/follow_child/documents/personal_ed.ppt.

Noddings, N. 2003. *Happiness and Education.* Cambridge: Cambridge University Press.

Noddings, N. 2005. *Educating Citizens for Global Awareness.* New York: Teachers College Press.

Noddings, N. 2006. *Critical Lessons: What Our Schools Should Teach.* New York: Cambridge University Press.

Northeast Foundation for Children. 2012. "Responsive Classroom." Accessed October 2, 2012. http://www.responsiveclassroom.org/about-responsive-classroom.

Northwest Evaluation Association. 2005. *RIT Scale Norms for Use With Achievement Level Tests and Measures of Academic Progress.* Lake Oswego, OR: Northwest Evaluation Association.

Odum, H. T. 1988. "Self-Organization, Transformity, and Information." *Science* 242: 1132–1139.

Ogden, C. L., Carroll, M. D., Kit, B. K., & Flegal, K. M. 2012. "Prevalence of Obesity and Trends in Body Mass Index Among U.S. Children and Adolescents, 1999–2010." *Journal of the American Medical Association* 307(5): 483–490.

Ormrod, J. E. 2011. *Essentials of Educational Psychology* (3rd ed.). Upper Saddle River, NJ: Pearson Education.

Orth, U., Robbins, R. W., & Widaman, K. F. 2012. "Life-Span Development of Self-Esteem and Its Effects on Important Life Outcomes." *Journal of Personality and Social Psychology* 102(6): 1271–1288.

Parjares, M. F. 1992. "Teachers Beliefs and Educational Research: Cleaning Up a Messy Construct." *Review of Educational Research* 62: 307–332.

Parjares, M. F. 1996. "Self-Efficacy Beliefs in Academic Settings." *Review of Educational Research* 66(4): 543–578.

Pastor, P. N., Reuben, C. A., & Duran, C. R. 2012. "Identifying Emotional and Behavioral Problems in Children Aged 4–17 Years: United States, 2001–2007." *National Health Statistic Report*, February 24. Atlanta, GA: Centers for Disease Control and Prevention, Office of Analysis and Epidemiology. http://www.cdc.gov/nchs/data/nhsr/nhsr048.pdf.

Patrick, H., Ryan, A. M., & Kaplan, A. 2007. "Early Adolescent Perceptions of the Classroom Social Environment, Motivational Beliefs, and Engagement." *Journal of Educational Psychology* 99(1): 83–98.

Pekrun, R. 1992. "The Impact of Emotions on Learning and Achievement: Towards a Theory of Cognitive/Motivational Mediators." *Applied Psychology: An International Review* 41(4): 359–376.

Pekrun, R. 2000. "A Social-Cognitive, Control-Value Theory of Achievement Emotions." *Advances in Psychology* 131: 143–163.

Pekrun, R., Goetz, T., Titz, W., & Perry, R. P. 2002. "Academic Emotions in Students' Self-Regulated Learning and Achievement: A Program of Qualitative and Quantitative Research." *Educational Psychologist* 37(2): 91–105.

Pennsylvania Department of Education. 2005. "Pennsylvania Department of Education Press Release." http://www.pdenewsroom.state.pa.us.

Peterson, L. E., Stahlberg, D., & Dauenheimer, D. 2000. "Effects of Self-Schema Elaboration on Affective and Cognitive Reactions to Self-Relevant Information." *Genetic, Social, and General Psychology Monographs* 26: 25–42.

Piaget, J. 1936. *Origins of Intelligence in the Child*. London: Routledge & Kegan Paul.

Piaget, J. 1957. *Construction of Reality in the Child*. London: Routledge & Kegan Paul.

Pintrich, P. R. 1999. "The Role of Motivation in Promoting and Sustaining Self-Regulated Learning." *International Journal of Educational Research* 31: 459–470.

Pintrich, P. R., & de Groot, E. 1990. "Motivational and Self-Regulated Learning Components of Classroom Academic Performance." *Journal of Educational Psychology* 82(1): 33–50.

Pintrich, P. R., Marx, R. W., & Boyle, R. A. 1993. "Beyond Cold Conceptual Change: The Role of Motivational Beliefs and Classroom Contextual Factors in the Process of Conceptual Change." *Review of Educational Research* 63: 167–199.

Pintrich, P. R., & Schunk, D. H. 2002. *Motivation in Education: Theory, Research, and Applications*. Upper Saddle River, NJ: Prentice-Hall.

Plato. 1993. *Phaedo*. New York: Oxford University Press.

Psychology Campus. 2011. "Existential Therapy Definition." Accessed October 2, 2012. http://www.psychologycampus.com/psychology-counseling/existential-therapy.html.

Public Broadcasting Service. 2012. "Finding Your Roots: Samuel L. Jackson, Condoleezza Rice, & Ruth Simmons." Accessed October 2, 2012. http://video.pbs.org/video/2225130612.

Putnam, R. 1993. *Making Democracy Work: Civic Tradition in Modern Italy*. Princeton, NJ: Princeton University Press.

Reeder, G. D., McCormick, C. B., & Esselman, E. D. 1987. "Self-Referent Processing and Recall of Prose." *Journal of Educational Psychology* 79(3): 243–248.

Republican Party of Texas. 2012. "Report of Platform Committee and Rules Committee." Accessed October 2, 2012. http://www.tfn.org/site/DocServer/2012-Platform-Final.pdf?docID=3201.

Resnick, L. B., & Resnick, D. P. 1992. "Assessing the Thinking Curriculum: New Tools for Educational Reform." In *Changing Assessments: Alternative Views of Aptitude, Achievement, and Instruction,* edited by B. R. Gifford & M. C. O'Connor, pp. 37–75. Boston: Kluwer.

Reyna, V. 2002. "What Is Scientifically Based Evidence? What Is Its Logic?" Paper presented at U.S. Department of Education Scientifically Based Research Conference. Accessed October 2, 2012. http://www.ed.gov/nclb/methods/whatworks/research/index.html.

Robinson, K. 2001. *Out of Our Minds: Learning to Be Creative*. West Sussex: Capstone.

Rogers, C. 1954. "Toward a Theory of Creativity." *ETC: A Review of General Semantics* 11: 249–260.

Rogers, C. 1961. *On Becoming a Person*. Boston: Houghton Mifflin.

Rogers, C. 1980. *A Way of Being*. Boston: Houghton Mifflin.

Rogers, C. 1986. *A Client-Centered/Person-Centered Approach to Therapy*. In *The Carl Rogers Reader*, edited by H. Kirschenbaum & V. Land Henderson. Boston: Houghton Mifflin.

Rogers, T. B. 1981. "A Model of the Self as an Aspect of the Human Information Processing System." In *Personality, Cognition, and Social Interaction*, edited by N. Cantor & J. F. Kihlstrom, pp. 193–214. Hillsdale, NJ: Lawrence Erlbaum.

Rogers, T. B., Kuiper, N. A., & Kirker, W. S. 1977. "Self-Reference and the Encoding of Personal Information." *Journal of Personality and Social Psychology* 35: 677–688.

Rosenbaum, P. R. 2002. *Observational Studies* (2nd ed.). New York: Springer.

Rotter, J. B. 1966. "Generalized Expectancies for Internal Versus External Control of Reinforcement." *Psychological Monographs* 80(1): 1–28.

Ryan, R. M., & Deci, E. 2000. "Self-Determination Theory and the Facilitation of Intrinsic Motivation, Social Development, and Well-Being." *American Psychologist* 55: 68–78.

Ryan, R. M., & Deci, E. L. 2001. "On Happiness and Human Potentials: A Review of Research on Hedonic and Eudaimonic Well-Being." *Annual Review of Psychology* 52: 141–166.

Ryff, C. D., & Singer, B. 1998a. "The Contours of Positive Human Health." *Psychological Inquiry* 9: 1–28.

Ryff, C. D., & Singer, B. 1998b. "The Role of Purpose in Life and Personal Growth in Positive Human Health." In *The Human Quest for Meaning: A Handbook of Psychological Research and Clinical Applications*, edited by P. T. P. Wong & P. S. Fry, pp. 213–235. Mahwah, NJ: Lawrence Erlbaum.

Ryff, C. D., & Singer, B. 2003. "The Role of Emotion on Pathways to Positive Health." In *Handbook of Affective Sciences*, edited by R. J. Davidson, K. R. Scherer, & H. H. Goldsmith. New York: Oxford University Press.

Ryff, C. D., Singer, B., Love, G. D., & Essex, M. J. 1998. "Resilience in Adulthood and Later Life: Defining Features and Dynamic Processes." In *Handbook of Aging and Mental Health*, edited by J. Lomranz. New York: Plenum.

Scheffler, I. 1985. *Of Human Potential*. Boston: Routledge & Kegan Paul.

Schroeder, S. 2007. "We Can Do Better: Improving the Health of the American People." *New England Journal of Medicine* 357: 1221–1228.

Schunk, D. H. 2000. *Learning Theories: An Educational Perspective* (3rd ed.). Columbus, OH: Merrill/Prentice-Hall.

Seligman, M. E. P. 2011. *Flourish: A Visionary New Understanding of Happiness and Well-Being*. New York: Free Press.

Seligman, M. E. P., & Csikszentmihalyi, M. 2000. "Positive Psychology: An Introduction." *American Psychologist* 55: 5–14.

Seligman, M. E. P., Schulman, P., & DeRubeis, R. J. 1999. "The Prevention of Depression and Anxiety." In *Prevention and Treatment* (Vol. 2). Accessed October 2, 2012. http://www.ppc.sas.upenn.edu/depprevseligman1999.pdf.

Senge, P., Cambron-McCabe, N., Lucas, T., Smith, B., Dutton, J., & Kleiner, A. 2000. *Schools That Learn*. New York: Doubleday.

Shanahan, M. J. 2000. "Pathways to Adulthood in Changing Societies: Variability and Mechanisms in Life Course Perspective." *Annual Review of Sociology* 26: 667–692.

Shaw, G. B. 1962. *Man and Superman*. New York: Heritage Press.

Shouse, E. 2005 "Feeling, Emotion, Affect." Accessed October 2, 2012. http://journal.media-culture.org.au/0512/03-shouse.php.

Sigel, I. E. 1985. "Parental Concepts of Development." In *Parental Belief Systems: The Psychological Consequences for Children*, edited by I. E. Sigel, pp. 83–105. Hillsdale, NJ: Lawrence Erlbaum.

Silko, L. M. 1996. *Yellow Woman and a Beauty of the Spirit Essays*. New York: Simon & Schuster.

Smith, E. R., Simpson, J. A., & King, L. A. 2012. "Life-Span Development of Self-Esteem and Its Effects on Important Life Outcomes." *Journal of Personality and Social Psychology* 77: 1271–1288.

# References

Snyder, C. R., & Lopez, S. J. 2002. *Handbook of Positive Psychology*. London: Oxford University Press.

Snyder, C. R., & Lopez, S. J., eds. 2005. *Handbook of Positive Psychology*. London: Oxford University Press.

Snyder, C. R., Rand, K. L., & Sigmon, D. R. 2005. "Hope Theory: A Member of the Positive Psychology Family." In *Handbook of Positive Psychology*, edited by C. R. Snyder & S. J. Lopez, pp. 257–276. London: Oxford University Press.

Sparks, S. D. 2012. "Neuroscientists Find Learning Is Not 'Hard-Wired.'" *Education Week*, June 6.

Speer, L. 2012. "2012 Kids Count Data Book." Accessed October 2, 2012. http://datacenter.kidscount.org/DataBook/2012/OnlineBooks/KIDSCOUNT2012DataBookFullReport.pdf.

Spiegel, D., Loewenstein, R. J., Lewis-Fernandez, R., Vedat, S., Simeon, D., Vermetten, E., Etzel Carden, E., & Dell, P. F. 2011. "Dissociative Disorders in DSM-5." *Depression and Anxiety* 28: 824–852.

Sternberg, L. 2007. "Who Are the Bright Children? The Cultural Context of Being and Acting Intelligent." *Educational Researcher* 36(3): 148–155.

Sternberg, R. J. 1999. *Handbook of Creativity*. New York: Cambridge University Press.

Sternberg, R. J., & Lubart, T. I. 1995. *Defying the Crowd: Cultivating Creativity in a Culture of Conformity*. New York: Free Press.

Strauss, A., & Corbin, J. 1998. *Basics of Qualitative Research: Techniques and Procedures for Developing Grounded Theory*. Thousand Oaks, CA: Sage.

Strauss, R. S. 2000. "Childhood Obesity and Self-Esteem." *Pediatrics* 105(1): e15. Accessed October 2, 2012. http://www.pediatrics.org/cgi/content/full/105/1/e15.

Substance Abuse and Mental Health Services Administration. 2011. "Results From the 2010 National Survey on Drug Use and Health: Summary of National Findings." NSDUH Series H-41, HHS Publication no. (SMA) 11-4658. Rockville, MD: Substance Abuse and Mental Health Services Administration.

Ternouth, A., Collier, D., & Maughan, B. 2009. "Childhood Emotional Problems and Self-Perceptions Predict Weight Gain in a Longitudinal Regression Model." *BMC Medicine* 7: 46.

Toffler, A. 1970. *Future Shock*. New York: Bantam Books.

Toffler, A. 1980. *The Third Wave: The Classic Study of Tomorrow*. New York: Bantam Books.

Tomasello, M. 2000. *The Cultural Origins of Human Cognition*. Cambridge, MA: Harvard University Press.

Twenge, J. M., & Campbell, K. W. 2009. *The Narcissism Epidemic: Living in the Age of Entitlement*. New York: Free Press.

Twenge, J. M., Gentile, B., DeWall, C. N., Ma, D. S., Lacefield, K., & Schurtz, D. R. 2010. "Birth Cohort Increases in Psychopathology Among Young Americans, 1938–2007: A Cross-Temporal Meta-Analysis of the MMPI." *Clinical Psychology Review* 30: 145–154.

Tyack, D., & Cuban, L. 1995. *Tinkering Toward Utopia*. Cambridge, MA: Harvard University Press.
University of Kansas Work Group for Community Health and Development. 2012. "The Community Tool Box." Accessed October 2, 2012. http://ctb.ku.edu/en/tablecontents/sub_section_main_1156.aspx.
University of Michigan. 2010. "Monitoring the Future, A Response to the Epidemic of Prescription Drug Use." Accessed October 2, 2012. http://www.whitehouse.gov/sites/default/files/ondcp/Fact_Sheets/prescription_drug_abuse_fact_sheet_4-25-11.pdf.
Urdan, T., & Schoenfelder, E. 2006. "Classroom Effects on Student Motivation: Goal Structures, Social Relationships, and Competence Beliefs." *Journal of School Psychology* 44: 331–349.
U.S. Congress. *Public Law 89–10/Elementary and Secondary Education Act of 1965*, 89th Cong., 1st sess. v. 79. Washington, DC: GPO.
U.S. Department of Education. 2002. "No Child Left Behind Fact Sheet." Accessed October 2, 2012. http://www.ed.gov/offices/OESE/esea/factsheet.html.
U.S. Department of Education. 2009. "Evaluation of Evidence-Based Practices in Online Learning: A Meta-Analysis and Review of Online Learning Studies." Accessed October 2, 2012. http://www2.ed.gov/rschstat/eval/tech/evidence-based-practices/finalreport.pdf.
U.S. Department of Education. 2010. "Learning Powered by Technology." Accessed October 2, 2012. http://www.ed.gov/technology/netp-2010.
U.S. Department of Education, National Center for Education Statistics. 2011. "The Condition of Education 2011." Accessed October 2, 2012. http://nces.ed.gov/programs/coe/indicator_scr.asp.
U.S. Department of Education, Office of Elementary and Secondary Education. 2001. *No Child Left Behind: A Desktop Reference*. Washington, DC: U.S. Department of Education.
U.S. Department of Health and Human Services. 2012. "Healthy People 2020." Accessed October 1, 2012. http://www.healthypeople.gov/2020/connect/webinars.aspx.
Van Geert, P., & Steenbeek, H. 2008. "Brains and the Dynamics of Wants and Cans in Learning." *Mind, Brain, and Education* 2(2): 62–66.
Vygotsky, L. S. 1978. *Mind in Society*. Cambridge, MA: Harvard University Press.
Vygotsky, L. S. 1987. "Thinking and Speech." In *The Collective Works of L. S. Vygotsky*, translated by N. Minick and edited by R. W. Weber & A. S. Caron. New York: Plenum Press.
Wallace, J. 2011. "Supt. Marple Lays Out Wide-Ranging Plans for Lawmakers." *The Legislature*, June 30. Accessed October 2, 2012. http://publications.wvsba.org/2011/06/30/news.
Wallis, C. 2005. "The New Science of Happiness." *Time Magazine*, January 17.

Wechsler, H., McKenna, M. L., Less, S. M., & Dietz, W. H. 2004. "The Role of Schools in Preventing Childhood Obesity." Accessed October 2, 2012. http://www.cdc.gov/healthyyouth/physicalactivity/pdf/roleofschools_obesity.pdf.

Weinert, F. E. 1987. "Introduction and Overview: Metacognition and Motivation as Determinants of Effective Learning and Understanding." In *Metacognition, Motivation, and Understanding*, edited by F. E. Weinert & R. H. Kluwe. Hillsdale, NJ: Lawrence Erlbaum.

Wells, G. 1986. *The Meaning Makers: Children Learning Language and Using Language to Learn*. Portsmouth, NH: Heinemann.

West Virginia State Legislature. 2011. *Senate Bill Number 516* (Requiring state board establish digital learning program). Accessed October 2, 2012. http://www.legis.state.wv.us/bill_status/Bills_history.cfm?input=516&year=2011&sessiontype=RS&btype=bill.

Wigfield, A., Eccles, J. S., Yoon, K. S., Harold, R. D., Arberton, A. J. A., Feedman-Doan, C., & Blumenfeld, P. 1997. "Change in Children's Competence Beliefs and Subjective Task Values Across the Elementary School Years: A 3-Year Study." *Journal of Educational Psychology* 89(3): 451–469.

Wolf, A. M., & Colditz, G. A. 1994. "The Cost of Obesity: The U.S. Perspective." *Pharmacoeconomics* 5(Suppl. 1): 34–37.

Wolf, A. M., & Colditz, G. A. 1998. "Current Estimates of the Economic Cost of Obesity in the United States." *Obesity Research* 6(2): 97–106.

Woolfolk, A. 2004. *Educational Psychology* (9th ed.). Boston: Pearson Education.

Yazzie-Mintz, E. 2010. "Schools Are Responding to Latest Findings From the High School Survey of Student Engagement." Indiana University, School of Education Feature Topic. Accessed October 2, 2012. http://education/indiana.edu/Feature_Topic_Detail/tabid/11553/Default.aspx?xmid=3554.

Zentner, M., & Renaud, O. 2007. "Origins of Adolescents Ideal Self: An Intergenerational Perspective." *Journal of Personality and Social Psychology* 92(3): 357–375.

# Index

Academic success, 99
Adverse Childhood Experiences (ACE), 5
Archimedes, 10

Bandura, Albert, 5, 30, 32, 57, 81, 90
Body mass index (BMI), 9, 165, 170
Borysenko, 12, 38, 117
Bullying, 8, 9, 14, 47, 50, 102, 185, 186, 187, 188, 189, 190, 191, 192, 193, 194, 195
    antibullying, 185, 190, 227

Career success, 5, 16, 133
Causal links/relationships, 5
    emotional profiles to health, 6
    relationship between self-esteem and Depression, 5
    relationship between self-esteem and obesity, 5
    self- and academic achievement, 5
    self, psychological, and physical well-being, 5
Centers for Disease Control and Prevention (CDC), 7, 9, 37, 164, 165, 169, 174, 175, 177, 181, 182, 183, 184, 189
Changing society, 30
Cognitive impairment, 5
Counseling
    Cognitive Behavioral Therapy (CBT), 75, 80
    as context for self-understanding, 3, 28, 50, 67, 69, 78, 122
    and first axiom of structural dynamics, 78, 79
    methods, 6, 25, 36, 63, 74, 123
    mental health/therapy, 3, 12, 14, 20, 76, 175
    private practice, 5, 14, 28, 111, 179
    as protective factor, 170, 171, 172, 173
    similarities between counseling and teaching, 79, 81, 87, 88, 91, 179
    strengths-based, 6, 75, 76, 160, 205
Curriculum
    best practices K–16, 115
    black box of teaching and learning, 115
    connecting academic content to self, 112, 113
    in language arts, 113
    in math, 114
    consciousness building through, 119–21
    contextual teaching and learning, 111
    creating realities through, 117, 118, 122
    critical thinking skills, 110
    curriculum versus teacher quality, importance of, 114
    direct transfer/near transfer of knowledge, 110
    emotions, 115
    epistemology, 116, 118
    far transfer/high road transfer of knowledge, 110

Curriculum (*continued*)
  fixed versus changing beliefs, 109, 110, 116, 117
  flourishing, 118
  happiness, 119, 126
  learning life purpose and dreams through, 111, 116
  meaningful connections, 123, 125
  motivation, 116, 131
  pedagogy for the good life, 109
  personalized learning, 112
  personalized learning plans, 116
  positive life course trajectory, 111
  potential in life, 117
  psychological well-being, 115
  Self Across the Curriculum (SAC), 110, 115
  Self Across the Curriculum applications
    in college educational psychology class, 123
    in high school social studies class, 125
    in middle school science class, 128
  Self Across the Curriculum and creating self, 110
  Self Across the Curriculum and iSelf model, 110, 122, 125, 127
    iSelf attributes as learning objectives, 127
  Self Across the Curriculum and policy, 115
  Self Across the Curriculum and 21st-century demands, 115
  Self Across the Curriculum and well-being outcomes, 115
  self-concept, 124, 125
  self-efficacy, 124, 130
  self-esteem, 116, 124
  self-other-all teaching and learning method, 127, 128
  self-referential teaching and learning method, 110, 112, 123, 129
  self-schema, 112
  structural tension, role of, 122
  subject-object dynamic, 118, 119
  Texas policy, 109
  transfer of knowledge, resistance to, 111
  transforming the self, process of, 122
  21st century versus 19th century, 109, 110, 111, 115
  whole-child focus, 109

Deci, E., 5, 13, 32, 36, 60, 82, 154
Depression
  and borderline personality disorder (BPD), 179
  and bullying, 192, 193
  emotions and, 63, 70, 162
  and the Great Depression, 178
  medication, 9
  mental health, 25, 77, 173, 178, 193
  adults and adolescents, percent with, 9, 176, 177, 178, 185
  and physical health/well-being, 5, 29, 164, 177
  programs, 174
  self as protective or risk factor and, 57, 59, 82, 84, 174, 177, 183
  stressors and, 14, 18, 70, 176
  and suicide, 174
  and well-being assessments, 182
DNA, ix, x, 11, 35, 81, 96, 161, 163
  inner life, ix

Emotions
  authentic, 5
  emotional healing, 70
  emotional intelligence, 35, 56, 63, 70, 71, 84, 134, 169, 176, 183, 187
  emotional profile, 6
  emotional well-being, 5, 29, 70, 72, 84, 105, 165
Epidemiologists, ix, 7, 10, 177

# Index

Flourishing/flourish, x, 3
  enabling conditions, 35, 36
  evolving beyond survival, 32, 206
  human flourishing as aim of education, 8, 109, 200
  as human potential, 13, 42, 118, 143, 150, 178, 185, 206
  personally and professionally, 4, 109
  purpose, dreams and, 34
  self and, 3, 34, 36, 56, 119, 204
  through schooling, 36, 37, 50, 109, 195, 200
  well-being and, 160, 178

Happiness/happy, 14
  bullying and, 194
  causal relationship with health, 26, 162, 204
  emotions and, 56, 63, 64
  and medications, 183, 184
  as outcome from schooling, 43, 115, 126, 143, 200
  personalized learning and, 151, 154
  positive psychology attributes, 35, 60, 61, 62
  self and, 14, 19, 48, 115, 154, 162
  well-being and, 206, 207
Harvard University's Mind-Body Clinic, 12
Health and Human Services (HHS), 7, 9, 102, 162, 165, 174, 175, 189, 193, 224
Health risk behaviors, 6
Health and well-being
  acute issues in society, 7, 36, 46, 161, 165
  behaviors: risk and protective, 13, 163, 169
  body of knowledge, 12
  counselors' and teachers' shared mission, 5, 173
  emotional/socioemotional, 84, 147, 167
  expenditures/prevention model, 38, 159
  outcomes from schooling, 36, 48, 82, 173
  personalized learning, 134, 169, 172
  physical, 82, 163, 167
  policies, 166, 201
  psychological, 46, 82, 167
  purpose of education, 93, 99, 173
  self and, 25, 104, 158, 163
  statistics, 8, 165, 184
Human potential
  antecedents/conditions for, 49, 100
  and flourishing, 13
  as purpose of education, 32, 105, 200
  self and, 105, 117
  Self Across the Curriculum and, 117
  transformed mind-set and, 43
  unique potential, 150

Integrated self-paradigm/model/iSelf
  academic performance/success, 91
  antecedent for flourishing, 36
  as aim of education, 36, 84, 88, 91, 97
  beliefs and, 88
  center of research and practice, 26, 199
  in counseling and teaching, 97, 113
  description of, 10, 49
  DNA of self, 81
  economic investment in, 199
  emotions/emotional intelligence, 63
  emotions and learning, 69, 83, 87
  emotional thought, 73
  focus in society, 13, 26, 199
  framework for epidemiologists, 10
  framework for counselors, 10
  framework for medical professionals, 10
  framework for parenting, 10
  framework for personalized learning, 10
  framework for prevention, 10
  framework for teachers, 10
  framework for 21st-century learning, 18

Integrated self-paradigm/model/iSelf (*continued*)
  meaning making, 61
  mediator between inner- and external self, 69, 88
  as mind, body, soul, brain, 11, 80
  mind, brain, and education (MBE), 55, 80
  nature–nurture, 67
  new kind of mind, 80
  pathway to change in counseling and teaching, 79, 88, 113
  risk and protective factor, 173, 185
  role in creating reality, 69
  self-schema, 59, 88
  self-esteem, 57
  structural tension, 79
  transformed mind-set and, 13
  well-being, 65, 84, 88, 91
Interdisciplinary view, 3, 5, 6, 30

K–16 schooling, 14, 37, 53, 122, 135, 170, 176

Maslow, Abraham, 4, 32, 35, 194, 195
Meaning
  construct, 118, 136
  creating meaning from academic content/subjects, 70, 101, 113, 119, 123, 136, 186
  culture creating/social construction, 30, 32, 90
  finding/creating, 14, 15, 30, 32, 59, 61, 64, 65
  life meaning as positive psychology attribute, 59, 60, 61, 65, 154
  loss of/lack of, 12, 77, 178, 191
  meaning of life, 77, 100, 126
  personal, 3, 7, 15, 66, 116, 119, 126, 206
  personally meaningful experiences, 4, 5, 32, 68, 134, 138, 194
  personal meaning and real world learning, 203, 204
  self and, 90, 116, 123, 206
  Self Across the Curriculum and, 116, 186, 194
  self-schema, role of, 59, 66
  and well-being, 64, 65
Medical care expenditures, 38
Medical professionals, ix, 5, 7, 10, 71, 72
  and iSelf model, 78, 84, 119, 122, 163, 176
  medical best practices, 167
  medical costs, 168, 169
  and mind, 96, 119
  and overwhelming problems, 161, 163, 165, 167
  and prescribing drugs, 182, 184
  and transforming the self, 122, 184
  and well-being, 35, 36, 85, 119, 161, 167, 176
Medical research, 12, 176
Medical theory, 17, 182, 183, 184
Mental well-being, 65, 170
  bullying as, 185
  mental health, 8, 20, 35, 54, 77
  mental health disorders and obesity, 65, 168, 175
  mental health and food, 163
  mental health indicators, 174
  mental health risk and protective factors, 175
  mental health and self, 79, 159, 160, 168, 174, 175
  mental health statistics, 173, 175, 177, 182, 189
  mental illness, 35, 170, 182
  mental illness and drug therapy, 182, 185
  mental illness and suicide, 174, 177
Mind, ix, 3, 9
  and bullying, 191, 193, 194
  changing minds, 79, 80, 117, 146

# Index

cultural influence, 30, 31, 59, 97, 191
demands upon/stressors, 29, 33, 167, 178, 187, 188, 190
dissociate from, 122, 187, 188
distinct from brain, 66, 97
equilibrium of mind, brain functions, 72, 161, 184, 191
evolution of, 30, 31, 106, 184
iSelf model and, 32, 33, 34, 52, 55, 56, 69, 70, 141
new kind of, model of, 6, 13, 14, 15, 29, 31, 32, 35, 48
new kind of mind and schooling, 41, 42, 52, 67, 70, 104, 148, 187
mind-body connection, 11, 12, 15, 70, 79, 82, 85, 104
mind and emotions, 82, 84, 120, 194
mind and health, 84, 85
mind as mediator, 22, 30, 31, 36, 59, 66
mind-set, 9, 11, 13, 19, 20, 28, 38, 43
mind-set and beliefs, 183, 201
as part of whole self, 3, 11, 15, 26, 31, 33, 41, 48, 67, 76
transformed, 11, 13, 19, 28, 43, 201
21st century versus 19th century, 48, 49, 95, 96, 97, 103, 178
Mind, brain, and education (MBE)
and emotional cognition, 72, 97
and emotions, 69
and learning processes, 6, 26, 69
and new kind of mind, 41
schooling, 72, 97

National Institutes of Health (NIH)
causal relationship, psychological states, and health research, 26, 84, 85
health and behavior, 85
National Institute of Mental Health (NIMH), 7, 179

No Child Left Behind (NCLB)
business model, 101
cognitive focus, 47, 99
and Common Core, 200
19th century versus 21st century, 98, 100, 144, 199
personalized learning, 143, 144, 147
reauthorization (ESEA) using iSelf model, 22, 199
standards versus well-being, 93, 148, 199
statistical measures and ineffectiveness, 47, 102, 110, 144, 199, 200
training for business/industry, 47, 100

Personalized learning
best practices, 6, 35, 96, 116, 135, 142, 146, 158
and flipped classrooms, 6, 204
individual, 96, 135
iSelf model as foundation/framework, 21, 26, 35, 133, 134, 142, 146, 150, 202
Khan Academy, 96, 151
learner-entered principles (LCP), 134, 135, 202
and personalized learning plans (PLP), 116, 135, 142, 151, 154–58
and potential, 21, 150
Quaglia's eight characteristics/conditions, 134, 150
Teachers' Unions perspectives, 143, 146, 148
technology, role of, 96, 133, 151, 153, 204
21st-century model, 199, 202
well-being portfolio, 181
whole-child, 142, 143, 146, 150, 158, 181

Physical well-being, 3
   aim of education, 13, 16, 46, 146, 163
   education and health policies, 161, 165, 166
   iSelf model and, 24, 25, 49, 63, 164, 204, 206
   obesity, 5, 6, 25, 84, 161
   obesity, cost of, 38, 163, 164, 168
   obesity, prevention of, 162, 163, 167, 169, 173
   obesity and mental health, 168, 169, 177
   obesity-related illness, 6, 38, 80, 163, 164, 173
   obesity statistics, 9, 37, 161, 162, 164, 165, 166
   personalized learning and, 133, 135
   problems/urgent needs, 7, 9, 106, 161, 163
   psychological causes/causal links, 5, 26, 29, 163, 169
   and schooling, 4, 10, 11, 84, 106, 133, 165, 169
   Self Across the Curriculum, 115, 160
   self-esteem, self-knowledge as protective factors, 29, 82, 160, 163, 169, 173
   stressors and obesity, 14, 29, 50, 166
Positive psychology, 34
   attributes, 29, 44, 60, 116, 126
   creativity, 44
   dreams/vision, 113, 116
   emotions, 29
   flourishing, 36
   happiness, 126
   high-impact college advising, 205
   and iSelf model, 10, 26, 29, 37, 51, 90, 179
   life purpose, 60, 153
   mental health, 35
   motivation, 116
   new mind, 6, 34
   personal meaning, 15
   and personalized learning, 6, 35
   and *Responsive Classroom*, 194
   in schooling and education, 35, 36, 50, 89, 113, 179
   and Self Across the Curriculum, 115
   self-determination, 116
   strengths-based counseling, 6, 75, 179
Potential, human
   academic, 49, 99, 100, 105
   aim of education, 35, 99, 105, 144, 187, 207
   beliefs about, 104, 117
   capabilities, capacities, propensities in self knowledge, 105
   capacity to grow, 57
   consciousness, levels of, 120, 121
   through counseling, 36, 79, 104
   dreams/visions as antecedent, 21, 79
   through education, 7, 36, 46, 99, 104
   empowering children and adults, ix, 79, 207
   importance in modern life, 4, 13, 23, 32, 99, 187
   iSelf model, 22, 23, 32, 49, 79, 91, 117, 178, 187
   through medicine, 36
   model of, 22, 105, 150
   and personalized learning, 21, 96, 133, 142, 143, 150
   primary motivator, 23, 24
   purpose in life, 104
   Quaglia's eights characteristics/conditions, 134, 150, 151
   schooling as obstacle, 23
   Self Across the Curriculum, 117, 130
   self-efficacy and, 57, 90
   through teaching and learning, 91, 104, 130
   under potentiality, 21
   unique, 4, 42, 46, 143
   well-being, 14, 143
Prescription drugs, 9, 102, 161
   abuse by 12th graders, 184

# Index

antidepressants, 182
statistics, 182, 184, 185
Protective factors
  broad-spectrum approaches (BSA), 159
  emotional intelligence, 174
  environmental factors, 162
  external versus internal, 24, 162, 169
  for health and well-being, 169
  iSelf model as, 60
  Michael Jackson case, 27
  pathways to flourishing life, 185
  personal protective factors, 161
  personalized learning, 171, 188
  purpose in life, 174
  self-esteem, 174
  self-esteem for obesity and physical illnesses, 29, 171
  self-knowledge, 29, 171, 174

Quality of life
  behaviors that impede or enhance, 13
  contributing to humankind, 65
  critical crossroads, 93
  good life, living, 63, 144
  healing children, 54
  importance of emotional well-being, 54
  importance of purpose and dreams, 54
  iSelf model, 37, 178, 206
  living purposefully, 65
  personal meaning, 4
  physical well-being, 4
  promise of K–16 education, 48, 144, 206
  psychological well-being, 4
  students through schooling, 4, 116, 144, 206
  well-being, 63

Ryan, R., 5, 13, 32, 36, 62, 154
Ryff, C., 5, 32, 65, 82, 134, 181

Self
  academics, 10, 36, 70, 112, 113
  achievement gap, 33, 34
  -actualization, 4, 11, 51, 93, 194, 206
  -affect, 55, 59, 60, 79
  attributions/attributes, 21, 27, 51, 55, 59, 75, 113
  -awareness, 11, 70, 77, 80, 103
  body/physical, 3, 52
  bullying, 191, 192
  causal link between self knowledge and well-being, 5, 6, 16, 57, 71, 82, 90, 115, 159, 168, 173, 176
  as center of education system, 10, 13, 22, 24, 25, 32, 48, 84, 94, 205
  -character, 52
  in classrooms, 3, 6, 16, 24, 67, 79, 112, 113, 124
  common to all, 11, 12
  concept, 55, 56, 70, 114, 116, 124
  construction of, 15, 49, 51, 66, 88, 89, 96, 115, 116, 187
  -control, 63
  core, 12
  -destructive behaviors, 21, 77, 180
  -determination, 16, 62, 97, 116, 126, 145, 154
  development across lifespan, 14, 89
  developmental psychology, 14, 89
  -directed, 33, 74, 75, 94, 121, 141
  -discipline, 52, 197
  DNA, ix, x, 11
  dreams/visions, 69, 114, 205
  -efficacy, 21, 55, 57, 87, 90, 124, 151, 205
  and emotions, 82, 83, 84, 88, 104
  -esteem, 5, 16, 19, 21, 29, 49, 55, 56, 57, 105, 151, 159, 160, 168, 180
  external, 22, 34, 61, 169
  as holistic system, 3, 52, 57, 67, 97
  at home, x
  -identity, 55, 58, 77, 88, 114, 205
  -image, 55, 179, 180, 192

## Index

Self (*continued*)
  inner-, 18, 22, 24, 27, 29, 34, 51, 55, 61, 74, 162, 169
  integrated self-paradigm/model/iSelf, 10, 12, 14, 18, 34, 49, 56, 61, 69, 79, 84, 115, 178, 179, 197
  -interest, 13, 61, 87, 89, 172
  -knowledge, 7, 10, 11, 16, 22, 27, 33, 89, 170, 176
  -learning, 14, 30, 33, 50, 87
  as lens, 22, 23, 24, 27, 34, 71
  lever for change, 10
  locus of control, 55, 58
  mediates inner and outer life, 3, 15, 22, 29, 32, 49, 59, 61, 69, 81, 90
  medicine/medical importance, 6, 14, 71, 161, 168
  modern life, demands upon, 12, 73, 97
  new kind of mind, 3, 7, 48, 49, 55, 67, 73
  -perceptions, 57
  personal meaning/role of, 15, 25, 61
  personalized learning/importance of, 34, 134, 150
  positive psychology, 36, 51, 89, 115
  as protective factor, 5, 6, 16, 50, 82, 90, 113, 159, 163, 169, 173, 175
  -psychology of, 5, 32
  -respect, 53, 120, 140
  -responsibility, 49, 65, 183
  as risk factor, 6, 159, 162, 168, 169, 173
  -schema, 55, 56, 59, 66, 87, 88, 89, 112, 167
  in schooling, x, 3, 4, 5, 6, 10, 15, 16, 25, 50, 89, 90
  self-other-all teaching method, 44, 61, 127, 130
  self-referential teaching method, 61, 89, 101, 110, 112, 123, 127, 130
  soul, 3, 12, 52
  -system, 10, 15, 20, 30, 50, 51, 55, 57, 90, 115
  theory of, 54, 128, 131
  in therapy (counseling), x, 3, 5, 15, 50, 65, 66, 67, 75, 79
  transfer, 33, 110
  transformation/transformed, 11, 13, 34, 45, 122, 161
  -understanding, 3, 5, 15, 18, 19, 55, 57, 116
  unique, 72, 97, 99
  well-being, 10, 11, 36
  whole, v, 11, 36, 52, 55, 67, 76, 97, 153, 174

United States Department of Education (DOE), 7, 37, 101, 133, 143, 152, 193, 198, 202, 205

Well-being
  abuse, 180
  assessments, 181
  beliefs about, 167
  borderline personality disorders (BPD), 179, 180
  broad-spectrum approaches (BSA), 159
  bullying, 185
    and emotions, 187
    Olweus Program, 193
    *Responsive Classroom*, 194
    and self-concept, 187
    and self-esteem, 187, 193
    signs of, 192
  cutting, 180
  Daimon, 161, 191
  definition, 160
  Depression/sadness, 176, 183
  dissociation, 188
  DNA, 161
  education policies and practices as cause, 165, 166
  emotional roots/causes, 160, 168, 175, 179, 180, 183, 194
  flourishing, 160
  happy/happiness, 160

# Index

HBO's *Weight of the Nation*, 164, 166, 167
Healthy People 2020 initiative, 174
identity, importance of, 180
inner-self versus external self factors, 162, 169
iSelf model, role of, 159, 163, 167, 178, 181, 183
medications, antidepressant and others, 182, 183, 184
mental/psychological, 160, 173, 179
mental health/psychological programs (SOS), 174
personal responsibility, 169
personalized learning, 181, 188
physical, 160, 161
    obesity epidemic, 161, 169
    obesity programs (CATCH), 162, 173
    overweight illnesses, 167
policies, 159, 163, 166, 176, 193
poor health, cost of, 168
prescription drug abuse, 184
prevention approaches, 159, 162, 163, 169, 173, 174, 181, 185, 193

protective factors
    environmental factors, 171–72
    personal factors, 170–71
    schooling as, 173
    self-esteem as, 159, 168, 169, 176
    self-knowledge, 169, 176
Self Across the Curriculum (SAC), 163
self-esteem, 159, 160, 174, 176, 179, 193
self-knowledge, 159, 174, 176, 193
self-mutilation, 180
socioeconomic considerations, 167
statistics, 163–65, 168, 173, 177, 180, 184, 189
suicide, 174, 175, 177–78
risk factors
    environmental factors, 171–72
    personal factors, 170–71
    poor self-esteem, 168, 169
    poor self-knowledge, 168, 169
    schooling as, 173
21st century versus 19th century, 178, 188

# About the Author

**Dr. Henry G. Brzycki** has more than 30 years of experience providing leadership to the fields of education and psychology. Dr. Brzycki challenges scholars and practitioners to expand their boundaries of understanding in order to impact the quality of children's lives. Dr. Brzycki founded *The Brzycki Group*, where his innovative counseling and psychoeducational programs pioneer positive psychology and strengths-based counseling methods. Dr. Brzycki consults schools, colleges, foundations, and policy makers on how to realize the potential of people. He recently founded *The Center for the Self in Schools*. The center's mission is to impact the psychological, socioemotional, and physical well-being of K–16 students through outreach programs, professional development, self-knowledge curricula, antibullying programs, and high-impact student advising assessments using strengths-based counseling methods.

Dr. Brzycki has a distinguished academic and scholarly career, having earned his PhD from Pennsylvania State University, his MA from Tufts University, and his BS from Babson College. Dr. Brzycki has served as a core faculty member in the teacher education program at Franklin Pierce University and earned the Teacher of the Year Award at Clarion University. He also taught at Pennsylvania State University. As Dean of the School of Education at American Public University, he transformed teacher and counselor education programs to reflect a visionary 21st century model of education.

Dr. Brzycki has provided leadership to the American Counseling Association (ACA) and the American Educational Research Association (AERA), where he has been invited to present his research on numerous occasions. As a researcher and author, Dr. Brzycki has published highly regarded research in peer-reviewed journals and an educational psychology textbook representing future directions in applying psychology to educational contexts. Dr. Brzycki served the U.S. Department of Education as a consultant on personalized learning methods and emerging 21st-century teaching and learning models.

Dr. Brzycki's most recent book captures his insights and experiences as a counselor, teacher, and thought leader, and offers a breakthrough model for transforming people's lives, teaching and learning best practices, and our society. *The Self in Schooling: Theory and Practice—How to Create Happy, Healthy, Flourishing Children in the 21st Century* is based on findings from his clinical experiences and scholarly research. This book provides teachers, school leaders, policy makers, and school and health psychologists with a comprehensive framework for personalized learning and 21st-century teaching and learning, fulfilling a growing need for both scholars and practitioners alike.

Dr. Brzycki is a sought-after speaker, consultant, and personal and professional development expert. Please visit The Brzycki Group website (http://www.brzyckigroup.com) to make your requests and inquiries.

www.ingramcontent.com/pod-product-compliance
Lightning Source LLC
Chambersburg PA
CBHW060949230426
43665CB00015B/2118